ADVERTISING MANAGEMENT AND THE BUSINESS PUBLISHING INDUSTRY

THE NEW YORK UNIVERSITY BUSINESS MAGAZINE PUBLISHING SERIES

Editorial Excellence in Business Press Publishing:
The Neal Awards
Edited by Frank C. Taylor and Albert N. Greco

Business Journalism: Management Notes and Cases
Albert N. Greco

The Business Press Editor
Edgar A. Grunwald

ADVERTISING MANAGEMENT AND THE BUSINESS PUBLISHING INDUSTRY

Marketing Notes and Cases

Albert N. Greco

NEW YORK UNIVERSITY PRESS
New York and London

Library of Congress Cataloging-in-Publication Data
Greco, Albert N., 1945–
Advertising management and the business publishing industry :
marketing notes and cases / Albert N. Greco.
p. cm. — (The New York University business magazine
publishing series)
Includes bibliographical references and index.
ISBN 0-8147-3040-X (cloth) — ISBN 0-8147-3041-8 (pbk.)
1. Advertising—Management.   2. Business literature—Publishing.
I. Title. II. Series.
HF5823.G695   1991
659.1'068—dc20   91-2451
                                                              CIP

New York University Press Books are printed on acid-free paper,
and their binding materials are chosen for strength and durability.

For Elaine, Albert, Timothy, John, and Robert

Contents

Foreword

You *could* publish an important business magazine without advertising *if* you had an enormous endowment, or a substantial body of readers who might be willing to pay one or two thousand dollars a year for subscriptions, or, better yet, if you had *both* an impressive endowment fund *and* multitudes of readers who were delighted to shell out thousand-dollar fees for copies. You could do this, and a few, a very few, magazines and newsletters manage it.

But the vast majority of business publications do not attempt to operate that way. They sell advertising; they are aware, as the bulletin of the Gallatin Division recently said, that "obviously, advertising is the fuel in any magazine's engine."

But advertising is not merely the income that pays most of the costs of magazine publishing; it is an extremely important part of any publication's value to its readers. It supplements and expands the editorial value by constantly bringing readers the essential information they need about products and services that they can use to improve thier business operations. And without advertising, the publication's editors, no matter how diligent and how efficient they might be, would lack the financial resources that enable them to build expert staffs, to initiate important investigations, and to turn out magazines that are vitally important to business executives and business staffs in all the myriad industrial, commercial, professional, and, indeed, educational and governmental activities of this vast economy.

Actually, the entire United States communications system depends heavily upon advertising. In the case of radio and television, all of the income that enables them to broadcast news, analysis, discussion, and entertainment comes from the sale of advertising; and while "pay television" of one sort or another is growing in importance and popularity, even it will be dependent upon advertising to enhance its ability to produce satisfactory program fare as time goes by.

In the case of print media, where readers mostly contribute to the publication expense, advertising revenue generally represents from one-half to two-thirds of income. Advertising accounts for 50 percent of the income of the average consumer magazine, according to an analysis of the Department of Commerce's figures, and some 65 percent or more of the average business or professional magazine. And the latter figure may be conservative; for example, in the case of *Advertising Age,* which we publish, and for which readers pay a relatively stiff subscription price, subscriptions only account for about fifteen cents of the income dollar, leaving eighty-five cents to be paid by advertisers.

So you may see why all of us with extensive personal knowledge of the business publication market consider advertising so important an element, one that requires tender, solicitous attention, and the most knowledgeable, expert sales personnel and operation.

I have tried in this Foreword to tell you why we at Crain Communications think the sale of advertising is so vitally important to the successful production of business publications and to explain how "advertising is the fuel in any business magazine's engine."

So go to it! And the best of luck and great success to you.

Sid Bernstein
Chairman of the Executive
Committee, Crain Communications

Preface

Charles Dillon (Casey) Stengel, perhaps the most famous and successful "old professor" of the twentieth century, had a remarkably simple rule about management. He once said, "I know I am a better manager when Joe DiMaggio is in center field."

I have tried to follow Stengel's approach, and I have certainly profited from the splendid advice and guidance of a number of people who "played center field" for me.

Colin Jones, Director of the New York University Press, provided invaluable advice about many different issues affecting the publishing industry. I was also aided by Despina Gimbel, a highly skilled, patient editor at NYU Press, who shared my admiration of Ronald Guidry and Donald Mattingly (two men who always exemplified Hemingway's notion of "grace under pressure").

Beth Luey, Editor of the *Book Research Quarterly*, offered exceptionally important editorial advice on the changing world of publishing. Part of the Introduction originally appeared in "Teaching Publishing in the United States: A Mix of the Practical and the Theoretical" in *Book Research Quarterly* 6 (Spring 1990); and an earlier version of chapter 4 originally appeared in "Mergers and Acquisitions in Publishing 1984–1988" in *Book Research Quarterly* 5 (Fall 1989).

Robert Jachino (from the Thomson Corporation) guided me through many discussions about the business publishing industry, especially ideas regarding mergers and acquisitions and the impact of global publishing.

Alberto Vitale (of Random House) offered invaluable advice on human resources management, as did Herbert I. London, Dean of the Gallatin Division.

Ann Cowan and Rowland Lorimer from Simon Fraser University and Basil Stuart-Stubbs from the University of British Columbia provided me with critically important information about the needs of publishing educators.

Lastly, I want to thank Joseph Kutner, the best manager I ever worked with, and Peter Maino and Jerry Wexler, thoughtful managers and fierce competitors.

The research for this book was made possible by a grant from Crain Communications and is dedicated to the memory of G. D. Crain. However, the ideas and positions contained within this book are those of this author and do not reflect the corporate position of Crain Communications.

All of the notes and cases in this book were prepared for class discussions rather than to illustrate either effective or ineffective ways to manage a problem. All of the names, addresses, places, dates, financial and statistical data, companies, corporations, and publications in *all* of the cases are fictional. *No* reference to any living or dead person is intended. This procedure was followed to protect the identity of the individuals and companies researched for these cases.

Introduction

TEACHING PUBLISHING: A MIX OF THE PRACTICAL AND THE THEORETICAL

Until quite recently publishing was perceived to be a small, cozy, "accidental" profession. The world of letters was firmly ensconced because of the impressive publishing efforts of a small group of talented individuals and magazine and book publishing houses, including, in the United States, Random House, Hearst, Harper and Row, Bantam Doubleday Dell, Macmillan, Norton, Simon and Schuster, Farrar Straus, McGraw-Hill, Viking, Scribner's, and the venerable Alfred Knopf; in Canada, McClelland and Stewart, Key Porter Books, Penguin, Nelson Canada, Grolier Ltd., the Thomson Corporation, and an impressive array of university presses at Toronto, Ottawa, and the University of British Columbia; and in England, William Collins, Hamish Hamilton, Faber, Weidenfeld, and the great presses sponsored by Oxford University and Cambridge University.

In 1987 Ted Solotaroff wrote about this "genteel profession" in the United States in a perceptive, highly controversial, and thought-provoking article entitled "The Literary-Industrial Complex."[1] Solotaroff began by describing the New York-based literary publishing environment as it existed in the early 1960s. At that time this nation's great publishing houses were "like the homes of the

[English] gentry, distinctive, stable, guided by tradition or at least precedent, inner directed in their values."[2]

Solotaroff wrote that Alfred Knopf helped to create (and perhaps best personified) this almost nineteenth-century world of publishing. According to Solotaroff, Knopf once said that he "did not want to publish any author he would not want to invite to dinner."[3] Yet to a substantial degree, the Knopfs of the world were really not responsible for publishing's great successes. The real credit belonged to a highly influential group of creative editors. An outstanding example is the famed Maxwell Perkins, who helped make Scribner's such a great book publishing house. These invaluable individuals acquired and edited the book manuscripts and magazine articles of Hemingway, Fitzgerald, and their peers and created the successes of *Time, Vanity Fair, Advertising Age*, and a host of other influential consumer and business publications in the years after 1920.

This cozy, fraternal world of publishing has changed. In the past few years, this industry has sustained a series of events (some unpleasant, most of them necessary, especially in the marketing and financial management areas) that transformed a significant number of specialized book or business magazine companies into publishing and information-processing corporations, many with global operations. These events include a plethora of international mergers and acquisitions of firms in the United States, Canada, England, France, and elsewhere; the rise in importance of specialized publishing products, including directories, annuals, newsletters, corporate publications, and buyer guides; the creation of economically and technically viable electronic publishing systems (for example, computer databases and CD-ROM products); the emergence of small independent publishers and university presses as major players in the mid-list book market; the development of the mass market hardback book; the rise of large "supermarket" chain bookstores; and the concomitant, inevitable displacement of many impressive and economically fragile business and consumer magazines and independent book companies and stores.

Perhaps the most crucial developments have yet to occur because international publishers now face two challenges that will test their mettle, resiliency, and resourcefulness. First, by 31 December 1992, trade restrictions within Europe's twelve Common Market nations will end. This means that a multibillion dollar-business market will be created overnight with over 324 million people, the largest consumer and business market in the world.

Second, the important Pacific Rim region in East Asia, which includes Japan, China, Korea, Taiwan, Indonesia, Australia, Hong Kong, and Singapore, will continue to need significant amounts of business publications and information services to support their impressive, far-reaching business and economic expansion plans. Recently, some international economists and politicians have discussed the possibility that these countries might join together and create a Pacific Rim version of Europe's Common Market, with all of the usual trade "guidelines" and regulations designed clearly to stimulate commerce within these Asian nations at the expense of non-Pacific Rim states.

In order to compete successfully in this new global, deregulated European market, and of course in a possible structured Pacific Rim economic community, publishing firms will need access to (1) effective global marketing and advertising expertise, (2) an impressive product mix, especially in the important business, medical-healthcare, financial services, pure science, and technology categories, and (3) access to most if not all of the currently available communications technologies, namely books, magazines, "free" television and cable television, feature films, electronic databases, newspapers, and miscellaneous publishing. Clearly, the ability to obtain adequate financing to support these endeavors is critical to their success.

The specialized "single product" publisher will continue to exist; yet as Theodore Levitt outlined in his perceptive article "Marketing Myopia," "product"-oriented companies will soon discover that there are strong, and at times hostile, market forces at work that just might doom many of these rugged entrepreneurs, even if they monitor cash flow and receivables efficiently, publish the best works in their field, provide more intelligent service, and stay in close contact with the wants and needs of their customers.[4] When Thomas Hobbes wrote that life was "nasty, brutish, and short," he might have been describing the professional futures of many of these people and corporations.

Will publishers and editors, eager to maintain a romantic, nine-teenth-century "Alfred Knopf" type of publishing environment be able to combat successfully these forces of change? I doubt it. Change is, after all, an inevitable fact of life thoroughly grounded in the laws of physics, nature, *and* business.

G. K. Chesterton (1874–1936) briefly touched on these feelings in "A Song of Defeat":

> And I dream of the days when work was scrappy,
> And rare in our pockets the mark of the mint,
> And we were angry and poor and happy,
> And proud of seeing our names in print.

In the 1990s the "names in print" are more likely to be those of large, diversified, global publishing and information corporations with a firm commitment to support financially diverse and excit-ing print and electronic publishing operations and able to release, for example, over fifty-four thousand books and fifteen thousand magazines in the United States alone! These firms are planning for the twenty-first century. They are not looking back to the publishing world that existed in the time of Dickens, but who really wants to return to such a time?

THE CHANGING WORLD OF PUBLISHING EDUCATION

What impact will this almost Kafkaesque metamorphosis within the global publishing industry have on the teaching of publishing? Clearly, professors of publishing, whether in departments offering academic degrees or in the highly important continuing education (noncredit, nondegree) programs that educate the vast majority of working publishing professionals in Canada, the United States, and Europe, are not immune to these major market forces. I do not believe that one can find many "Mr. Chips" types, those terri-bly impressive, erudite, but isolated individuals, teaching publish-ing in North America. However, academicians must consider the need to reevaluate their research projects, courses and seminars, faculty development programs, and their professional ties to the publishing community if their training is to remain meaningful to both students and employers.

TEACHING PUBLISHING: THE THEORETICAL FRAMEWORK

What *theoretical* framework might we work within to train the next generation of publishing leaders? What will publishers need to know in order to become and remain effective executives? What problems are inherent in trying to be effective within large, global publishing and information-processing corporations?

Whenever I need answers to complex questions associatedwith management or marketing, I always consult the writings of Peter Drucker. I do this not because Drucker is a professor emeritus of management at New York University; rather, I am motivated by the unassailable fact that Drucker, a German emigrant who became a citizen of the United States and indeed the world, is considered to be the foremost authority on management theory and practice.[5]

DRUCKER ON MANAGEMENT

Drucker's key ideas on management development were developed in *Management: Tasks, Responsibilities, and Practices.*[6]

Drucker maintained that *the* key area of managerial concern was, and will always be, "effectiveness." To Drucker effectiveness cannot be taken for granted, especially within large, convoluted organizations.[7] Instead of supervising manual workers, publishing managers today must deal with "knowledge workers," those creative authors and editors who supply the end product, whether it is a directory, a scholarly journal, or a business magazine article, and who ultimately make money for the firm. Creative people cannot be supervised in the traditional way. They work at intellectually complex tasks and make key decisions that affect directly the performance and financial results of the entire firm; and all of this work is done at their own special, unpredictable rate of "production." Consequently, the effective manager must make a major commitment to help and not hinder these people.[8]

TEACHING PUBLISHING: THE PRACTICAL FRAMEWORK

With Drucker's ideas in mind, I tried to create a practical framework to train the next generation of publishing leaders. I will not pretend for one second that the publishing program at New York University is flawless; the opposite is the truth. However, I want to mention a few of the steps we have taken to create a realistic, workable publishing program for our graduate students; and I will also point out some of the problems and failures we have encountered, and still face.

When we first started to plan a comprehensive publishing curriculum, we began with the idea that educated publishers needed to have a solid foundation in the liberal arts, the humanities, and the sciences.[9] So we sought M.A. candidates with undergraduate concentrations in these areas. This academic foundation would then be augmented by a significant exposure to the fundamental ideas of management, marketing, international marketing, finance, accounting, and business law, as well as a working knowledge of statistics. Finally, a would-be publisher should be exposed to the unique characteristics of the publishing industry.

At first we tried to do this by creating our own publishing courses that were built in reality on a foundation of traditional business administration courses. From the start we believed that management was an *art* and *not* a science; if it were a science, there would be no bankruptcies, companies with faltering market shares, or necessity to close archaic operating units. However, we felt that it was very important intellectually for students to be aware of the impressive body of managerial theories. So we created many courses on such subjects as communications management, business magazine advertising, and accounting for the publisher.

This was an error. We forgot what Theodore Levitt said years ago about being "product" and not "market" oriented. We were, after all, reinventing the wheel. Accounting is accounting, regardless of the industry. So we changed this approach. Now we have a multitier system of courses in which all of our graduate students are sent to our school of business for their training in business. The second part of this system is composed of courses and seminars that deal with *specific* problems and areas of concern to publishers (for example global publishing, mergers and acquisitions, business and scholarly publishing, or trends in the book industry).

The case method of instruction is utilized in our core publishing courses. We could not turn over management of a viable publishing firm to students. Yet we can allow them to read and digest real case studies of successful and unsuccessful publishing companies to ascertain how *real* managers dealt with *real* concerns and crises. Drucker once wrote that Thomas Watson of IBM "saw that what mattered was *not* what the computer could do *but* what the user could get from it." The spirit of Watson motivated us to research effective case studies of publishing companies.[10]

Augmenting the cases was a series of hands-on internships with a cross-section of publishing firms, from a daily business newspaper covering the banking industry (*American Banker*) to a weekly trade magazine tracking trends in the mercurial fashion industry (*Women's Wear Daily*) to large global trade book companies (Random House, Bantam, Hearst, and Harper and Row). These highly structured experiences allowed students to determine what managerial theories do and do not work in the real world of publishing. Thus students exposed to, for example, theoretical economic models of the business magazine marketing environment in Korea would be able to determine whether such a model had any bearing on what really happens in the world of commerce.

ADVISORY BOARD MEMBERS

We also came to realize that a superb publishing program needs an advisory board of industry leaders to give timely, practical advice to university-based academicians. When we established our publishing program, we created two different boards, one from the trade book industry and the second from the specialized business magazine industry.

After a few years, we discovered that too many (but certainly not all) of the members on each board were "product" and not "market" oriented. *Some* of the book publishers thought only about mass-market trade books and did not want us to provide much if any training in other areas such as university presses. *Some* of the business magazine publishers, on the other hand, viewed the world of publishing as defined solely by trade magazines, and they were vocal in their opposition to teaching or doing research about database publishing, scholarly publishing, newsletters, and so forth.

We were genuinely concerned about this type of response. We were well aware of the fact that since 1984 the U.S. publishing industry had experienced a period of rapid mergers and acquisitions that led ultimately to the creation of a small number of corporations active in most if not all aspects of publishing and information processing. Yet *some* members on our boards were still acting as if no product diversification existed, as if Dickens were still the number one author on their latest list, or as if the United States's manufacturing industries were still the primary concern of "business" papers.

To address this, we approached a small group of key executives who had a global view of publishing. We told them how we viewed the changing world of publishing, and we asked them for their support. We believe that this new board will be helpful in arranging for funded internships and research projects in these key areas and in aiding our overall efforts to provide them with the best-trained candidates for their industry.

A TEACHING AND RESEARCH FACULTY

Recruiting and keeping a faculty has also been a major challenge. Although we are fortunate to be located in the publishing capital of the United States, most of the best individuals with publishing industry experience who were candidates for full-time teaching appointments could not afford to take a sizable cut in wages in order to join the university. So we have relied on adjuncts, who provide an invaluable overview of what is going on today in the eclectic publishing world.

However, you cannot develop a first-rate educational program based on the work of adjuncts. We approached our new advisory board with this problem and then discussed the idea of establishing an endowment so that we could attract and keep a key leader (or leaders) from the industry at New York University. This matter is still not resolved; and until it is, we remain concerned about this issue.

PROFESSIONAL PUBLISHING ASSOCIATIONS

We have been very active in developing effective relations with the key industry trade associations. The past president of the Association of American Publishers (AAP) and the chief executive officer of the American Booksellers Association (ABA) both served on our book advisory board. The past president of the Association of Business Publishers (ABP) was a member of our business press board. In addition I was a judge for the ABP Neal Editorial Prize for four years, which assisted me in keeping in touch with editors and academicians throughout the United States.

RESEARCH ON THE PUBLISHING INDUSTRY

To aid us in the pivotal area of research, we established a business magazine book series. Books have been issued on *Business Journalism: Management Notes and Cases* (which contains thirty-five management cases about the business press industry in the United States), *The Business Press Editor* (which analyzes the pivotal role of the business press editor as manager), and *Editorial Excellence in Business Press Publishing: The Neal Awards*, which we believe will be of help to professors teaching feature- writing courses.

However, we are very concerned about the lack of attention paid within the academic community to the world of publishing. The two principal scholarly journals covering publishing are the impressive *Book Research Quarterly* and the internationally renowned *Scholarly Publishing*. However, both journals are somewhat "product" and not publishing oriented. The *Journal of Communications* is at the other end of the spectrum in that all forms of communication are covered and little attention is paid each year to publishing. *Journalism Quarterly* has been and is likely to remain a journal devoted primarily to newspaper and television journalism.

What is needed is a scholarly journal that addresses the key areas of concern to professors teaching about the entire publishing and information-processing fields. Getting published in the existing referred journals is not easy because each journal must provide a service to its product-oriented readership, which in each instance is not primarily publishing professors. The principal "magazine for magazine managers" in the United States is the critically acclaimed *Folio* magazine; yet *Folio* tends to publish "how-to" articles, and professors seeking tenure generally have little interest in researching and writing articles of this type.

A SCHOLARLY PUBLISHING ASSOCIATION

Finally, there is no scholarly organization just for publishing professors. I am a member of the Society for Scholarly Publishing, the Association for Education in Journalism and Mass Communications, and the International Communication Association. So I understand firsthand the inability of each one of these fine organizations to publish many articles on publishing or to allocate many sessions at their annual meeting to publishing. They must serve other markets.

Perhaps the time has come to prod professors in Canada, the United States, and Europe to create a scholarly journal and professional organization to address the unique research and teaching needs of publishing professors.

TEACHING

Teaching about the publishing industry is an exciting endeavor. In the last few years, publishing has been covered extensively in the business press because of the numerous multibillion-dollar global mergers and acquisitions that engulfed this eclectic industry *and* of course the complex issues related to the publication of *The Satanic Verses*.

We are deeply involved in the transmission of knowledge and the preparation of the next generation of publishing executives. We are witnessing a global transformation of the entire communications industry. In spite of all of the serious problems related to the creation and implementation of a publishing program, I cannot think of a more exciting responsibility or a better place to be than in the academic community researching and teaching about this ever-changing publishing industry.

DEVELOPING TEACHING MATERIALS FOR PUBLISHING EDUCATION PROGRAMS

Since 1985 publishing has received a significant amount of attention in both the consumer and specialized business press. For example, Rupert Murdoch's $3 billion acquisition of Triangle Publications (which includes *TV Guide, Seventeen* magazine, and the *Racing Form*) and Robert Maxwell's + $2.52 billion purchase of Macmillan, to list only two of the more visible global publishers, sparked the interest and imagination of a plethora of people who had never paid very much attention to the world of publishing.

However, in spite of this recent media attention and the inevitable proximity professors of mass communications have to the book and magazine industry, college professors have an exceptionally difficult time obtaining usable and historically reliable materials about the highly diversified global publishing industry.

This fact hit home hard during the fall of 1988. I was doing some research on the history of publishing in the United States, and I discovered that John Tebbel's critically important multi-volume history of the book publishing industry in the United States was out of print, as was Frank Luther Mott's definitive five volume history of the magazine industry in the U.S., Kenneth C. Davis's *Two-Bit Culture: The Paperbacking of America*, and David Forsyth's study of the business press industry in the United States.[11]

As I continued to dig into the published literature on special market niches, it also became obvious that there was no single volume available on the history of scholarly, technical, professional, or database publishing in the United States; and, regrettably, most of the existing corporate histories of book or magazine companies in the United States were flawed or at least suspect because of their methodological approach to the corporations and individuals under study.[12]

Ironically, the publishing community has given the world exciting, high-quality works in a variety of formats on everything from managerial theories to agricultural economics, from fission and fusion to the films of Alfred Hitchcock; yet publishers and editors have not spent the time and allocated the necessary resources to help interested and concerned scholars study their own industry!

Obviously there are scholarly communications journals in the United States. Yet they have a highly specialized "product" (and not "market") orientation. So what can publishing professors do to obtain needed information about the industry they study? In this chapter I will address some of the research obstacles I faced and describe the steps I took to overcome these roadblocks. However, I do not want to imply for one moment that my own experiences in coping with these situations are illustrative of *the* methodological theory that must be followed in order to do publishing research. The following material must be viewed merely as a personal description of what proved to be somewhat successful for my research.

RESEARCH FOR A MANAGEMENT CASEBOOK

Several years ago I decided to create and teach a management course for business publishing students. I was surprised to discover a shortage of suitable teaching materials for graduate students about the industry and its problems. I followed the standard research techniques that I learned in graduate school, namely, reading through several years worth of *Folio* magazine articles (the "magazine for magazine managers") and the various publications issued by the Association of Business Publishers (ABP).[13] I also worked my way through several years of articles from major business publications, including the *New York Times*, the *Wall Street Journal, Fortune*, etc. I evaluated all sixteen publishing cases available through the Harvard Business School.

However, I quickly discovered a few interesting facts. Only a few of these Harvard cases dealt with business magazines. Harvard discontinued the circulation of some of the best, most exciting general-interest publishing cases because of lagging sales; and most of the remaining cases were really not that useful.

I did not have enough substantive material; so I decided to research and write my own cases, which would be at the center of all class discussions.

I selected cases because I believed that the most effective form of management training, whether it is done in a college, a continuing education program, or an in-house program, was the case method of instruction.[14] The case method is based on a remarkably simple premise: management is an art and not a science; it is not merely a collection of theories or techniques to be replicated endlessly in the editing room or in advertising meetings. Management is a skill that can be learned, and the best way to learn something is through constant observation and practice. Business cases allowed a student to "manage" a problem or crisis as if he or she were the publisher. This method of teaching had been employed successfully for decades in law and business schools, even medical residents study case histories.

The problem was how to find useful, timely material and then prepare written cases. I began by reviewing all of the statistical data I could find about the general publishing and the highly specific business press industry. I read through studies released by the United States Department of Commerce and its Bureau of the Census and International Trade Administration. Unquestionably, Commerce's statistical studies covering the *U.S. Industrial Outlook*, the *Census of Manufacturers*, *County Business Patterns*, the *Survey of Current Business*, *Economic Indicators*, and the *Annual Survey of Manufacturers* formed the cornerstone of my research on various macroeconomic issues.[15] I also found the *Folio 400* ranking of key business magazines and the invaluable *Business Publication Rates and Data* to be of immense importance in my work.[16] Regrettably, *Folio* has not issued its ranking since 1986, and, apparently because of the steep costs associated with this compilation, it is unlikely that another study will be published.

However, in 1988 the editors of *MagazineWeek*, which started out as a newsletter and then grew into an impressive weekly tabloid, released its highly useful ranking of the top consumer and business periodicals in the United States; and Oxbridge Communications's *National Directory of Magazines*, along with the invaluable reports issued by *Advertising Age*, also provided detailed and useful historical and contemporary information about the diverse magazine industry.[17]

These studies provided me with a detailed overview of real business magazine trends (especially in relation to successful and unsuccessful magazines and various major market niches). I reviewed all of the key management books and articles written by the important people in this field, including Peter Drucker, Theodore Levitt, Robert H. Hayes, William Abernathy, Henry Mintzberg, Michael E. Porter, etc.[18] I prepared a tentative syllabus of topics addressed in these cases, which in the end included corporate strategy; the legal and social context of business; organizational strategy; and human resources management. I was able to review these topics with colleagues in our business school for their input.

This procedure produced, ultimately, some important revisions in the list of topics and the general structure of the course. A second edition of this book will certainly contain useful comments from both students and colleagues about the course.

I also decided to talk with some key industry leaders in the business publications industry. This was unquestionably the most difficult part of the entire research process. As you might imagine, a significant number of publishing executives were not eager to tell me all about their problems just so I could write a book about them; and those individuals who were anxious to inform me about their grand successes and acquisitions were often unable to remember key facts, further proof that the old adage "those who say do not know; and those who know do not say" is indeed accurate.

So I had to change my approach. I was originally trained to be a historian (with a specialty in twentieth century U.S. economic and intellectual history). Because of the problems I confronted, I was forced to develop new research skills that borrowed extensively from the procedures followed by investigative newspaper reporters and private detectives; and I also quickly discovered that I needed the tenacity of a divorce lawyer or a used-car salesperson. "Never take no for an answer" became my modus operandi.

I read through corporate annual reports, quarterly financial statements, "tombstones" (financial display advertisements placed by investment bankers in the business papers), the *Wall Street Journal*, the *New York Times*, all of the available databases, and various U.S. Government industry projections.[19] I talked to as many people as possible to check facts and details. I attended the highly useful *Folio* magazine seminars, something which all professors of publishing really should do each year, as well as trade association meetings.

Ironically, some of the best information about current managerial problems was collected during monthly business luncheons of a professional association of business press editors that I joined. I was elected to this group's board of directors and volunteered to be the luncheon program chairperson; so I selected the topics and the main speakers. These small meetings gave me a tremendous opportunity to discuss in some detail current management and marketing problems with the very editors, assistant editors, and publishers who had to develop reasonable and timely answers to a grand variety of vexing situations.

For example, at one of these luncheons an editor I knew casually mentioned that she was having some difficulty attracting experienced editorial people to her publication's new office, which had just moved out of New York City to New Jersey. I asked about the move, and I discovered that this internationally known publishing firm needed access to the horizon for the satellite transmission of information; the tall buildings in New York City interfered with this type of transmission. Clearly, this was going to be a major area of concern for a significant number of publishing corporations located in congested cities.

So I undertook some research, including several discussions with current and past employees of this company, to ascertain the nature of the problem in terms of finances, real estate issues, highly technical issues related to the satellite transmission of data and electronic databases, human resources, etc.

In the mid-1980s, I worked as a consultant with a variety of New York City agencies in the area of economic development. So I called some people I knew in City Hall and in Albany to determine what New York City and State were doing to address this issue and to keep and/or attract publishing concerns.

The spontaneous remark of a colleague gave me some insight into an intriguing predicament that I turned into a pretty interesting case for class use.

Before I wrote any cases, I established two non-negotiable positions regarding teaching methodology and confidentiality. First, I would try to present usable material in each case. Second, I decided not divulge the real identity of any person or firm in a case. This meant that all of the names, dates, locations, financial data, etc., used in every case were changed. Getting hundreds of names for the three dozen cases in this book was an exciting challenge. I relied on lists of popular song authors, old friends, and, ultimately, baseball players!

After I wrote about a dozen cases, I tried them out in my class. This was unquestionably "trial by fire"; but it was the best approach to ironing out those little wrinkles that appeared inevitably in every case, for example, missing or incomplete financial statements, dates that did not correspond, etc. Student input was invaluable during my numerous rewrites.

When I felt comfortable with these cases, I asked some colleagues to read them for their suggestions. Additional problems were identified, and another round of rewriting took place. However, I swiftly discovered that Murphy was indeed an optimist; if typographical errors could emerge between the time the manuscript was submitted and the appearance of the final printed book, they would and did.

RESEARCHING ARTICLES

About two years ago an acquisitions editor at the *Book Research Quarterly* asked me to address an interesting problem. Were university presses publishing more books in the mid-list book market? If so, why?

When I started my research, I discovered that no clear definition existed for *mid-list books*. I read through *Publishers Weekly*, and I also talked to people in the New York book community to ascertain what this term really meant.

After coming up with an acceptable definition, I then discovered that no one tracked statistics on mid-list books. The Commerce Department monitored trade books; the Book Industry Study Group had detailed data on trade and university press unit and dollar sales. However, no one knew very much about the market and actual (or even estimated) sales revenues.

I visited the Association of American University Presses to see if they knew anything about this alleged phenomenon. Of course they did; but they also did not have any numbers about marketing trends. However, they had a marvelous collection of recent book catalogs from their members, so I read through these catalogs to see what these presses were selling in the spring of 1987. In addition I went through the special "Spring 1987 Announcement" issue of *Publishers Weekly*, and I counted the total number of advertisements placed by university presses (and the number of trade books listed in these ads).

I then reviewed all of the articles published in the 1980s about university presses and their books, authors, and concerns. This led me to a question I never expected to explore, namely, What is the proper domain of scholarly publishing? In addition I had to deal with the economic underpinnings of the academic publishing market and how it interfaced with the general state of the economy in the United States.

All of this exciting and painful research reinforced within me the notion that the scholarly analysis of the publishing industry has to be improved upon if this area of specialization within the mass communications field will ever attract more than a handful of academicians.

At times I became concerned about doing only narrowly focused research. So since 1985 I have been writing a series of feature articles about the printing and publishing industry in the United States for a leading weekly business magazine; and this experience has proven to be invaluable. For example, I discovered rather quickly that the nonacademic reader had a specific orientation and need for timely information and suggestions. So material on, for example, the importation of books into the United States, had to be written and analyzed without the use of any detailed statistical tables. References to intellectual theories or the major mass communications or publishing writers on this topic were of little or no practical use to the reader. In addition, suggestions about this complex, global problem had to be constructed in a pragmatic manner, unless I wanted to lose the interest of my reader. I came to believe that this experience helped me to become a more patient teacher and writer.

SUMMATION

On the basis of my experiences, I have come to believe that the shortage of published materials about this industry and the apparent indifference, whether intentional or not, within the world of publishing toward attempts to write either scholarly books and articles or classroom materials makes it exceptionally difficult to prepare useful teaching documents for student use. Researchers must develop skills more appropriate for the Central Intelligence Agency or M.I. 5. Too often needed data is proprietary or unavailable.

One way to address this critical problem would be to marshall the formidable influence and resources of the leading research universities in Canada, the United States, and Europe (and ultimately the Pacific Rim) and initiate the creation of an international association of publishing studies professors devoted to promoting effective teaching and research about this industry. These institutions of higher learning must also take the initiative and develop effective working relationships with the publishing industry and attack directly and quickly a problem that adversely affects every one of us, namely the inability to transmit accurate, timely knowledge about the publishing industry to the next generation of leaders of this industry. Unless a bold step is taken, we will continue to struggle in both the classroom and the seminar room; and this is hardly an exciting prospect.

NOTES

1. Ted Solotaroff, "The Literary-Industrial Complex," *New Republic,* 8 June 1987. Also see Solotaroff's *A Few Good Voices in My Head* (New York: Harper & Row, 1987).
2. Ibid., 28.
3. Ibid., 28.
4. Theodore Levitt, "Marketing Myopia," *Harvard Business Review* 54 (September-October 1975): 26–37.
5. Alan M. Kantrow, "Why Read Peter Drucker?" *Harvard Business Review* 59 (January-February 1980): 74–82. Also see Tony H. Bonaparte and John E. Flaherty, eds., *Peter Drucker: Contributions to Business Enterprise* (New York: New York University Press, 1971).

6. Peter Drucker, *Management: Tasks, Responsibilities, and Practices* (New York: Harper & Row, 1974). Also see *The Effective Executive* (New York: Harper & Row, 1967), 1–24; *Managing in Turbulent Times* (New York: Harper & Row, 1980), 10–40; *Innovation and Entrepreneurship: Practice and Principles* (New York: Harper & Row, 1985), 243–51; and "Behind Japan's Success," *Harvard Business Review* 59 (January-February 1981): 83–90.

7. Drucker, *Management*, 465–80.

8. Drucker, *Management*, 176, 170–72, 177–79.

9. Edwin Diamond, "The New (Land) Lords of the Press," *New York*, 27 February 1989, 33–38.

10. Drucker, *Management*, 125–28, 530–41, 611.

11. John Tebbel, *Between Covers: The Rise and Transformation of Book Publishing in America* (New York: Oxford University Press, 1987); *A History of Book Publishing in the United States, vol. 1, The Creation of an Industry, 1630–1865* (New York: R. R. Bowker, 1972); *A History of Book Publishing in the United States, vol. 3 The Golden Age between Two Wars, 1920–1940* (New York: R. R. Bowker, 1978). Frank Luther Mott, *A History of American Magazines, vol. 1, 1741– 1850* (Cambridge, Mass.: Harvard University Press, 1966); *A History of American Magazines vol. 2, 1850–1865* (Cambridge, Mass.: Harvard University Press, 1957). David Forsyth, *The Business Press in America: 1750– 1865* (Philadelphia: Chilton, 1964). Kenneth C. Davis, *Two-Bit Culture: The Paperbacking of America* (Boston: Houghton Mifflin, 1984).

12. See Roger Burlingame, *Of Making Many Books* (New York: Scribner's, 1946); *Endless Frontiers: The Story of McGraw-Hill* (New York: Mc-Graw-Hill, 1959); Charles Morgan, *The House of Macmillan, 1842– 1942* (New York: Macmillan, 1944).

13. Some of the more useful articles include William Abbot, "Planning a Trade Ad Campaign," *Folio*, April 1983, 106; Slade R. Metcalf, "Libel: Staying out of Trouble," *Folio*, November 1983, 70–71; Taylor J. Ogdin and Betty Cannes, *Guidelines to Editorial Interviewing, Hiring, and Firing* (New York: Association of Business Publishers, 1982), 1– 10; and David P. Forsyth, *Guidelines to Editorial Research* (New York: Association of Business Publishers, 1980), 1–8.

14. C. Roland Christensen, *Teaching and the Case Method* (Cambridge, Mass.: Harvard Business School, 1987), 7–59.

15. U.S. Department of Commerce, International Trade Administration, *1989 U.S. Industrial Outlook* (Washington, D.C.: GPO, 1988); U.S. Department of Commerce, *Annual Survey of Manufacturers, 1986* (Washington, D.C.: GPO, 1988); U.S. Department of Commerce, *1982 Census of Manufacturers: Newspapers, Periodicals, Books, and Miscellaneous Publishing* (Washington, D.C.: GPO, 1985);

16. *Folio 400, 1986* (Stamford, Conn.: Folio Publishing, 1987), 175–86;

Business Publications Rates and Data (Wilmette, Ill.: Standard Rate and Data Service, 1988).

17. Matthew Manning, ed., *The National Directory of Magazines: 1989* (New York: Oxbridge Communications, 1989); Peter Jacobi, "Judging the Business Press," *Advertising Age*, 16 May 1983, M12–13.

18. Peter Drucker, *Management: Tasks, Responsibilities, and Practices* (New York: Harper & Row, 1974); Robert H. Hayes and William J. Abernathy, "Managing Our Way to Economic Decline," *Harvard Business Review* 58 (July-August 1980): 67–77; Theodore Levitt, "Marketing Myopia," *Harvard Business Review* 53 (September-October 1975): 26–48; Michael E. Porter, *Competitive Strategy* (New York: Free Press, 1980).

19. Examples include annual reports from International Thomson, News Corporation, Harcourt Brace Jovanovich, Capital Cities/ABC, and so forth.

Syllabus and Suggested Readings

The purpose of this book is to provide effective, realistic notes and cases that can be used in an advertising management class in a college or in a continuing education program sponsored by a publishing company or a university.

The purpose of original research is to expand the known frontiers of knowledge, to ask key questions, and to provide answers to problems. Frequently, this approach leads to "reinventing the wheel" rather than writing the definitive study of a selected topic. A review of the current marketing literature indicates clearly that others have gone down this road and made precisely this mistake. In this book I have tried to avoid this pitfall. Accordingly, while the notes and cases in this book can be used alone in a class for discussion purposes, it was written, in all candor, to be used as a *companion* to a standard textbook on marketing or advertising management.

The following syllabus is merely a model that could be followed. While I decided to use Philip Kotler's *Principles of Marketing* (3rd ed., Englewood Cliffs, N.J.: Prentice-Hall, 1986) as the primary text, other textbooks or readings can be substituted.

A SAMPLE SYLLABUS

1. Introduction to Marketing and Advertising in the Business Publishing Industry
   (a) Social Foundations of Marketing
   (b) The Marketing Management Process
   (c) Strategic Planning
   (d) Marketing Research
   (e) The Marketing Environment
   (f) Organizational Markets
   (g) Readings:
      (1) Kotler, chapters 1, 2, 3, 4, 5, 8.
      (2) Theodore Levitt, "Marketing Myopia," *Harvard Business Review* 53 (September-October 1975): 26–48.
      (3) Greco, chapters 1, 2 (including all seventeen cases), 3, and the following cases in 6: *Journal of Industrial Accident Prevention* A, B, and C; *Oxbridge Journal, Green's Book News,* the Stein Publishing Company A and B, *U.S. Wine,* and *The Mall.*
      (4) Robert H. Hayes and William J. Abernathy, "Managing Our Way to Economic Decline" *Harvard Business Review* 58 (July-August 1980): 67–77.
2. Measuring and Forecasting
   (a) Market Segmentation
   (b) Readings:
      (1) Kotler, chapters 9, 10.
      (2) Greco, chapter 4.
3. The Marketing and Promotion Mix
   (a) Strategies
   (b) Sales Promotions
   (c) Publicity
   (d) Sales Management
   (e) Readings:
      (1) Kotler, chapters 17, 18, 19.
      (2) Greco, chapter 6 (*Clinton Construction Products,* the Morrison Publishing Company, *Olivares Supermarket Digest, Carew's Hardware Weekly* A and B).

4. Competitive Marketing Strategies
   (a) Controlling Marketing Programs
   (b) International Marketing
   (c) Readings:
       (1) Kotler, chapters 20, 21, 22.
       (2) Greco, chapter 5.
5. The Legal and Social Context of Marketing
   (a) Readings:
       (1) Kotler, chapter 24.
       (2) Greco, chapter 6 (*Grocery Store Business, Fosse's Industrial Purchasing Digest, Fowler's Beverage Times, McRae Business Times, Domingo's Fashion News* A and B, and *Retaining Industry News.*
       (3) Sarah Hardesty and Nehama Jacobs, *Success and Betrayal: The Crisis of Women in Corporate America* (New York: Watts, 1986).

ONE

The Publishing Industry in the United States

INTRODUCTION

This chapter was prepared to provide the reader with an overview of all aspects of the publishing industry in the United States. In this way anyone seeking a clear understanding of the existing advertisement management functions within the world of business publications will comprehend the critically important role business periodicals play within the U.S. economy and the highly specialized world of magazine publishing.

For the purposes of this book, the term *publishing* will refer specifically to books of all kinds, business and consumer periodicals (including scholarly and professional and technical journals), electronic databases and CD-ROM products, and miscellaneous publishing (for example, annuals, directories, loose-leaf supplements, etc.). Newspapers will be excluded from all analyses, unless specifically identified and addressed; periodicals issued in tabloid format will be considered magazines, which is the generally accepted view of the industry toward these publications.

Table 1.1 / The Periodical Industry in the United States: 1967–1982 (in millions of dollars)

Category	1967	1972	1977	1982	Percent Change 1967–1982
Establishments	2,510.0	2,456.0	2,863.0	3,328.0	+32.6
Employees	79,100.0	66,500.0	69,900.0	94,000.0	+18.8
Payroll	$ 633.7	708.5	1,019.8	1,986.1	+213.4
Value Added by					
Manufacturing	$1,868.7	2,109.9	3,762.7	6,910.9	+269.8
Value of					
Shipments	$3,095.9	3,510.6	6,056.5	11,478.0	+270.7
New Capital					
Expenditures	$ 58.0	56.8	78.9	194.8	+235.9

Source: U.S. Department of Commerce, Bureau of the Census, *1982 Census of Manufactures* (Washington, D.C.: USGPO, 1984), 27A-6.

THE CHANGING WORLD OF PUBLISHING

Researchers interested in obtaining detailed historical data must rely on the *Census of Manufactures,* issued every five years. The following data was obtained from these sources. However, an excellent source of publishing industry information is the *U.S. Industrial Outlook,* issued each year by the United States Department of Commerce.[1]

The first three tables (1.1, 1.2, and 1.3) outline general developments in the publishing industry between 1967 and 1982; historical data on electronic databases and CD-ROM products for the 1960s and 1970s and most of the 1980s is not available from the United States Department of Commerce.

Table 1.1 deals with the complex periodical industry during the years 1967–1982, a period when this part of the publishing industry posted an impressive 32.6 percent growth in the number of establishments, a strong 18.8 percent increase in the number of employees, and a decisive 270.7 percent surge in shipments.

Between 1967 and 1982, the number of book-publishing establishments grew at a strong 108.4 percent pace while increasing the work force by a modest 29.0 percent. Dollar shipments remained

Table 1.2 / The Book Industry in the United States: 1967–1982 (in millions of dollars)

Category	1967	1972	1977	1982	Percent Change 1967–1982
Establishments	1,022.0	1,205.0	1,745.0	2,130.0	+108.4
Employees	52,000.0	57,100.0	59,500.0	67,100.0	+29.0
Payroll	$ 389.9	557.7	830.2	1,327.3	+240.4
Value Added by Manufacturing	$1,456.6	1,935.8	3,261.9	5,291.5	+263.3
Value of Shipments	$2,134.8	2,856.8	4,793.9	7,740.0	+262.6
New Capital Expenditures	$ 55.1	48.4	79.8	174.1	+216.0

Source: U.S. Department of Commerce, Bureau of the Census, *1982 Census of Manufactures* (Washington, D.C.: USGPO, 1984), 27A-6.

behind the periodical industry, although its impressive 262.6 percent increase was a harbinger of good times in the late 1980s.

The ubiquitous miscellaneous publishing industry lagged significantly behind both the periodical and book industries in total dollar shipments; however, this niche's truly remarkable 374.4 percent growth in shipments indicated that it had a bright future.

Table 1.3 / The Miscellaneous Publishing Industry in the United States: 1967–1982 (in millions of dollars)

Category	1967	1972	1977	1982	Percent Change 1967–1982
Establishments	1,493.0	2,041.0	2,352.0	2,057.0	+37.8
Employees	31,100.0	38,800.0	42,100.0	45,300.0	+45.7
Value Added by Manufacturing	$ 417.5	775.8	1,290.7	1,958.2	+369.0
Value of Shipments	$ 605.3	1,070.2	1,850.9	2,871.3	+374.4
New Capital Expenditures	$ 10.0	22.7	39.1	67.1	+571.0

Source: U.S. Department of Commerce, Bureau of the Census, *1982 Census of Manufactures* (Washington, D.C.: USGPO, 1984), 27A-6.

Table 1.4 / The Periodical Industry: 1987–1990 (in millions of dollars)

Item	1987	1988	1989	1990	Percent Change 1987–1990
Value of Shipments	$17,559	19,149	20,726	22,168	+26.2
Total Employment	111,000	116,000	122,000	127,000	+14.4
Dollar Value of Imports	$ 107	108	123	142	+32.7
Dollar Value of Exports	$ 446	496	431	483	+8.3

Source: U.S. Department of Commerce, International Trade Administration, *1990 U.S. Industrial Outlook*, (Washington, D.C.: USGPO, 1990), 48–1 through 48–13.

The following table (1.4), covering the years 1987 through 1990, provides an overview of recent trends in the periodical industry. Periodicals' record in shipments was rather uneven during these years. They etched out a strong 9.1 percent increase in total shipments between 1987 and 1988; however, shipments slipped to an 8.2 percent pace in 1988–1989 and a 7.0 percent rate between 1989 and 1990. Steep declines in total advertising allocations clearly adversely affected this industry.

Books, on the other hand, generated better growth rates during this same time period (as outlined in Table 1.5). Between 1987 and 1988, this niche achieved an impressive 8.9 percent growth in shipments; the following year they surged to 10.4 percent, dropping to a still-strong 9.3 percent pace in 1989–1990. As for the

Table 1.5 / The Book Industry 1987–1990 (in millions of dollars)

Item	1987	1988	1989	1990	Percent Change 1987–1990
Value of Shipments	$11,642	12,680	14,000	15,300	+31.4
Total Employment	70,300	71,500	74,000	75,500	+7.4
Dollar Value of Imports	$ 744	801	760	795	+6.9
Dollar Value of Exports	$ 739	925	1,090	1,250	+69.1

Source: U.S. Department of Commerce, International Trade Administration, *1990 U.S. Industrial Outlook*, (Washington, D.C.: USGPO, 1990), 48–1 through 48–13.

Table 1.6 / The Miscellaneous Publishing Industry: 1984–1988 (in millions of dollars)

Item	1984	1985	1986	1987	1988	Percent Change 1984–1988
Value of Shipments	$3,223	4,437	4,995	5,620	6,175	+91.6
Total Employment	42,000	52,000	52,700	57,300	60,000	+42.9
Value of Imports	38	51	63	66	70	+86.8
Value of Exports	22	19	17	12	15	−31.8

Source: U.S. Department of Commerce, International Trade Administration, *U.S. Industrial Outlook 1988* (Washington, D.C.: USGPO, 1988), 29–11.

critically important export arena, the book industry achieved tremendous successes during this three-year period. In 1987–1988 exports grew at a blistering 25.2 percent rate, dropping to more normal rates of 17.8 in 1988–1989 and 14.7 percent in 1989–1990.

Periodicals were able to generate an impressive amount of cash, much of it in the form of paid-up subscriptions; the total value of shipments grew at an impressive 26.2 percent rate between 1987 and 1990.

Yet in spite of these positive numbers, a critical review of key import-export data revealed a structural weakness that could haunt the magazine industry. Between 1987 and 1990 there was a gigantic 32.7 percent increase in imports; exports grew at a languid rate of 8.3 percent. Aside from contributing to the nation's embarrassing balance-of-trade fiasco, market share for domestic magazines was lost to foreign titles, a situation clearly warranting additional research by the periodical industry.

Material on the miscellaneous publishing industry for the years after 1988 was rather difficult to obtain. Yet the Department of Commerce's studies indicated clearly that this niche posted impressive growth rates in total value of shipments and employment between 1984 and 1988. The following table (1.6) illustrates this strong pattern of growth.

Table 1.7 / Operating Ratios in the Periodical Industry in the United States: 1967–1982 (in millions of dollars)

Operating Ratios	1967	1972	1977	1982	Percent Change 1967–1982
Payroll per Employee	$8,011	10,654	14,587	21,129	+163.7
Cost of Materials as a Percent of the Value of Shipments	40	40	38	40	n/a
Value Added per Employee	$23,625	31,728	53,830	73,520	+211.2

Source: U.S. Department of Commerce, Bureau of the Census, *1982 Census of Manufactures* (Washington, D.C. USGPO, 1984), 27A-7 through 27A-8.

Did operating ratios vary for employees in these three niches? The following three tables (1.7, 1.8, and 1.9) provide insight on this issue.[2]

While periodicals consistently paid higher average wages, this industry lagged behind the book industry in the critically impor-

Table 1.8 / Operating Ratios in the Book Industry in the United States: 1967–1982 (in millions of dollars)

Operating Ratios	1967	1972	1977	1982	Percent Change 1967–1982
Payroll per Employee	$ 7,498	9,767	13,953	19,781	+163.8
Cost of Materials as a Percent of the Value of Shipments	36	34	32	31	n/a
Value Added Per Employee	$28,012	33,902	54,822	78,860	+181.5

Source: U.S. Department of Commerce, Bureau of the Census, *1982 Census of Manufactures* (Washington, D.C.: USGPO, 1984), 27–A7 and 27A-8.

Table 1.9 / Operating Ratios in the Miscellaneous Publishing Industry in the United States: 1967–1982 (in millions of dollars)

Operating Ratios	1967	1972	1977	1982	Percent Change 1967–1982
Payroll per Employee	$ 6,347	8,536	11,948	15,583	+145.6
Cost of Materials as a Percent of the Value of Shipments	30	28	31	32	N/A
Value Added per Employee	$13,424	19,995	30,658	43,227	+220.0

Source: U.S. Department of Commerce, Bureau of the Census, *1982 Census of Manufactures* (Washington, D.C.: USGPO, 1984), 27–A7 and 27A-8.

tant "[dollar] value added by each employee" category (see Table 1.7).

In Table 1.8 it is clear that the book industry's cost of materials as a percentage of the total value of shipments ran below those of the periodical industry but higher than those recorded by miscellaneous publishing.

The next table (1.9) reveals the important fact that the average payroll for miscellaneous publishing employees was well below that of both the book and periodical industries, a trend that could adversely affect the ability of publishers in this niche to attract and keep qualified employees.

It is important to have an understanding of the geographical areas with large concentrations of publishing activity. The leading states, in terms of the total number of establishments, employment, annual payroll, and the total value of shipments in this product category are listed in the following three tables (1.10, 1.11, and 1.12; based on the 1982 *Census of Manufactures*).[3] "N/A" indicates that data was not available.

In Table 1.10 one can see the overwhelming superiority enjoyed by New York State, which is the unquestioned center of the periodical industry in the United States. Illinois was second, while California was a distant third.

Table 1.10 / The Publishing Industry and Major States: Periodicals 1982 (in millions of dollars)

State	Total Number of Establishments	Total Number of Employees	Annual Payroll	Value of Shipments Percent of Total U.S.
California	455	7,400	$ 146.4	7.4
Connecticut	92	1,600	33.1	1.4
Florida	182	1,800	30.5	1.5
Illinois	217	10,700	228.5	8.6
Massachusetts	115	2,800	65.3	2.3
Michigan	78	1,100	19.7	1.2
New Jersey	109	2,500	46.2	1.9
New York	603	34,800	853.4	47.9
Ohio	86	3,100	56.4	2.5
Pennsylvania	109	4,500	80.3	6.1
Texas	174	2,200	42.4	1.6
U.S.A.	3,238	94,000	1,986.1	—

Source: U.S. Department of Commerce, Bureau of the Census, *1982 Census of Manufactures* (Washington, D.C.: USGPO, 1984), 27A-10 through 27A-14.

The book industry (as indicated in Table 1.11) was totally entrenched in New York in terms of the number of employees (with 20.6 percent of the nation's total), annual payroll (with a staggering 34.6 percent of the U.S. total), and the value of shipments (43.9 percent).

New York also dominated the miscellaneous publishing niche (Table 1.12) with a 21.1 percent share; California trailed with 10.4 percent and Illinois was 10.3 percent.

NEW YORK CITY

A review of the material contained in the above tables indicates conclusively that more periodical publishing was done in 1982 in New York State than anywhere else in the United States. New York City held a commanding 19 percent share of the country's establishments; and its record in the other three major niches was truly staggering, with 37 percent of the individuals toiling in this

Table 1.11 / The Publishing Industry and Major States: Books 1982 (in millions of dollars)

State	Total Number of Establishments	Total Number of Employees	Annual Payroll	Value of Shipments Percent of Total U.S.
California	329	5,300	$ 94.1	5.9
Connecticut	57	1,300	30.0	1.5
Florida	78	600	8.8	0.6
Illinois	137	6,600	136.8	11.7
Massachusetts	109	4,400	90.5	7.4
Michigan	35	400	5.8	0.7
New Jersey	109	4,900	97.7	5.2
New York	438	21,900	459.3	43.9
Ohio	44	4,100	82.9	4.5
Pennsylvania	73	2,500	45.6	2.7
Texas	87	1,200	20.9	1.1
U.S.A.	2,130	67,000	1,327.3	—

Source: U.S. Department of Commerce, Bureau of the Census, *1982 Census of Manufactures* (Washington, D.C.: USGPO, 1984), 27A-10 through 27A-14.

industry, 43 percent of the total annual payroll, and a "Ruthian" 48 percent market share of total shipments!

Citizens from Chicago, Boston, and Los Angeles might view their own geographical area as the "hub" of the publishing universe. However, an extensive analysis of this data reveals the fact that this tiny piece of land legally known as New York County but commonly called Manhattan was at the very heart of the entire magazine industry in 1982 in this nation. This is made clear by three intriguing statistics: it held an overwhelming 83 percent market share of all magazine publishing jobs in New York State, a blistering 87 percent of the total annual payroll, and an impressive 65 percent of the state's periodical establishments.

How does this magazine industry compare with other industries operating in Manhattan, New York City's principal county? After all, Manhattan is the home of a significant number of major corporations. Is magazine publishing overshadowed by the showy real estate industry, large, attractive retail chain stores, or the

Table 1.12 / The Publishing Industry and Major States:
Miscellaneous Publishing 1982 (in millions of dollars)

State	Total Number of Establishments	Total Number of Employees	Annual Payroll	Value of Shipments Percent of Total U.S.
California	310	5,400	$78.5	10.4
Connecticut	45	1,100	15.6	2.2
Florida	103	2,100	31.6	3.1
Illinois	109	2,700	46.7	10.3
Massachusetts	50	600	8.2	1.2
Michigan	71	2,400	40.1	5.4
New Jersey	73	1,800	28.0	3.4
New York	326	9,600	174.2	21.1
Ohio	53	1,200	17.5	2.4
Pennsylvania	64	n/a	n/a	n/a
Texas	100	n/a	n/a	n/a
U.S.A.	2,057	45,300	705.9	—

Source: U.S. Department of Commerce, Bureau of the Census, *1982 Census of Manufactures* (Washington, D.C.: USGPO, 1984), 27A-10 through 27A-14.

gigantic credit service and reporting agencies that so greatly influence the financial service component of this nation's economy?

A detailed analysis of the U.S. Department of Commerce's *County Business Patterns, 1986: New York* reveals the magnitude of the publishing industry in this urban center. The following table (1.13), based on the rankings of total annual payroll as calculated by the author, outlines clearly the significant economic role played by periodical publishing in Manhattan.[4] Although ranked sixth in terms of the largest number of establish ments, publishing paid the third highest average salary, $34,050, trailing only the high-paying but cyclical securities industry's ($67,765) and the legal services component of Manhattan's economy (with $37,170). The other three industries ranked in the top six seriously lagged behind publishing. Banking paid an average of $28,638, health services hovered at the $23,331 mark, and the retail sales industry, loaded with panache, trailed badly with an average annual wage of $16,391.

Obviously magazine publishing has carved out an impressive

Table 1.13 / Top Twenty-Eight Major Industries in Manhattan: 1986 (in millions of dollars)

Rank	Industry	Number of Employees	Annual Payroll	Number of Establishments
1	Security, Commodity Brokers, and Services Banking	131,410	$ 8,905	2,184
2	Banking	145,506	4,167	1,145
3	Retail Trade	197,675	3,240	16,584
4	Health Services	106,083	2,475	4,989
5	Legal Services	58,139	2,161	3,759
6	Publishing	62,875	2,141	1,114
7	Insurance Carriers	65,154	2,098	685
8	Miscellaneous Services	62,278	1,942	3,660
9	Real Estate Services	72,834	1,809	9,792
10	Advertising Agencies	41,003	1,648	1,167
11	Educational Services	64,814	1,145	714
12	Credit Agencies Other Than Banks	27,323	1,001	422
13	Telephone Communication	28,636	915	106
14	Eating and Drinking Places	74,565	912	5,369
15	Radio and Television Broadcasting	17,606	875	158
16	Membership Organizations	41,006	832	2,122
17	Holding and Other Investment Offices	16,449	740	1,175
18	Women's and Misses' Outerwear	36,816	709	1,486
19	Personnel Supply Services	47,572	687	1,005
20	Motion Pictures	24,064	631	1,468
21	Services to Buildings	30,915	629	349
22	Amusement and Recreation Services	22,044	598	1,920
23	Machinery, Equipment and Supplies	17,347	580	1,055
24	Miscellaneous Retail	30,430	542	4,595
25	Social Services	36,850	538	1,138
26	Computer and Data Processing	15,303	509	758

Table 1.13 / Continued

Rank	Industry	Number of Employees	Annual Payroll	Number of Establishments
27	Hotels and Lodging Places	26,555	514	344
28	General Contractors and Operative Builders	14,935	514	649
Manhattan's Totals		2,027,647	60,785	102,522
Manhattan's Average Wage			$29,978	

Source: U.S. Department of Commerce, Bureau of the Census, *County Business Patterns 1986: New York* (Washington, D.C.: USGPO, 1986), 122-31.

niche in the constantly changing business battlefield that is New York City.

PUBLISHING IN THE UNITED STATES'S ECONOMY

How do the various components of the publishing industry compare with other sectors in the United States's economy? The U.S. Department of Commerce monitors economic and business activity in this nation, and according to the detailed data contained in the *1989 U.S. Industrial Outlook*, publishing's track record in the 1980s was rather impressive in terms of its growth rate, as the following two tables (1.14 and 1.15) indicate.[5]

Table 1.14 reveals the strength of the miscellaneous publishing industry.

Of special interest in Table 1.15 is the impressive track record posted by electronic databases, which overshadowed the gains of several key components of the U.S. economy, including entertainment, transportation, and equipment leasing, always a favorite of individuals interested in taking advantage of the U.S. income tax code.

Publishing is considered to be a "manufacturing nondurable industry" by the U.S. Department of Commerce (Standard Industrial Code SIC 27). When compared with other manufacturing

Table 1.14 / U.S. Industries with the Greatest Rate of Change:
1984–1989

Rank	Industry	Greatest Percentage Rate of Growth
1	Semiconductor Devices	+22.6
2	Missiles/Space Vehicles	+14.1
3	Particleboard	+11.0
4	Paper Industry Machinery	+10.7
5	Miscellaneous Publishing	+9.3
6	Wines and Brandies	+9.2
7	Surgical and Medical Equipment	+9.1
8	Aircraft Engines/Parts	+8.9
9	Engineer/Science Equipment	+8.9
10	Metal-Forming Machines	+8.6

Source: U.S. Department of Commerce, International Trade Administration, *1989 U.S. Industrial Outlook* (Washington, D.C.: USGPO, 1989), 17–20.

Table 1.15 / U.S. Industrial Growth Rates: 1988–1989

Rank	Industry	Unit of Measure	1988–1989 Percent Change
1	Space Commercialization	Revenues	+50.0
2	Computer Software	Receipts	+24.0
3	Electronic Databases	Revenues	+20.0
4	Computer Professional Services	Revenues	+15.5
5	Prerecorded Music	Manufacturers' Value	+15.0
6	Operations and Maintenance Security	Expenditures	+15.0
7	Airlines	Revenues	+14.5
8	Data Processing	Revenues	+13.0
9	Equipment Leasing	Equipment Cost Added	+12.0
10	Operations and Maintenance Airlines	Expenditures	+11.5

Source: U.S. Department of Commerce, International Trade Administration, *1989 U.S. Industrial Outlook* (Washington, D.C.: USGPO, 1989), 17–20.

Table 1.16 / U.S. Manufacturing Industries: Changes in Employment and Shipments, 1972–1986 (in billions of dollars)

Industry	Changes in Employment	Industry Shipments
Food and Kindred Products	− 160,000	$193.5
Tobacco Manufacturers	− 20,000	13.2
Textile Mill Products	− 308,000	27.3
Apparel	− 352,000	30.1
Lumber and Wood Products	− 72,000	34.3
Furniture and Fixtures	+ 5,000	21.8
Paper and Allied Products	− 31,000	69.6
Printing and Publishing	+ 320,000	88.4
Chemicals/Chemical Products	− 35,000	139.7
Petroleum/Coal Products	− 15,000	96.2
Rubber/Plastic Products	+ 124,000	52.5
Leather and Products	− 144,000	2.0
Stone, Clay, and Glass	− 109,000	35.7
Primary Metals	− 453,000	47.2
Fabricated Metal	− 74,000	86.2
Machinery, Excluding Electric	+ 35,000	142.7
Electrical/Electronic Equipment	+ 281,000	142.9
Transportation Equipment	+ 51,000	219.1
Instruments	+ 132,000	46.4
Miscellaneous Manufacturing Equipment	− 120,000	15.0
All Manufacturing Totals	− 946,000	1,503.8

Source: U.S. Department of Commerce, International Trade Administration, *1989 U.S. Industrial Outlook* (Washington, D.C.: USGPO, 1989), 21.

industries, publishing's positive achievements during the period 1972–1986 were truly remarkable. During these years the United States sustained two major recessions (1973–1975 and 1981–1982) and a severe, debilitating period of high inflation rates and equally grotesque interest rates. The following table (1.16) outlines publishing's record.[6]

However, there are some major problems with this data. The Commerce Department groups many industrial units into exceptionally large categories. Consequently, all publishing operations (including newspapers) are combined with printing activities, which is unquestionably a manufacturing operation. Publishing really should be classified by the Commerce Department in the service sector since only a handful of publishing companies print, that is manufacture, their final product.

This classification procedure makes it exceptionally difficult for the reader to obtain a concrete overview of the real role played by periodicals, books, and miscellaneous publishing in the U.S. economy. However, this author's calculations indicate that publishing accounts for 53 percent of the total value of shipments in this consolidated category; and this percentage has remained essentially constant for the last ten years. This knowledge should assist the reader in evaluating the following data.

Nevertheless, some analysts might argue that even partial data illuminates the picture better than no data at all. With this in mind, the following table (1.16), based on the SIC code hierarchy, is presented.

CONSUMER MAGAZINES

Consumer magazine publishing is a large, financially successful, and dynamic component of the diverse publishing industry in the United States. A review of key statistical indices indicates clearly that most Americans primarily purchase and read those ubiquitous weekly consumer mass market periodicals that are easily available at unusually high retail prices at newsstands and supermarket checkout counters throughout this nation, plus the vintage dated ones found in the offices of the nation's dentists. Deeply discounted subscriptions for consumer magazines are also readily available; and the annual early January "publishing clearing house" parade of hundreds of millions of direct-marketing (mail) pieces that seem to engulf every known bastion of civilization certainly sells hundreds of thousands of consumer magazine subscriptions in every town and village in this nation.

Consumer periodicals, which range from the sophisticated *New Yorker* to *Yachting*, report on the ever-changing American landscape. Clearly, consumer periodicals have had a major impact upon the cultural, educational, political, and social history of the United States. While a number of media critics have analyzed the role played by consumer magazines in our society, additional scholarly research on this aspect of consumer magazine publishing is critically needed.

BEST-SELLING PERIODICALS

According to a 1988 Publishers Information Bureau (PIB) list of the *Top 50 PIB Publications* in the United States, only two general business publications (*Fortune* and *Business Week*) were on their "Top Ten" magazine list. Advertising linage figures for 1988, which appeared in *Advertising Age* (the business publication serving the eclectic, highly charged, and creative advertising industry) essentially confirmed these findings. The definitive rankings available in the 1988 *MagazineWeek 500*, which is similar in both approach and content to *Fortune* magazine's ranking of the five hundred largest industrial corporations in the United States, is an exceptionally important, reliable barometer of the state of the entire magazine industry. The following table (1.17) lists the top forty consumer magazines in the United States.[7]

Are there strong regional magazine-reading preferences in the United States? Young & Rubicam, the largest advertising agency in the U.S., investigated this question in a major study; and, when *TV Guide* and *Reader's Digest* were excluded in their research study, the results were absolutely intriguing.[8]

While it could be argued that only a sociologist or a cultural historian could make any sense out of these findings, a review of the most popular magazines in some of the largest cities in this nation clearly sheds some light on the intellectual predilections of an interesting cross-section of Americana. After all, it must be meaningful that *International Combat*, rarely found in supermarkets or newsstands, makes the top five list in both Los Angeles and Houston, that *The Star* dominates Pittsburgh, and that *Penthouse* sells so well in Minneapolis.

The findings of the Young and Rubicam study, which list the five top-selling magazines in each city, are listed in Table 1.18.

BUSINESS PERIODICALS: A WORKING DEFINITION

What is a realistic working definition of the term *business magazine* or *business publication?* I believe that a "business publication"

Table 1.17 / Top Forty Consumer Periodicals in the United States: 1988 (in millions of dollars)

Rank	Publication	Total Circulation	Total Revenues	Percent of Total Revenues of Top Forty Periodicals
1	TV Guide	16,955,943	$945.50	12.7
2	Time	5,026,183	476.60	6.4
3	People	3,434,396	456.99	6.2
4	Sports Illustrated	3,536,562	402.42	5.4
5	Readers Digest	17,126,474	328.09	4.4
6	Newsweek	3,353,267	263.15	3.5
7	Better Homes & Gardens	8,237,909	228.18	3.1
8	National Geographic Magazine	10,590,083	226.53	3.1
9	Business Week	945,094	221.56	3.0
10	Good Housekeeping	5,166,060	216.12	2.9
11	Family Circle	5,984,996	211.84	2.9
12	Parade	33,354,000	205.51	2.8
13	National Enquirer	4,298,820	202.68	2.7
14	Woman's Day	5,373,857	182.58	2.5
15	US News & World Report	2,439,501	163.48	2.2
16	Cosmopolitan	2,940,331	162.44	2.2
17	Ladies' Home Journal	5,307,510	158.57	2.1
18	Redbook	4,016,711	155.47	2.1
19	Star	3,660,060	151.53	2.0
20	PC Magazine	597,394	151.41	2.0
21	McCall's	5,148,809	140.56	1.9
22	Playboy	3,647,075	135.07	1.8
23	Forbes	793,550	126.43	1.7
24	Fortune	724,822	122.70	1.7
25	Money	1,951,300	116.33	1.6
26	Vogue	1,233,755	115.71	1.6
27	Glamour	2,194,225	112.83	1.5
28	Penthouse	2,093,994	111.72	1.5

Table 1.17 / Continued

Rank	Publication	Total Circulation	Total Revenues	Percent of Total Revenues of Top Forty Periodicals
29	New York Times Magazine	1,589,290	102.34	1.4
30	Southern Living	2,309,661	92.05	1.2
31	Rolling Stone	1,333,490	83.91	1.1
32	Modern Maturity	19,562,539	81.75	1.1
33	USA Weekend	15,080,059	80.93	1.1
34	Smithsonian	2,419,747	79.23	1.1
35	Parents Magazine	1,880,946	75.62	1.0
36	Golf Digest	1,359,829	70.72	1.0
37	Bride's Magazine	444,574	68.33	1.0
38	Travel & Leisure	1,232,514	67.23	1.0
39	Woman's World	1,424,707	67.12	1.0
40	Globe	1,522,027	65.89	0.9

Source: "MagazineWeek 500" *MagazineWeek*, 23 October 1989, 26.

is a "magazine" written by and for specialists in their field. In reality it need not be printed, audited, or issued by a tax-paying legal entity. It can appear annually, semiannually, only during trade shows or annual conventions, or even irregularly, such as every other year.

The vast majority of all business publications are issued in typical magazine format (9" x 11"). Yet a significant number are printed in tabloid form (newspaper style; ranging from 10" x 13 1/2" up to 11" x 14"). Others appear using the scholarly or professional journal format (6" x 9" up to 9" x 12"). Ironically, publications issued in these myriad of forms are called "books" by American industry insiders.

Some of the most successful and notable business publications are released in loose-leaf form as supplements for the accounting, legal, and medical-healthcare professions. Other key publications appear only once a year or on an irregular schedule as annuals, directories, buyers' guides, or special supplements (often for a

Table 1.18 / Regional Magazine Preferences: 1988

City	Top Five Consumer Periodicals
Boston	*New Yorker, Atlantic Monthly, Gourmet, Yachting, Ski*
New York	*New York, Natural History, New Yorker, Atlantic Monthly, Business Week*
Philadelphia	*W, Colonial Homes, Essence, M, Boating*
Washington	*Navy Times, Federal Times, Smithsonian, Black Enterprise, Army Times*
Pittsburgh	*Star, National Examiner, Parade, Dirt Rider, Grit*
Detroit	*Detroit Monthly, Essence, Jet, Black Enterprise, Ebony*
Chicago	*Jet, Essence, Venture, Business Month, Ebony*
Minneapolis-St. Paul	*Outdoor Life, Nation's Business, Penthouse, Sports Afield, Field & Stream*
Kansas City	*Army Times, Weight Watchers, Scouting Federal Times, Boy's Life*
Miami	*Skin Diver, Motor Boating & Sailing, Boating, W, Vogue*
Atlanta	*Southern Accents, Southern Living, World Tennis, Black Enterprise, Jet*
Houston	*Southern Living, Food & Wine, Travel & Leisure, Southern Accents, International Combat*
Denver	*Outside, Skiing, Ski, Back-Packer, World Tennis*
Salt Lake City	*Scouting, Boy's Life, Skiing, Outside, Ski*
Los Angeles	*Sea, Sunset, International Combat, Architectural Digest, Vanity Fair*
San Francisco	*Sunset, Sea, Bon Appetit, Gourmet, Vanity Fair*
Seattle-Tacoma	*Sea, Sunset, INC., Navy Times, Army Times*

Source: "Ideas & Trends: Who Buys . . . *Navy Times? Dirt Rider?" New York Times,* 29 October 1989, section 4, 29.

convention, trade show, or annual conference). Still others are never printed; they are available only through computer databases, CD-ROM discs, or on floppy discs (both the 5 1/4" and the more handy 3 1/2" types).

In June 1988 this author conducted an exhaustive analysis of all of the publications listed in the 24 May 1988 issue of Standard Rate and Data's (SRDS) *Business Publications Rates and Data,* part 1.[9] While 4,143 different publications (excluding "action packs") were cataloged, only 1,682 (40.6 percent) of them were audited. The remaining 2,461 titles (59.9 percent) were unaudited, and, consequently, not eligible to join the Association of Business Publishers (ABP), America's most important business press trade association. ABP also insists that a member firm must be a taxpaying legal entity, thereby excluding a plethora of publications issued by universities or nonprofit organizations. For example, one title excluded from membership in ABP is the *New England Journal of Medicine*, the principal scholarly publication in the medical-healthcare field in the United States (and one of the three most influential ones in the world), with a weekly paid circulation of 223,420. This journal has been published continuously since 1826 by the Massachusetts Medical Society (a nonprofit medical society).

BUSINESS MAGAZINE CATEGORIES

On the basis of this extensive review of existing business publications, this author believes that there are nine distinct categories of business publications issued in the United States: (1) trade [e.g., *Advertising Age* or *Folio*], (2) business [*American Banker, Medical Economics, Printing News East,* and *CableVision*], (3) professional [the *Chronicle of Higher Education* or *Corporate Accounting*], (4) scholarly [*Book Research Quarterly, Scholarly Publishing, Journalism Quarterly,* or the *Journal of Communication*], (5) loose-leaf supplements [issued by the Thomson Corporation, Prentice-Hall, Commerce Clearing House, Matthew Bender, or the Bureau of National Affairs; areas served include medical, accounting, legal, or U.S. Internal Revenue Service tax series], (6) newsletters or bulletins [the *Bulletin of the Association for Business Communication*], (7) directories, annuals, buyers' guides, or special supplements [*Printing Impressions Master Catalog, Computers in Accounting: Tax Prep '89*], (8) electronic databases or services [InFiNet, Nexis, or Lexis], and (9) in-house periodicals [*NYU Today*].

THE NUMBER OF BUSINESS PUBLICATIONS

The 4,143 business publications listed in the 24 May 1988 issue of *Business Publications Rates and Data*, part 1 (which is owned by Robert Maxwell's Macmillan) were placed into 180 separate groups. The author sorted through all of these titles and determined the fifteen largest categories of business periodicals, which listed 1,793 books (43.28 percent of all the titles in SRDS). The results are listed in Table 1.19.

Any reader of Frank Luther Mott's definitive five-volume *History of American Magazines*, or any of the other important studies of this industry, will rather quickly perceive the fact that magazine publications have a distinct lifespan. Each month SRDS reports on the birth and death of literally dozens of business publications in this nation.

Again on the basis of a review of SRDS, this researcher discovered that in June 1988 thirty-one new publications were issued and eight terminated operations. The following month an additional thirty-seven new business titles appeared and eight more went out of business. The net result was that the total number of business publications listed in the 24 July 1988 issue of SRDS was 4,195, up from 4,143 (+1.26 percent) in May 1988.

However, in reality no one knows how many periodicals (business or consumer) are issued each year in the United States. The U.S. Department of Commerce's Bureau of the Census and the International Trade Administration collect and analyze more data than most agencies in this nation, if not the world. Yet even the Commerce Department relies on *Gale's Directory of Publications* (a commercial directory of periodical titles) in Commerce's definitive *1989 U.S. Industrial Outlook. Gale's* (which is published by the Thomson Corporation) listed 11,593 different magazine titles in 1987, up 250 magazines (+2.2 per cent) over 1986.[10]

Yet another close analysis of the May 1988 issue of SRDS revealed that many titles, perhaps in the hundreds in several key categories, were not listed, including (1) publications issued by most of America's scholarly and professional societies and organizations; for example, the widely read *Journal of American History*, the *American Historical Review*, and the *Journal of Communica-*

Table 1.19 / Business Magazine Categories: 1988

SRDS Category Number	Category	Total Number of Business Publications	Number of Audited Titles	Number of Unaudited Titles
87	Medical-Surgical	484	129	355
5A	Automatic Data Systems	164	91	73
20A	Business: Metro, State, and Regional	143	91	52
1	Advertising and Marketing	109	54	55
38	Education	104	13	91
20	Business	96	47	49
41	Engineering and Construction	91	41	50
6	Automotive, Automobiles, Tires, Batteries, Accessories, Service Stations, Garages	90	45	45
40	Electronic Engineering	86	53	33
122	Radio and Television	81	41	40
132A	Science, Research, and Development	78	24	54
88	Metal, Metalworking, and Machinery	71	36	36
19A	Building Management and Real Estate	68	10	58
102	Nursing and Health	64	4	60
16	Brewing, Distilling, and Beverages	64	10	54

Source: Standard Rate and Data Service, *Business Publications Rates and Data, part 1* (Wilmette, Ill.: Standard Rate and Data Service, 24 July 1988), A28–A37.

tion are not carried by SRDS, (2) loose-leaf supplements, (3) newsletters and bulletins, (4) nonprint business "publications" (databases, floppy discs, or CD-ROM), and (5) the vast network of in-house publications.

In spite of these problems, can one determine precisely how many business publications exist in the United States? It would be an exciting albeit impossible quest. Executives at ABP told this author in 1988 and again in 1989 that the real number of business titles is somewhere "near" the five thousand mark, with a net annual increase of new periodicals somewhere in the "250–375" range. These numbers (estimates) were "confirmed" by other industry experts, although hard statistical data substantiating this estimate just does not exist.

THE MARKET SHARE OF BUSINESS PUBLICATIONS IN THE UNITED STATES

As imprecise as current data collection systems may be, some sense of order must be made out of this information in order to determine the market share held by business publications in the United States. Accordingly, using the generally accepted numbers issued by both *Gale's* and SRDS (in order to utilize consistent data), one could make the argument that the business publications share of the total magazine market is 35.74 percent (that is, SRDS's 4,143 business titles divided by Gale's total of 11,593).

How accurate is this number (35.74 percent)? Since 1985 this author has had a significant number of lengthy discussions on precisely this topic with key individuals in the United States Department of Commerce (as recently as February 1989), ABP, and industry executives. It is the unscientific impression of these individuals that business publications hold about a one-third market share of the American periodical market. Therefore, it appears that the 35.74 percent figure is a realistic working number.

TOTAL REVENUES AND MARKET SHARE

What are the total revenues generated by business publications? Obviously the 35.74 percent figure is of little value in addressing this question. The best source of data is the United States Department of Commerce's *Census of Manufactures*, which is issued every five years. The last year for which data is available is 1982; while rough preliminary data covering 1987 has been issued, it appears that the final 1987 statistics will be released sometime in late 1990, although the Commerce Department had difficulty throughout the 1980s reaching its scheduled publication dates because of reductions in staffing.

A review of the important economic indices in the 1977 and 1982 censuses provided this researcher with some interesting insight into total revenues. The following table (1.20) illustrates the business publication market share of the total value of shipments for all periodicals in 1977 and 1982.[11]

Of the business publication total, farm titles generated $109.3 million in subscription, sales, and advertising revenues in 1977. By 1982 this increased to $334.9 million, a staggering 206 percent increase during these years. Farm publications captured a 1.8 percent market share in 1977 but reached 2.92 percent in 1982.

As for business publications, subscription revenues reached $333.3 million in 1977 and topped $744.4 million in 1982, an impressive increase of 123.34 percent. Advertising revenues topped $1.039 billion in 1972 and increased 98.63 percent by 1982, reaching $2.064 billion.

Consumer magazines posted strong increases, but they were unable to keep pace with business publications during this critical five-year period. Revenues generated by subscriptions and sales grew at a modest rate of 41.72 percent ($1.573 billion in 1977 and $2.229 billion by 1982). Advertising dollars increased a strong 83.62 percent ($2.19 billion in 1977; $4.02 billion as of 1982).

However, the U.S. government's numbers were not completely accurate. The Commerce Department reported total periodical revenues of $6.056 billion in 1977; yet an exhaustive analysis by this author of their individual tallies as listed in the *Census of Manufactures* totaled only $5.475 billion. Somewhere $581.5 million (9.6 percent of the total) was unaccounted for in their calculations. This problem resurfaced in 1982, but the discrepancy topped $1.598 billion (13.92 percent of the total). Unfortunately this prob-

Table 1.20 / Business Magazine Market Share (in millions of dollars)

Periodical Category	Value of Shipments		Percent of Total Value of Shipments		Percent Change, 1977–1982
	1977	1982	1977	1982	
All Periodicals	$6,056.5	$11,478.0	100.00	100.00	+89.52
All Business Publications (including Farm)	1,481.7	3,143.3	24.46	27.39	+112.14
All Consumer Publications	3,762.4	6,249.6	62.12	54.45	+66.11
"Other"	230.9	487.1	3.81	4.24	+110.96

Sources: U.S. Department of Commerce, Bureau of the Census, 1982 Census of Manufactures: Newspaper, Periodicals, Books, and Miscellaneous Publishing (Washington, D.C.: USGPO, 1985), 27A6–27A11; 1977 Census of Manufactures: Newspaper, Periodicals, Books, and Miscellaneous Publishing (Washington, D.C.: USGPO, 1980), 27A6–27A11.

lem was not addressed in any of the Commerce Department's appendices or footnotes.[12]

Aside from this troubling miscalculation, several interesting patterns were evident. The total value of shipments for consumer magazines in relation to the entire periodical industry declined dramatically, from a strong 62.12 percent market share in 1977 to only a 54.45 percent share in 1982.

Business publications, on the other hand, strengthened their market position in both total dollars (+112.14 percent) and share, growing from a 24.46 percent mark in 1977 to 27.39 percent by 1982.

Lastly, consumer magazines' total income for subscriptions and newsstand sales declined precipitously, from a 25.97 percent market share to 19.42 percent. During these years the average cost of a single copy of the typical consumer title skyrocketed, prompting many individuals to curtail newsstand purchases. This quickly became the magazine publishing industry's equivalent of the "sticker shock" syndrome that adversely affected the American automobile industry during this same period of time.

ADVERTISING REVENUES AND NICHES

By 1987 total advertising revenues for business and farm publications reached $2.698 billion (up 30.72 percent from 1982).[13] Consumer titles captured $5.5 billion (up 36.78 percent from 1982). This meant that of the total $8.198 billion placed in magazine advertising, business publications held a 32.91 percent market share, perhaps another indication that the commonly held idea that business books hold a one-third market share of the periodical market just might be true. Consumer magazines' posi tion retained a strong 67.09 percent of the total. The following table (1.21) outlines trends between 1977 and 1982 in this critically important source of magazine income.[14]

The following table (1.22) isolates advertising revenues for business (but not farm) publications for the years 1977–1988.[15]

In 1987 the United States experienced a 2.9 percent increase in its Gross National Product (GNP) while advertising revenues for business publications (excluding farm titles) grew 3.77 percent.[16]

Table 1.21 / Advertising Revenues: 1977–1982 (in millions of dollars)

Periodical Category	Total Advertising Revenues		Percent of Total Advertising Revenues		Percent Change, 1977–1982
	1977	1982	1977	1982	
All Periodicals	$3,361.1	$6,367.5	100.00	100.00	+89.45
All Business Periodicals	1,122.4	2,210.8	33.39	34.72	+96.97
Business	1,039.1	2,064.0	30.09	32.41	+98.63
Farm	83.3	146.8	2.48	2.31	+76.23
All General and Consumer Periodicals	2,189.8	4,020.9	65.15	63.15	+83.62
"Other" Periodicals	53.9	135.9	1.60	2.13	+152.13

Source: U.S. Department of Commerce, International Trade Administration, 1988 U.S. Industrial Outlook (Washington, D.C.: USGPO, 1988), 29-5–29-7.

Table 1.22 / Advertising Revenues for Business Publications: 1977–1988 (in millions of dollars)

Year	Advertising Revenues	Percent Change from Previous Year
1977	$1,221	—
1978	1,400	+ 14.66
1979	1,575	+ 12.50
1980	1,674	+ 6.29
1981	1,841	+ 9.98
1982	1,876	+ 1.90
1983	1,990	+ 6.07
1984	2,270	+ 14.07
1985	2,375	+ 4.62
1986	2,382	+ 0.02
1987	2,458	+ 3.19
1988	2,610	+ 6.18
Total	23,672	—

Source: Robert J. Coen, "Ad Spending Outlook Brightens," *Advertising Age*, 15 May 1989, 24; and "Media Muscle: The Power of Numbers," *Advertising Age*, 9 November 1988, 66–67.

Table 1.23 / Advertising Revenues for all U.S. Media: 1980–1988 (in millions of dollars)

Year	Total Dollars	National Advertising Dollars	Local Advertising Dollars	Total Percent Change From Previous Year
1980	$53,550	$29,815	$23,735	+ 9.8
1981	60,430	33,890	26,540	+ 12.7
1982	66,580	37,785	28,795	+ 10.2
1983	75,850	42,525	33,325	+ 13.9
1984	87,820	49,690	38,130	+ 15.8
1985	94,750	53,355	41,395	+ 7.9
1986	102,140	56,850	45,290	+ 7.7
1987	109,650	60,625	49,025	+ 7.4
1988	118,820	66,350	52,470	+ 8.4
Total	769,590	430,885	338,705	—

Sources: Robert J. Coen, "Ad Spending Outlook Brightens," *Advertising Age*, 15 May 1989, 24; and "Media Muscle: The Power of Numbers," *Advertising Age*, 9 November 1988, 66–67.

Table 1.24 / Business Magazine Market Share: 1982–1988 (in millions of dollars)

Year	Total U.S. Advertising Dollars	Total Business Publications Advertising Dollars	Percent Share Held by Business Publications of Total Advertising Expenditures
1982	$66,580	$2,211	3.32
1985	94,750	2,114	2.23
1986	102,140	2,150	2.11
1987	109.650	2,231	2.03
1988	118,820	2,698	2.27
Total	491,940	11,404	—

Sources: Robert J. Coen, "Ad Spending Outlook Brightens," *Advertising Age*, 15 May 1989, 24; and "Media Muscle: The Power of Numbers," *Advertising Age*, 9 November 1988, 66–67.

The following table (1.23) lists total advertising dollars for all media in the United States.[17]

Using the data contained in the statistical tables listed above, it is possible to ascertain the market share held by business and farm publications of the total advertising dollars spent in the United States. The following table (1.24), based on calculations by the author, outlines these market shares.

This information reveals conclusively that in the mid- to late-1980s business publications experienced a sharp decline in both general American advertising expenditures *and* the total market share held by these periodicals in this nation. Why has this vibrant segment of the nation's communications industry sustained such a dramatic reversal? Was it due to intense competition from other media (for example, videocassettes, telemarketing, or various electronic forms)? Are there too many business titles in certain market niches, thereby allowing the inevitable law of supply and demand to reduce advertising page rates? Perhaps advertisers have grown disenchanted with the effectiveness of business magazines to reach clearly defined target audiences? Is this merely a cyclical phenomenon? Or is this problem a mirror of the general malaise affecting the entire advertising industry?

Liz Horton addresses this problem in an important article in

Folio entitled "Business Titles Slip As Consumer Books Gain."[18] Horton focused on the marked decline in advertising revenues by business books. She remarked that as recently as 1984 business magazines maintained an average operating cashflow margin hovering near the 20 percent mark. Consumer magazines lagged behind at a 13.2 percent pace. By January 1990 the balance had shifted precipitously.

Horton pointed out that profit margins for consumer books in "1988 were lower than in 1987 but still higher than in 1984. Operating cashflow margins dropped 0.9 percent, to 14.7 percent, and pretax operating income margins also dropped 0.9 percent, to 13.1 percent."[19] Yet because consumer titles maintained a low asset base, they continued to churn out the highest relative cashflow in the entire media industry.

Business periodicals continued their downward spiral. While total revenues topped $2.6 billion in 1988 (up 7.7 percent), much of this growth was due primarily to the impact of acquisitions on the balance sheet rather than to real growth. A review of key financial data revealed that "operating income margins dropped 1.3 percentage points, to 12.6 percent; cashflow margins were down 1.4 points, to 15.9 percent."[20] Since 1984 pretax operating income margins dipped a staggering 5.4 points; operating cashflow margins declined a distressing 3.9 percent.

What is the prognosis for the early 1990s? According to Veronis, Suhler & Associates, the leading investment banking firm servicing the magazine industry, "business magazine advertising has grown at only half the rate of the overall economy since 1985." The end result is not very encouraging; Veronis, Suhler anticipates that "it will take another two or three years [that is, till 1992 or even 1993] before business-to-business advertisers are on the upswing."[21]

Neal Weinstock of *Advertising Age* also addresses this phenomenon in a perceptive article. He writes that

although many advertisers maintain trade-oriented campaigns in publications targeting their customers in lean times, business publications tend to boom primarily when vendors [advertising agencies and their clients] think a product category or industry can or should grow. . . .[22]

Unfortunately, no serious study has been undertaken to address this apparently complex problem, so impressions but not scientific observations abound. Clearly some of these opinions are interesting and worth some comments.

One of the most astute observers of the American business magazine field is William O'Donnell. After four years as President of the Association of Business Publishers, O'Donnell resigned his position in mid-1989, and the entire industry lost an eloquent leader and a caring person.

In 1988 O'Donnell remarked that business periodicals "normally either follow the economy or lead it by about six months."[23]

Weinstock followed up on O'Donnell's comment, and he reviewed key SRDS data. He discovered that among all market groups with at least $20 million in advertising expenditures, the following industries experienced strong business gains in 1987: food processing (+18.8 percent); building trades (+15.7 percent); trucking (+14.8 percent); waste management (+14.6 percent; a major campaign issue during the U.S. presidential election of 1988); and drug packaging (+14.5 percent). Reversals were evident in the paper (−26.8 percent), glue (−20 percent), oil (−19.1 percent), and real estate industries (−17.7 percent).

Banking publications are an interesting case study of this phenomenon since they sustained a deep decline in total revenues and advertising linage after the devastating October 1987 stock market crash. The following table (1.25) lists percent changes in monthly advertising pages, covering the period between April 1987 and April 1988, for some of the nation's leading banking titles.[24]

American Banker certainly rebounded from the crash, posting an impressive 278.35 advertising pages in April 1988 (up 95.68 percent over April 1987). The rest of these business titles were not so fortunate.[25]

Ironically, business publishers are somewhat reluctant to announce publicly the state of their own businesses, although they are dependent on collecting this type of data for their readers. Consequently, it is exceptionally difficult to obtain reliable data on the many privately held business publishing corporations in the United States.[26]

Table 1.25 / Percent Changes in Advertising Pages in Banking Publications: 1987–1988

Month	Savings Inst.	American Banker	ABA Banking Journal	US Banker	Mortgage Banking	Computers in Banking
Apr. '87	79.83	142.25	81.67	40.75	97.53	97.08
May	+3.84	+34.99	+53.08	+19.00	−3.45	−23.41
June	+12.25	+35.40	+1.00	+5.07	−15.70	+20.92
July	+7.67	−3.69	−10.64	+20.42	−21.28	−52.30
Aug.	+3.17	−53.63	−20.42	−9.50	−22.03	−50.75
Sept.	+27.50	+50.87	+15.66	+27.92	−12.41	−38.89
Oct.	+30.00	+58.29	+62.50	+38.00	+34.25	−13.08
Nov.	+11.50	+8.03	−2.34	+31.17	−17.50	−17.83
Dec.	−15.16	−26.07	−11.59	−2.50	−41.28	−43.41
Jan. '88	−8.66	−40.58	−14.34	−5.25	−48.91	−69.91
Feb.	+2.67	−42.78	−18.50	−4.22	−43.45	−64.25
Mar.	−24.16	−2.26	−12.50	+7.25	−15.70	−61.58
Apr.	−5.00	+136.10	−10.34	−4.94	−15.36	−52.58

Source: "Bank Magazines Still Bear Scars from October 19," *Publishing News*, Pilot Issue (July 1988), 13.

On occasion a private company will issue a press release dealing with recent earnings. In 1988, for example, Penton (with a strong collection of thirty-two impressive business titles in 1988) stated that it had posted strong gains in total advertising revenues for the first half of 1988. Edgell Communications, one of the largest business publishing companies in the United States with over one hundred business publications and created out of the sale of the Harcourt Brace Jovanovich business magazine division, posted a 7 percent increase in first quarter 1988 sales revenues.[27] Yet concern must be exercised whenever evaluating these "unaudited" press releases.

MAJOR BUSINESS PUBLICATIONS

What were the major business publications in the United States in 1988? The following table (1.26), again utilizing the definitive statistical results contained in the 1988 *MagazineWeek 500*, lists the top forty key business periodicals in the United States.[28]

The rankings utilized in Table 1.26 are from the top five hundred, which gives the reader some indication of the actual placement of these major business books within the entire periodical market. In determining a publication's inclusion in this table (1.26), the author compared all of the entries in the *MagazineWeek 500* with the titles contained in SRDS's *Business Publication Rates and Data*, part 1; if a book was in SRDS's business directory, then it was a business periodical. In this way all of those useless, petty points raised in a dozen asinine debates this author witnessed since 1985 about what is a *real* business magazine were nullified.

Certain industries covered by business publications are worth some brief attention. The following tables (1.27, 1.28, 1.29, and 1.30), utilizing data drawn from the *MagazineWeek 500*, highlight four of these interesting markets: (1) advertising and marketing, (2) specialized business industry publications, (3) medical and healthcare titles, and (4) farm magazines. The *MagazineWeek 500* rankings were again utilized.

The term "average CPM" refers to the cost to the advertiser to reach one thousand readers of the magazine in question.

Advertising and marketing is a key category for advertising managers, and this niche is serviced by five books (see Table 1.27). *Advertising Age* is the number one periodical in this category in terms of revenues and average CPM. It also dominates the general advertising niche.

Four specialized publications covering the world of business made the top five hundred (see Table 1.28). In this category the results were a bit cloudy, and no single magazine emerged as the total number one book, a situation directly affected by the major roles played by the general consumer business titles (*Fortune, Forbes, Business Week,* and *Money*) in U.S. society.

Another interesting collection of titles is the impressive list of medical journals and publications that can be seen in any medical college library in the United States (see Table 1.29). While the *Journal of the American Medical Association* posts better figures regarding total advertising revenues and average CPM, the *New*

Table 1.26 / Top Forty Major Business Publications in the United States: 1988 (in millions of dollars)

Rank	Publication Title	Total Circulation	Total Revenues	Percent of Total Revenues of Top Forty Publications
42	PC Week	151,112	$64.86	5.53
44	Architectural Digest	712,556	62.63	5.34
45	Computerworld	123,010	62.48	5.33
74	PC World	503,205	43.77	3.73
75	Personal Computing	546,018	43.71	3.73
79	Restaurants & Institutions	138,064	41,82	3.57
85	Travel Weekly	42,281	40.51	3.46
98	EDN	137,213	33.51	2.86
100	Computer Reseller News	57,406	33.20	2.83
101	HFD	32,792	33.18	2.83
103	Electronic Engineering Times	121,537	32.97	2.81
104	Advertising Age	97,810	32.95	2.81
108	Institutional Investor	139,347	31.48	2.69
109	Professional Builder	140,988	30.60	2.61
112	Journal of the AMA	371,408	30.06	2.56
114	Infoworld	160,595	29.57	2.52
118	MacUser	212,646	27.47	2.34
119	Design News	170,027	27.42	2.34
124	New England Journal of Medicine	225,908	25.75	2.20
126	Financial World	343,206	25.64	2.19
129	Data Communications	55,028	24.79	2.11
131	Nation's Restaurant News	93,106	24.29	2.07
132	Medical Economics	173,547	22.26	2.06
135	Datamation	180,217	23.23	1.98
136	Nation's Business	903,515	23.13	1.97
140	Billboard	50,717	22.09	1.88
142	Builder	180,764	21.86	1.86
143	Drug Store News	41,956	21.74	1.85
147	Computer Shopper	219,035	21.21	1.81
148	Scientific American	663,683	21.20	1.81
149	Machine Design	187,240	20.90	1.78
155	Restaurant Business	115,212	20.04	1.71
163	Farm Journal	836,470	19.66	1.68
165	Nursing 88	442,529	19.52	1.67
168	Automotive News	74,866	19.26	1.64
169	Electronic Design	137,191	18.92	1.61
172	Computer Systems News	80,000	18.60	1.60
176	Information Week	117,418	17.85	1.59
178	Electronic Buyers' News	61,272	17.72	1.51
181	American Banker	20,695	17.55	1.50

Source: "MagazineWeek 500," MagazineWeek, 23 October 1989, 26.

Table 1.27 / Advertising and Marketing Business Periodicals: 1988
(in millions of dollars)

Rank	Publication	Total Revenues	Total Advertising Pages	Average CPM	Revenue Market Share Percent
101	Advertising Age	$31.49	3,179	$92.16	42.27
180	Adweek	17.10	1,473	145.23	22.95
195	Broadcasting	13.25	3,259	122.20	17.79
382	Adweek's Marketing Week	6.96	1,615	385.40	9.34
469	Marketing & Media Decisions	5.70	803	202.03	7.65
	Grand Total	74.50	10,329	189.40	—

Source: "MagazineWeek 500," MagazineWeek, 23 October 1989. 26.

England Journal of Medicine is the definitive number one book in the largest business magazine category in the United States.

The *MagazineWeek 500* created a special ranking system for farm titles, and these rankings were incorporated into the following table (1.30).

Table 1.28 / Business Industry Periodicals: 1988
(in millions of dollars)

Rank	Publication	Total Revenues	Total Advertising Pages	Average CPM	Revenue Market Share Percent
218	Industry Week	$13.96	1,053	$40.25	32.80
243	Journal of Accountancy	12.79	1,056	21.83	30.10
343	Sales & Marketing Management	8.12	877	127.94	19.09
359	High Technology Business	7.67	214	53.29	18.03
	Grand Total	42.54	3,200	60.83	—

Source: "MagazineWeek 500," MagazineWeek, 23 October 1989. 26.

Table 1.29 / Major Medical Publications: 1988 (in millions of dollars)

Rank	Publication	Total Revenues	Total Advertising Pages	Average CPM	Revenue Market Share Percent
113	New England Journal of Medicine	$28.09	3,380	$17.79	16.97
149	Medical Economics	21.02	2,873	40.95	12.70
164	Journal of the AMA	18.26	3,892	12.81	11.03
257	Diversion	12.10	1,855	43.80	7.31
285	Annals of Internal Medicine	10.42	2,048	28.66	6.30
290	Hospital Practice	10.16	2,006	29.22	6.10
313	American Family Physician	9.25	2,335	29.68	5.60
315	Post-Graduate Medicine	9.18	2,126	28.61	5.60
363	MD Magazine	7.61	1,500	41.50	4.60
380	Physician's Management	7.03	1,971	32.38	4.20
399	Medical Aspects of Human Sexuality	6.56	1,200	36.44	3.98
402	Emergency Medicine	6.50	1,827	27.26	3.90
451	Hospital Medicine	5.39	1,218	31.17	3.26
482	Consultant	4.76	1,098	35.10	2.89
486	Medical World News	4.61	1,006	37.79	2.80
491	Modern Medicine	4.60	1,240	30.83	2.78
	Grand Total	165.54	31,575	31.50	—

Source: "MagazineWeek 500," MagazineWeek, 23 October 1989. 26.

Table 1.30 / Farm Periodicals: 1988 (in millions of dollars)

Rank	Publication	Total Revenues	Total Advertising Pages	Average CPM	Revenue Market Share Percent
1	Farm Journal	$24.50	554	$45.68	24.00
2	Successful Farming	19.16	628	37.06	18.78
3	Progressive Farming	18.17	583	36.16	17.81
4	Lancaster Farming	11.69	6,986	36.42	11.46
5	Prairie Farmer	6.74	700	58.84	6.60
6	High Plains Journal	6.08	9,095	8.92	6.00
7	Wallace's Farmer	5.61	627	108.55	5.50
8	Hoard's Dairyman	5.34	384	79.71	5.23
9	Farmer	4.72	587	56.23	4.63
	Grand Total	102.01	20,144	51.95	—

Source: "MagazineWeek 500," MagazineWeek, 23 October 1989. 26.

THE BUSINESS OUTLOOK OF THE MAGAZINE INDUSTRY IN THE UNITED STATES

What is the business outlook of the magazine industry, and specifically business periodicals, in the 1990s in the United States?

It is not an easy task to make sense, much less make intelligent projections, about the eclectic periodical industry in the United States. All magazine titles depend on advertising revenues; paid circulation books augment advertising income with earnings generated through subscriptions or newsstand sales in order to earn after-tax profits.

The only exception to this rule is, ironically, *Mad* magazine, the iconoclastic periodical that has never sold advertising space in any issue since it was first launched in 1952 by the intrepid William Gaines. This title is currently owned by Time Warner, which certainly has an impressive track record selling advertising space; yet this large corporation has not tinkered with what is an almost "sacred" institution, at least to millions of gradeschool children in this nation. It remains free of all advertisements, except those plugging *Mad* products (namely book versions of the comic book).

This inevitable dependence on the economic health and stability of the nation as a whole remains the characteristic of general consumer magazines, for example *Time* and *Newsweek*. Publishers of specialized business titles, on the other hand, know all too well that their business future is tied inextricably to the state of affairs in their particular product niche; for example, *Billboard* magazine's future is tied unquestionably to the business stability of the music industry in this nation.

MAJOR PUBLISHING COMPANIES

Perhaps the best way to approach this question is to obtain a general overview of the current state of the periodical industry and then review the business projections of specialists who have studied this dynamic industry. Consequently, the first step is to identify the largest media companies in the U.S. according to total magazine revenues. The following table (1.31) outlines the major firms active in this niche.[29]

How much magazine advertising revenues did these publications generate? The following table (1.32) outlines total advertising revenues (in millions of U.S. dollars) covering the period 1987–1988.[30]

BUSINESS PROBLEMS

So are magazines (both business and consumer) in the United States "healthy"? According to Robert J. Coen, a senior vice president at McCann-Erickson Worldwide and unquestionably the leading advertising forecaster in the United States, the outlook does not appear promising. Total advertising expenditures in 1989 fell short of an earlier projection of 6.9 percent, which Coen made in mid-1989. In reality the actual growth rate hovered at a lackluster 5.8 percent pace. Coen's outlook for 1990 is equally dismal; he projected a 6.2 percent increase, barely above the anticipated increase in the nation's inflation rate and the announced increases in postage and magazine manufacturing costs. In essence there was little or no real growth in 1989, and Coen does not view 1990 as being any better.

Table 1.31 / The Top Thirty-Five U.S. Publishing Corporations
Ranked by Magazine Revenues: 1988 (in millions of dollars)

Rank 1988	Rank 1987	Company	Magazine Revenues 1988	Percent Change in Revenues 1987–1988
1	1	Time Inc.	$1,752	+8.1
2	2	Hearst Corp.	919	+5.3
3	3	Advance Publications	745	+10.0
4	5	Reader's Digest	600		14.9
5	4	Thomson Corp.	596	+12.9
6	13	News Corp.	510	+53.2
7	8	Cahners Publishing Corp.	420	+23.6
8	6	McGraw-Hill	414	+9.8
9	7	Capital Cities/ABC	370	−1.3
10	11	Hachette Group	366	+14.0
11	9	Meredith Corp.	365	+10.9
12	12	International Data Group	352	+13.3
13	10	Washington Post Co.	328	+1.9
14	16	Times Mirror Co.	299	+47.3
15	14	New York Times Co.	249	+10.2
16	15	National Geographic Society	245	+9.9
17	19	Ziff Communications	200	+37.9
18	17	Petersen Publishing Co.	187	+15.4
19	18	Forbes Inc.	175	+9.4
20	21	General Media International	150	+7.1
21	20	Edgell Communications	148	+2.8
22	23	U.S. News & World Report	142	+14.5
23	22	Crain Communications	137	+7.0
24	24	Playboy Enterprises	120	+3.4
25	n/a	Whittle Communications	97	+44.8
26	25	Maclean Hunter	70	+2.9
27	28	Affiliated Publications	62	+100.0
28	36	Macfadden Holdings	45	—
29	29	Cowles Media Co.	42	+50.0
30	27	Warner Communications	40	+5.3
31	26	Dow Jones & Co.	36	−7.6
32	30	Times Publishing Co.	25	+8.7
33	31	LIN Broadcasting	21	+10.5
34	32	CMP Publications	20	+25.0
35	33	Media General	14	−10.9
		Total	10,260	+11.9

Source: "100 Leading Media Companies by Revenues," Advertising Age, 26 June 1989, S2.

Magazine Company	Total Advertising Revenues		Percent Change, 1987–1988
	1988	1987	
1 Time Inc.	$622	$522	+ 12.6
2 Hearst Magazines	254	250	+ 1.8
3 Conde Nast Publications	205	185	+ 10.9
4 Triangle Communications	183	179	+ 1.9
5 New York Times Co.	159	142	+ 12.3
6 Meredith Corp.	130	117	+ 11.7
7 Newsweek Inc.	111	116	− 4.2
8 Times Mirror Magazines	103	89	+ 16.9
9 Hachette SA	103	98	+ 5.0
10 McGraw-Hill	102	97	+ 4.8
11 Reader's Digest Association	72	64	+ 11.6
12 Murdoch Magazines	66	54	+ 23.4
13 U.S. News and Atlantic	64	50	+ 26.6
14 Forbes Inc.	59	55	+ 6.4
15 Working Women and McCall's	50	52	− 3.9
16 Knapp Communications	41	35	+ 16.7
17 Gannett	41	30	+ 34.7
18 Straight Arrow Publishers	36	28	+ 27.3
19 Petersen Publishing	33	27	+ 20.0
20 American Express Publishing Co.	28	26	+ 7.8
21 Family Media	27	22	+ 20.7
22 Rodale Press	26	22	+ 17.1
23 Goldhirsh Group	23	21	+ 9.4
24 Penthouse International	22	22	− 0.5
25 Playboy Enterprises	18	17	+ 4.8
Grand Total	2,578	2,320	+ 11.1

Source: "100 Leading Media Companies by Revenues," Advertising Age, 26 June 1989, S2.

Are all magazine segments sustaining losses or at best generating small increases in revenues? A close look at recent developments in a number of major niches will shed some light on this question.

Publishing News (an impressive tabloid launched by *Folio* magazine in 1988) reported that advertising by magazines in the major business and consumer publications had declined. *Advertising Age, Adweek, Marketing & Media Decisions, Inside Print,* and the bellwether Standard Rate and Data Services all reported that ad space sales dropped sharply in 1987 and again in 1988, apparently proof that the old adage that "the children of shoemakers go barefoot" still has some measure of truth to it!

Advertising pages purchased by magazine companies in consumer books dipped −3.5 percent (off almost 142 pages) in 1988. Business books experienced an even more dramatic decline of −7.2 percent (down 245 pages).[31]

A careful review of circulation statistics indicates that some business titles stagnated, and, in far too many instances, slipped, in 1988. The following table (1.33) lists figures for the top fifteen business periodicals in total circulation in 1988.[32]

ADVERTISING REVENUES

What happened to advertising revenues in 1988? An analysis of the fifteen leading business publications in total ad revenues indicated that four publications registered declines, three posted either no increase or very modest growth in 1988, and the rest achieved positive results. Over all, 1988 was not a spectacular year for business titles. The following table (1.34) outlines advertising revenues for these leading titles.[33]

Why has there been a decline in advertising in specialized business magazines? Scott Donaton addressed this issue in one of the most important articles on the business magazine industry, published in 1989. He wrote that business titles are caught in the grip of a tight vise that will lead ultimately to a "classic shakeout as the [business magazine] industry rides a swelling tide of new trade titles and an eroding base of ad pages."[34]

Donaton reported that on the average 154 new business peri-

Table 1.33 / The Top Fifteen Business Publications in Total Circulation: 1988

Rank	Publication	Total Circulation	Percent Paid	Percent NonPaid	Percent Change, 1987–1988
1	ABA Journal	393,427	92.7	7.3	+3.0
2	Journal of the American Medical Association	358,916	74.4	26.6	+3.0
3	American Medical News	356,470	2.6	97.4	+4.9
4	Physician's Travel & Meeting Guide	339,238	1.0	99.0	+7.4
5	Top Shelf Barkeeping At Its Best	300,353	0.0	100.0	n/a
6	Industry Week	300,183	0.6	99.4	−8.0
7	RN Magazine	284,817	95.5	4.5	+3.0
8	Farm Issue News	270,436	0.0	100.0	n/a
9	CFO	251,109	0.0	100.0	n/a
10	Air Force Magazine	229,109	81.9	18.1	−5.5
11	New England Journal of Medicine	225,986	99.3	0.7	+1.1
12	New Equipment Digest	213,099	0.0	100.0	+2.2
13	Industrial Equipment News	211,376	0.0	100.0	+0.6
14	Soybean Digest	204,791	0.0	100.0	+2.0
15	Industrial Product Bulletin	200,055	0.0	100.0	0.0
	Grand Total	4,139,365	—	—	—

Source: "MagazineWeek 500," MagazineWeek, 23 October 1989, 26.

odicals were launched between 1984 and 1988, all seeking their share of the market's lucrative rewards. Few survived. The Standard Rate and Data Service announced that 128 business titles failed in 1987; it is possible that upwards of 240 will cease operations in 1989, hardly a positive sign for the 1990s.[35]

With a decline in advertising pages in business periodicals (dropping another 1.5 percent in 1989) and a growth in the num-

Table 1.34 / The Fifteen Top Business Magazines in Gross Advertising Revenues: 1988 (in millions of dollars)

Rank	Periodical	Gross Advertising Revenues		Percent Change, 1987–1988
		1988	*1987*	
1	PC Magazine	$105.5	$78.0	+35.3
2	PC Week	75.3	72.3	+4.2
3	Computerworld	51.4	51.9	−0.1
4	Restaurants & Institutions	39.7	39.9	−0.4
5	EDN	34.8	30.8	+13.0
6	Design News	27.6	25.3	+9.5
7	Advertising Age	26.9	26.8	0.0
8	Electronic Engineering Times	26.8	22.7	+17.9
9	Computer Reseller News	26.6	22.8	+16.4
10	PC World	26.3	28.0	−6.3
11	Medical Economics	25.3	24.5	+3.2
12	Mac User	22.8	11.9	+91.1
13	Journal of the American Medical Association	22.6	19.5	+15.7
14	Institutional Investor	22.3	29.0	−23.0
15	InfoWorld	20.7	16.7	+24.0
	Grand Total	554.6	500.1	+10.9

Source: "Tops in the Trade," *Advertising Age*, 12 June 1989, 158.

ber of business periodicals, chaos looms on the horizon. To Donaton "chaos" is spelled "rate negotiation."

Donaton interviewed a plethora of industry experts to gauge the seriousness of this phenomenon. Bernard Kovach, President of Bill Communications in New York City, told Donaton that "the [rate negotiation] practice is growing because we hit the ad page wall, and there are publishers foolish enough to just throw away rate cards."[36] Ned Borowsky, President of North American Publishing in Philadelphia, offered a pithy comment: "Where companies were buying four books [in a four or five book business maga-

Table 1.35 / Advertising Revenues for Business Periodicals: Computer Titles, 1986–1988 (in millions of dollars)

1988 Rank	Title	Advertising Revenues 1988	1987	1986	Percent Change, 1986–1988
1	Computer World	$96.8	$99.3	$105.0	− 7.8
2	Datamation	52.0	50.0	49.0	+ 6.1
3	Information Week	15.0	13.0	12.0	+25.0
4	MIS Week	9.0	9.9	11.5	−21.7
5	Computer Decisions	2.5	7.1	10.5	−76.2
6	Infosystems	0.3	2.3	4.5	−93.3
	Grand Total	175.6	181.6	192.5	− 8.8

Source: "MagazineWeek 500," MagazineWeek, 23 October 1989, 26.

zine niche], they are now buying two." This meant to Borowsky that "in the past you could be the number three book, the number four book, and you could hold your position or grow a little each year because markets were expanding." In the early 1990s, few if any markets will expand; so those periodicals in the bottom of a category now face fiscal disaster.

Computer titles occupy perhaps the most competitive niche in the entire periodical industry. Table 1.35 presents an analysis of advertising revenues in this category plus additional calculations by the author; clearly life in the fast lane can indeed be dangerous.[37]

BUSINESS VERSUS CONSUMER PERIODICALS

Have former (or potential) business magazine advertisers decided to place their advertisements in selected consumer and/or general business periodicals instead of specialized business magazines? All of the available evidence indicates that this has happened. Why?

In the 1980s many U.S. corporations were purchased by foreign companies eager to penetrate the highly competitive U.S. market. Some of these new owners apparently fell under the seductive spell of a number of internationally known and respected publishers of consumer and general business magazines. These experienced publishing executives carefully and aggressively convinced many foreign chief executive officers that traditional specialized business books lacked the panache, style, grace, and effective advertising "reach" (that is, to reach existing or potential customers) long associated with the "classic" consumer or general business magazines in the United States, which included *Time, Newsweek, Forbes, Fortune,* or *Business Week.*

Therefore many foreign business leaders decided to purchase advertising space in publications that had, at least to more than a few foreign executives, more "glitz" than the typical business book, perhaps the ultimate proof that David Ogilvy's maxim, "You do not sell the steak; you sell the sizzle," still works!

This was not a cavalier decision; advertisements for these foreign companies were designed carefully to generate interest for specific products (for example, computers or office system equipment) and to act as "image pieces" for these new "American" companies. Many foreign business leaders felt this was rather important if they were to create an effective business beachhead in this nation.

One of the most interesting business-to-business campaigns was first launched by *Newsweek* in 1983. In order to convince executives of the merit of allocating business-to-business advertising dollars in *Newsweek,* which was clearly one of this nation's premier consumer books, the marketing department at *Newsweek* created a sophisticated campaign that was evaluated by this author.

The obligatory media kit contained a personal letter (obviously produced on a computer) emphasizing the fact that recent research documented *Newsweek*'s media strength vis-a-vis specialized business books.

A detailed, stylish brochure addressed the following key points:

(1) two-thirds of all investors owning stock in three or more publicly traded companies in the United States are regular *Newsweek* readers;
(2) nearly half of all U.S. investors read newsweeklies but only 21 percent of investors read business magazines of any type; and

(3) *Newsweek* readers are corporate decision-makers who make *the* final decisions to purchase office machines, computers, etc.

Newsweek even created a special *Newsweek* "Gold" demographic edition (with a base exceeding 650,000 individuals). To qualify to receive this controlled paid version of *Newsweek*, an executive must have a personal income exceeding $78,000 (as of 1986) and pass *Newsweek*'s rigorous screening procedure.

In addition, *Newsweek* included a special brochure listing over 170 recent *Newsweek* business-to-business advertisers. A significant number of these companies (14 percent) were foreign-based corporations, including AEG Aktiengellschaft, Canon, Epson, Hitachi, Japan Shipbuilding, Konishiroku Photo, Matsushita Electric, Mitsui Manufacturers Bank, NEC, Nihon Tetra, and Toshiba.[38]

For those individuals who required detailed statistical data about *Newsweek*'s study, *Newsweek* also provided a detailed and useful seventy-two page booklet filled with material about their statistical methodology, an executive summary, a technical appendix, and an interesting selection of "field materials," namely copies of the actual questionnaires and advertisements utilized in their study.[39]

The major findings listed in this booklet were as follows: (1) "business ads perform as well in the major newsweeklies as they do in the major business books," (2) professionals and managers "are more likely to read newsweeklies from cover to cover, while they are more likely to spot-read business maga zines, first looking at the table of contents or cover and then going to specific articles," (3) "a greater proportion of pages is read in a newsweekly, compared to a business magazine," and (4) there is a greater likelihood that an ad in an average issue of a newsweekly, compared to a business magazine, will be seen and read by professionals and managers.

THE LONG-TERM OUTLOOK OF BUSINESS PUBLICATIONS IN THE U.S.

Robert Coen expects to see additional dramatic declines in total magazine advertising and usage patterns. "The magazine's share of expenditures of all media, which was about five percent in 1988, will be eroded over the next decade."[40] Business publications, which experienced a sharp, dangerous decline in their market share of the total advertising pie in the United States in the 1980s, will not be spared the agony of this projected decline.

What happened to the specialized business periodical industry in the United States? It seems as if it were just yesterday that new business publications were appearing as if by wizardry at a mind-boggling pace. Every conceivable niche had one or more titles servicing real or expected customers; and the long-term business projection for this industry was unquestionably optimistic.

Did the soft economy of the late 1980s adversely affect these books? Were they victimized by mindless overexpansion? Did postage rates finally catch up with reality and cut deeply into profit margins? Or did other, more aggressive media formats, consumer and general business periodicals, television, direct marketing (mail), and trade shows capture such a large and "unreasonable" market share that declines in specialized business magazine advertising and usage were inevitable?

According to Coen, the magazine industry was directly affected by eight key and conflicting business changes in the 1980s, and not all of which had a positive impact on magazines.

Magazines experienced wildly uneven, cyclical business conditions that made planning difficult. At times advertising revenue streams at periodicals surged ahead as if they were trying to match or exceed the nation's Gross National Product (the GNP; the sum total of all goods and services produced in the United States in one year minus depreciation). All of this may have lulled the sensibilities of some business magazine publishers into believing that increases in advertising and circulation revenues were inexorable.

Some publishers might have been fooled by statistics indicating that the growth rate of magazine advertising income outpaced advertising revenues generated by the three major national television networks. These networks sustained losses in viewers and advertising income because of the seductive appeal of cable television and VCRs and not because of the lure of periodicals, a point that some publishers must have overlooked.

The rapid increase in the cost of television advertising apparently alarmed many media buyers, who began to incorporate shorter, fifteen-second commercials and print campaigns into their advertising plans. These alternative formats were designed clearly to curtail, or at least reduce substantially, the direct impact of these radical increases in total television advertising billings.

Another interesting development was the emergence of a plethora of consumer and business periodicals, many with clearly defined niches. This feature appealed to media buyers who seemed enchanted with the possibility of finally discovering a realistic way to target their expensive efforts to reach just the right audience.

Yet troubles quickly appeared on the horizon that made the 1980s a "dog-eat-dog" decade, with one type of media feasting on, and later being attacked by, other advertising formats.

For example, in the 1980s the sharp decrease in total advertising expenditures by tobacco and alcohol companies cut deeply into advertising budgets, which directly and ultimately eroded already thin profit margins at many magazines.

The rise in importance in the early 1980s of consumer and general magazine advertising affected traditional advertising patterns in television, radio, and the business press. In addition, the development of alternative advertising mediums, namely free-standing inserts, sophisticated direct marketing campaigns that incorporated the latest in computer technology with advances in business and demographic research, plus the adoption of "pre-prints," all helped to reduce the role of business periodicals.

Finally, the establishment of a viable, exciting cable television medium, sophisticated independent television stations that employed innovative programming techniques that challenged effectively the national network affiliates, and the introduction of first-run television syndication formats all attracted scarce advertising dollars normally placed in magazines.[41]

The following three tables (1.36, 1.37, and 1.38), based essentially on the statistical forecasting work of Robert J. Coen, outline the cyclical nature of the advertising industry and the uneven performance of the periodical industry between 1977 and 1988.[42]

Table 1.36 / The Growth in Advertising: 1977–1981 (in millions of dollars)

Format	1977	1978	1979	1980	1981	Percent Change 1977–1981
Newspapers	$10,751	$12,214	$13,863	$14,794	$16,528	+53.7
Magazines (Consumer)	2,162	2,597	2,932	3,149	3,533	+63.4
Magazines (Farm)	90	104	120	130	146	+62.2
Television	7,612	8,955	10,154	11,474	12,886	+69.9
Radio	2,634	3,052	3,310	3,702	4,230	+60.6
Direct Marketing	5,164	5,987	6,653	7,596	8,944	+73.2
Magazines (Business)	1,221	1,400	1,575	1,674	1,841	+50.8
Outdoor	418	466	540	578	650	+55.5
Miscellaneous	7,388	8,555	9,633	10,453	11,672	+58.0
Grand Total	37,440	43,330	48,780	53,550	60,430	+61.4

Source: Robert J. Coen, "A Mixed-Bag Future," Advertising Age. 24 May 1989, 68.

Table 1.37 / The Growth in Advertising: 1982–1986 (in millions of dollars)

Format	1982	1983	1984	1985	1986	Percent Change 1982–1986
Newspapers	$17,694	$20,582	$23,522	$25,170	$26,990	+52.2
Magazines (Consumer)	3,710	4,233	4,932	5,155	5,317	+43.3
Magazines (Farm)	148	163	181	186	192	+29.8
Television	14,716	16,842	20,090	21,290	22,881	+55.5
Radio	4,670	5,210	5,817	6,490	6,949	+48.8
Direct Marketing	10,319	11,795	13,800	15,500	17,145	+66.1
Magazines (Business)	1,876	1,990	2,270	2,375	2,382	+27.0
Outdoor	721	794	872	945	985	+36.6
Miscellaneous	12,726	14,241	16,336	17,639	19,299	+51.7
Grand Total	66,580	75,850	87,820	94,750	102,140	+53.4

Source: Robert J. Coen, "A Mixed-Bag Future," Advertising Age. 24 May 1989, 68.

Table 1.38 / The Growth in Advertising: 1987–1988 (in millions of dollars)

Format	1987	1988	Percent Change 1987–1988
Newspapers	$29,142	$31,197	+7.1
Magazines (Consumer)	5,607	6,072	+8.3
Magazines (Farm)	196	196	—
Television	23,904	25,686	+7.5
Radio	7,206	7,798	+8.2
Direct Marketing	19,111	21,115	+10.5
Magazines (Business)	2,458	2,610	+6.2
Outdoor	1,025	1,064	+3.8
Miscellaneous	20,731	25,774	+24.3
Grand Total	109,650	118,050	+7.7

Source: Robert J. Coen, "A Mixed-Bag Future," *Advertising Age*. 24 May 1989, 68.

Table 1.39 / The Growth in Advertising: 1978–1988 (in millions of dollars)

Format	1977–1988 Change in Total Dollar Expenditures	1977–1988 Percent Change in Total Dollar Expenditures
Newspapers	$20,446	+190.18
Magazines (Consumer)	3,910	+180.85
Magazines (Farm)	106	+117.78
Television	18,074	+237.44
Radio	5,164	+196.05
Direct Marketing	15,951	+308.89
Magazines (Business)	1,389	+113.76
Outdoor	646	+154.55
Miscellaneous	18,386	+248.87
Grand Total	80,610	+215.31

Source: Robert J. Coen, "A Mixed-Bag Future," *Advertising Age*. 24 May 1989, 68.

The following table (1.39), utilizing Coen's data and calculations of the author, outlines clearly the changes in dollar expenditures, including data on the percentage change in these advertising allocations for each of the media formats. Business magazines posted the smallest percentage increase in revenues, barely surpassing farm periodicals. Consumer magazines recorded a healthy growth, as did newspapers and radio.

Direct marketing exhibited the greatest growth rate, a fact that impressed media buyers, who turned to this format instead of ads in business publications.

Perhaps the best method to gauge real growth is to evaluate the market share held by these media formats. The following three tables (1.40, 1.41, and 1.42) are based on original calculations by the author based on Coen's yearly data figures.

Consumer magazines' market share fell from a 5.77 share to barely 5.14. This dangerous decline of 10.92 percent has certainly alarmed publishers of these books, many of whom now plan to go on the offensive to recoup the advertising revenues that they formerly held, which will directly, and possibly adversely, affect business periodicals.

Business periodicals were decimated. They dipped from a barely respectable 3.26 share to 2.21, off −32.2 percent. If this trend continues into the early- to mid 1990s, it is likely that many business books will be unable to withstand the intense pressure of having an advertising "sword of Damocles" hanging over them. Additional declines in the total number of business periodicals would have to be anticipated unless bold, innovative ideas are followed within this beleaguered business publishing industry.

MANAGING IN TURBULENT TIMES

The only possible way for intelligent business publishers to survive in what has become a hostile, highly competitive marketplace is to review and try to follow (or at least try to adapt) the managerial ideas of Peter Drucker, America's preeminent management

Table 1.40 / Market Share Held by Various Media: 1978–1981

Format	1977	1978	1979	1980	1981
Newspapers	28.70%	28.18%	28.42%	27.63%	27.35%
Magazines (Consumer)	5.77	5.99	6.01	5.88	5.85
Magazines (Farm)	0.24	0.24	0.25	0.24	0.24
Television	20.33	20.67	20.82	21.43	21.32
Radio	7.04	7.04	6.79	6.91	6.99
Direct Marketing	13.79	13.82	13.62	14.18	14.80
Magazines (Business)	3.26	3.23	3.22	3.13	3.05
Outdoor	1.11	1.08	1.10	1.08	1.08
Miscellaneous	19.73	19.74	19.75	19.52	19.31

Sources: Robert J. Coen, "Ad Spending Outlook Brightens," *Advertising Age*, 15 May 1989, 24; "Media Muscle: The Power of Numbers," *Advertising Age*, 9 November 1988, 66–67; and "A Mixed-Bag Future," *Advertising Age*, 24 May 1989, 68.

consultant and author. Drucker literally wrote the book on this subject (*Management: Tasks, Responsibilities, Practices*), and it worth commenting on his most basic ideas since they have a direct application in the besieged world of business publishing.

Table 1.41 / Market Share Held by Various Media: 1982–1986

Format	1982	1983	1984	1985	1986
Newspapers	26.58%	27.14%	26.78%	26.56%	26.42%
Magazines (Consumer)	5.57	5.58	5.62	5.44	5.21
Magazines (Farm)	0.22	0.21	0.21	0.19	0.19
Television	22.10	22.20	22.88	22.47	22.40
Radio	7.01	6.87	6.62	6.85	6.80
Direct Marketing	15.49	15.55	15.71	16.36	16.79
Magazines (Business)	2.82	2.62	2.58	2.51	2.33
Outdoor	1.08	1.05	0.99	0.99	0.96
Miscellaneous	19.11	18.78	18.60	18.62	18.89

Sources: Robert J. Coen, "Ad Spending Outlook Brightens," *Advertising Age*, 15 May 1989, 24; "Media Muscle: The Power of Numbers," *Advertising Age*, 9 November 1988, 66–67; and "A Mixed-Bag Future," *Advertising Age*, 24 May 1989, 68.

Table 1.42 / Market Share Held by Various Media: 1987–1988

Format	1987	1988
Newspapers	26.58%	26.43%
Magazines Consumer	5.11	5.14
Magazines Farm	0.18	0.17
Television	21.80	21.76
Radio	6.57	6.61
Direct marketing	17.43	17.89
Magazines business	2.24	2.21
Outdoor	0.93	0.90
Miscellaneous	18.91	21.83

Sources: Robert J. Coen, "Ad Spending Outlook Brightens," *Advertising Age*, 15 May 1989, 24; "Media Muscle: The Power of Numbers," *Advertising Age*, 9 November 1988, 66–67; and "A Mixed-Bag Future," *Advertising Age*, 24 May 1989, 68.

THE PURPOSE OF A BUSINESS

In his celebrated book on management, Drucker, as is his style, starts with the most basic question imaginable: What is the purpose of a business? His response is equally simple.

There is only one valid definition of business purpose: to create a customer. Markets are not created by God, nature, or economic forces but by businessmen. . . . It is the customer who determines what a business is.[43]

What then is the essential function of a business? To Drucker "the business enterprise has two, and only these two, basic functions: marketing and innovation. Marketing and innovation produce results; all the rest are 'costs.' "[44]

If Drucker is correct, if the most important task of the effective executive is marketing, then what is "marketing"? He defined it in simple but elegant terms. Marketing "is the whole business seen from the point of view of its final result, that is, from the customer's point of view. Concern and responsibility for marketing must, therefore, permeate all areas of the enterprise."[45]

Some individuals have equated marketing with selling. Drucker disagrees strongly with this position.

Selling and marketing are antithetical rather than synonymous or even complementary. There will always, one can assume, be need for selling.

But the aim of marketing is to make selling superfluous. The aim of marketing is to know and understand the customer so well that the product or service fits him [or her] and sells itself.[46]

As for innovation, Drucker has written extensively on this topic. His thoughts are worth considering.

The second function of a business is, therefore, innovation, the provision of different economic satisfactions. It is not enough for the business to provide just any economic goods and services; it must provide better and more economic ones. It is not necessary for a business to grow bigger; but it is necessary that it constantly grow better.[47]

APPROACH TO MARKETING TRAINING

These ideas of Peter Drucker, a professor emeritus at New York University, form the essential thesis of this book. The only way for the business publishing industry to survive in the 1990s is to adopt effective marketing procedures, to seek to understand the wants and needs of the customer, and to abandon the idea that the primary function of an advertising manager is to sell space.

The business magazine industry is at a crossroads; all of the key economic indicators are negative. Unless bold, intelligent steps are taken, the market share held by the business periodical industry will continue to shrink, leaving an emaciated industry unable or unwilling to respond to the exciting business challenges and opportunities of the 1990s. Those who reject this approach, those industry "dinosaurs" who pine for the glory days of the 1940s and 1950s, are doomed to fail, bringing with them countless thousands of people employed in this industry.

Drucker also says over and over again that management is a rational activity. Effective executives must set goals, priorities, and objectives. The marketing notes and cases that follow have been designed specifically to stimulate thinking and discussion on a wide variety of important ideas. This author hopes that these written materials will prove helpful in preparing the next generation of business publishers in the United States.

NOTES

1. U.S. Department of Commerce, Bureau of the Census, *1982 Census of Manufactures* (Washington, D.C.: GPO, 1984), 27A-6; U.S. Department of Commerce, International Trade Administration, *1990 U.S. Industrial Outlook* (Washington, D.C.: GPO, 1990), 48-1–48-13. For additional information about employment projections for the publishing industry, see *Employment Projections for 1995: Data and Methods* (Washington, D.C.: GPO, 1986), 39, 41–56; and *Occupational Employment in Manufacturing Industries* (Washington, D.C.: GPO, 1985), 45–50.

2. *1982 Census*, 27A-7, 27A-8.

3. *1982 Census*, 27A-10–27A-14.

4. U.S. Department of Commerce, Bureau of the Census, *County Business Patterns, 1986: New York* (Washington, D.C.: GPO, 1986), 122–31.

5. U.S. Department of Commerce, International Trade Administration, *1989 U.S. Industrial Outlook* (Washington, D.C.: GPO, 1989), 17–20.

6. Ibid., 21.

7. "*MagazineWeek* 500," *MagazineWeek*, 23 October 1989, 26.

8. *1988 MagazineWeek 500* (Natick, Mass.: MagazineWeek Partners, 1988), 1; "Ideas & Trends: Who Buys . . . *Navy Times? Dirt Rider? New York Times*, 29 October 1989, sec. 4, 29. Also see Publishers Information Bureau, *PIB: Magazine Advertising Pages and Dollars Gain in First Six Months of 1988* (New York: PIB, 1988), no page numbers. Also see *The Folio: 400/1986* (Stamford, Conn.: Folio Publishing, 1987), 29; and the advertising linage statistics in *Advertising Age*, 18 July 1988, 42. For a detailed statistical analysis of the American business publishing industry, see Albert N. Greco, *Business Journalism: Management Notes and Cases* (New York: New York University Press, 1988). For additional data about markets, see Martin Greenberger ed., *Electronic Publishing Plus* (White Plains, N.Y.: Knowledge Industry Publications, 1985); Joost Kist, *Electronic Publishing* (London: Croom Helm, 1987); Judith S. Duke, *The Technical, Scientific, and Medical Publishing Market* (White Plains, N.Y.: Knowledge Industry Publications, 1985); "Legal Publications: A New Growth Industry," *New York Times*, 19 August 1988, B5. Also see Gary Levin, "Industry Back on the Right Track," *Advertising Age*, 15 June 1987, S-1.

9. Standard Rate and Data Service, *Business Publications Rates and Data, Part I* (Wilmette, Ill.: Standard Rate and Data Service, July 24, 1988).

10. U.S. Department of Commerce, International Trade Administration, *1988 U.S. Industrial Outlook* (Washington, D.C.: GPO, 1988), 29–5–29–7; Gale Research, *The Gale Directory of Publications* (Detroit, Mich.: Gale Research, 1987).

11. U.S. Department of Commerce, Bureau of the Census, *1982 Census of Manufactures: Newspapers, Periodicals, Books, and Miscellaneous Publishing* (Washington, D.C.: GPO, 1985), 27A-6, 27A-11; *1977 Census of Manufactures: Newspapers, Periodicals, Books, and Miscellaneous Publishing* (Washington, D.C.: GPO, 1980), 27A-6, 27A-11.

12. Ibid. For some stimulating ideas, also see Irving Louis Horowitz, *Communicating Ideas: The Crisis of Publishing in a Post-Industrial Society* (New York: Oxford University Press, 1986).

13. U.S. Department of Commerce, *1988 U.S. Industrial Outlook*, 29–5–29–7.

14. Ibid.

15. Robert J. Coen, "Ad Spending Outlook Brightens," *Advertising Age*, 15 May 1989, 24; "Media Muscle: The Power of Numbers," *Advertising Age*, 9 November 1988, 66–67; and additional calculations by the author.

16. Council of Economic Advisors, *Economic Indicators, January 1988*, (Washington, D.C.: GPO, 1988), 1. Also see Pamela Sebastian, "Data Likely to Signal Mounting Inflation," *Wall Street Journal*, 8 August 1988, 18; Martin F. Feldstein, ed., *The U.S. in the World Economy* (Cambridge, Mass.: National Bureau of Economic Research, 1987), 49–53.

17. Coen, "Media Muscle . . . ," 66–67.

18. Liz Horton, "Business Titles Slip as Consumer Books Gain," *Folio*, January 1990, 16.

19. Ibid., 16.

20. Ibid., 16.

21. Ibid., 16.

22. Neal Weinstock, "Leaner Times Bedevil Business Magazines," *Advertising Age*, 20 June 1988, S-24–S-25; Joanne Lipman, "Estimate for '88 U.S. Ad Spending Is Sliced by Prominent Forecaster," *Wall Street Journal*, 16 June 1988, 28; Philip H. Dougherty, "Smaller Gain for Ads in '88 Is Predicted," *New York Times*, 16 June 1988, D23; Johnnie L. Roberts, "Forecast Lowered for '88 Spending on Newspaper Ads," *Wall Street Journal*, 3 August 1988, 24.

23. Weinstock, "Leaner Times . . . ," S-24.

24. Ibid., S-25.

25. "Bank Magazines Still Bear Scars from October 19," *Publishing News*, Pilot Issue (July 1988), 13. For additional data see Tom Herman, "Economists Expect Expansion to Continue for at Least a Year Despite a Faster Inflation Pace and Increase in Interest Rates," *Wall Street Journal*, 5 July 1988, 3; "A Sampling of Interest-Rate and Economic Forecasts," *Wall Street Journal*, 6 July 1988, 37; Pamela Sebastian, "Robust Economy Raises Inflation Fears," *Wall Street Journal*, 11 July 1988, 22; Alan Murray, "Greenspan Signals Higher Interest Rates," *Wall Street Journal*, 14 July 1988, 2; Lindley H. Clark, Jr., and

Alfred Malabre, Jr., "Economists Fret Over Consumer Outlays," *Wall Street Journal*, 3 August 1988, 6; and Victor Zarnowitz, "Economic Outlook Survey: Second Quarter 1988," *NBER* [National Bureau of Economic Research] Reporter, Summer 1988, 11–14.

26. Patrick Reilly, "Trade Journals Riding Rebound of U.S. Industry," *Advertising Age*, 16 May 1988, 50.

27. "Ad Revenues by Group Publisher," *Advertising Age*, 21 November 1988, S17.

28. "MagazineWeek 500," *MagazineWeek*, 23 October 1989, 26.

29. "100 Leading Media Companies by Revenues," *Advertising Age*, 26 June 1989, S2.

30. Ibid.

31. "Bank Magazines Still Bear Scares from October 19 [1987]," *Publishing News*, Pilot Issue (July 1988), 13.

32. "MagazineWeek 500," *MagazineWeek*, 23 October 1989, 26.

33. "Tops in the Trades," *Advertising Age*, 12 June 1989, 158.

34. Scott Donaton, "Business Publishers Caught in Vicious Rate-Cutting Trap as Big Shakeout Looms," *Advertising Age*, 12 June 1989, S1.

35. Ibid., S1.

36. Ibid., S1.

37. "MagazineWeek 500," *MagazineWeek*, 23 October 1989, 26.

38. Audits and Survey Department, *Newsweek*, "How Professionals/Managers Read Business and Newsweekly Magazines: A Landmark Study-Phase II," *Newsweek*, 1986.

39. Ibid.

40. Robert Coen, "A Mixed-Bag Future," *Advertising Age*, 24 May 1989, 68.

41. Ibid.

42. Robert Coen, "Ad Spending . . .," 2.

43. Peter Drucker, *Management: Tasks, Responsibilities, Practices* (New York: Harper & Row, 1974), 61.

44. Ibid., 61.

45. Ibid., 63.

46. Ibid., 64.

47. Ibid., 65.

TWO

Business Publishing History and Case Studies

INTRODUCTION

Business publications have an intriguing history; yet most citizens of the United States are unaware of the role these periodicals have played in the evolution of this nation. To address this situation, a *brief* history of the industry is presented. It is followed by a comprehensive review of the major United States and foreign business publishers active within the U.S. as of January 1990, although financial records for these firms is based on 1987 and 1988 data.

A BRIEF HISTORY OF BUSINESS PUBLICATIONS IN THE UNITED STATES

Calvin Coolidge, who was president of the United States in the 1920s, once remarked that the business of America was business. Many academicians would agree with him. Yet, ironically, the very first two magazines issued in North America in 1741 (in the days before the thirteen American colonies revolted against the rule of Great Britain and became the United States) were political and not business periodicals.

Andrew Bradford's *American Magazine* was the first American title, issued on 13 February 1741. Three days later Benjamin Franklin, one of the founding fathers of the United States and a *philosophe* of the first rank, published his *General Magazine*.

According to Franklin scholar J. A. Leo Lamay, Franklin had announced on 13 November 1740, in his illustrative *Gazette*, plans to launch America's first magazine. Franklin later accused Bradford of stealing his plan for this periodical. Franklin was piqued, and he undercut the newsstand price of Bradford's magazine by three shillings (selling it for only nine shillings), thereby establishing the time-honored U.S. tradition of rate-cutting!

Frank Luther Mott, the foremost historian of the American magazine industry, remarked that Franklin's *General Magazine* "had more pages and more variety than its rival."[1] Yet these two publishers, ironically both working in the important colonial port city of Philadelphia, entered into America's first wrenching circulation war, and both of these titles failed within months of each other. Franklin's magazine was the "victor" in this circulation confrontation, lasting all of six months; his rival's magazine died after only three months!

Three other magazines were issued in 1743, and all of them quickly perished in what was a rather hostile business environment. It was not until 1752 that another magazine was born, and it soon followed the same well-worn path of its predecessors into oblivion.

If modern-day publishers believe that it is exceptionally difficult to survive, much less dominate a market niche today, then they would be appalled at the business conditions confront ing editors and publishers in North America in the mid-eighteenth century.

All of the American colonies at that time lacked an effective typesetting and printing infrastructure; and the quality of almost all of the early titles was embarrassingly low, if not downright marginal. There was no distribution network, since these British colonies lacked both a reliable postal system and an efficient transportation network. Consequently, if a magazine were made available to individuals in a restricted geographical region, for example, business executives in lower New York City near Wall Street or on the developing Hudson River side of the city, publishers faced the horrible specter of not having any efficient advertising, fulfillment, and collection support services. Compounding these obviously severe problems were reader indifference and a lack of people who could read.

This author reviewed the list of all magazines published in the United States in the eighteenth and nineteenth centuries, and this study revealed that only seventeen periodicals were issued in what became the United States between the years 1741 and 1776, the year the American Revolution began.[2]

However, once independence was achieved, this nation experienced a virtual explosion of economic activity. The industrial revolution had begun in England in 1760, and the ideas, technology, and equipment associated with this cultural, social, and economic metamorphosis eventually filtered into the United States, often "borrowed" from Great Britain without proper permission.

As might be expected, there was a corresponding increase in general magazine publishing activity. Between 1776 and 1800, sixty-five new titles emerged. Many of them dealt with medical, scientific, and religious issues, clearly a reflection of the new nation's concerns.

However, in the years after the inauguration of George Washington as president of the United States in 1789, the outburst of new periodical titles was truly astounding. The following table (2.1), based entirely on the historical scholarship of Mott and calculations by this author, lists the total number of new titles released between 1741 and 1869.[3]

The very first American business "publication" was issued in 1752 in Halifax, Nova Scotia, then an important maritime center and now part of Canada. This crudely printed broadside listed the buying and selling prices for various commodities (for example, beer, honey, mustard, tobacco, and wheat). Dubbed "price-currents," these documents were issued irregularly in North America throughout the 1750s.

By the end of the eighteenth century, after the formation of the

Table 2.1 / U.S. Periodicals: 1741–1869

Decade	Number of New Titles Issued in That Decade	Total Number of New Periodicals Issued since 1741	Percentage Increase over Previous Decade
1741–1749	5	5	—
1750–1759	7	12	+140.0
1760–1769	1	13	+ 14.3
1770–1779	5	18	+500.0
1780–1789	15	33	+300.0
1790–1799	49	82	+326.7
1800–1809	56	136	+114.3
1810–1819	58	196	+103.6
1820–1829	98	294	+169.0
1830–1839	122	416	+124.5
1840–1849	133	549	+109.0
1850–1859	321	870	+241.1
1860–1869	377	1,247	+117.4

Source: Frank Luther Mott, *A History of American Magazines, vol. 1, 1741–1850* (Cambridge, Mass: Harvard University Press, 1966), 13–17, 24.

United States of America, "price-currents," could be found in every major maritime center, including Boston, New York, Philadelphia, and Charleston. Because of the peace, the United States experienced a period of economic activity, which enabled the Republic to develop an effective public school system. All of this allowed the nation to support other types of business publications.

The following table (2.2), based on a detailed statistical analysis of Forsyth's studies, outlines the developmental patterns of these early business publications.[4]

Between 1800 and 1865, a significant number of medical, scientific, technical, and what would be perceived today as "hard business" magazines (as opposed to mere lists of commodity prices) emerged, some of which were still published in 1990!

In the medical-healthcare fields, some of these early busi ness publications included the *Journal of the Philadelphia College of Pharmacy* (first issued in 1835; published today as the *American Journal of Pharmacy*); *American Druggists' Circular and Chemical Gazette* (1857; published today as *Drug Topics*); and *New England Journal of Medicine, the* internationally respected medical journal

Table 2.2 / Business Publications: 1752–1869

Decade	Number of New Titles Issued	Total Number of New Periodicals Issued Since 1752	Percentage Change Previous Decade
1752–59	1	1	—
1760–69	0	1	—
1770–79	2	3	+200
1780–89	3	6	+100
1790–99	4	10	+40
1800–09	4	14	+40
1810–19	8	22	+57
1820–29	8	30	+36
1830–39	11	41	+30
1840–49	16	57	+39
1850–59	42	99	+73
1860–69	25	125	+25

Source: David Forsyth, *The Business Press in America: 1750–1865* (Philadelphia, Penn: Chilton, 1964), 20–87.

(first issued in 1826; still published today by the Massachusetts Medical Society).

Scientific titles were also popular, and a few of the more interesting ones included *Scientific American* (1844; still published); the *American Mineralogical Journal* (1810); and the *Journal of the Franklin Institute* (1826; still issued).

Technology was, perhaps, the most active publishing market niche at that time. Some of these early titles included *Rail-Road Advocate* (1831); the *American Railroad Journal* (1832); *American Telegraph, Aerial Reporter,* and the *Ink Fountain* (all first issued in 1852); and the *National Petroleum Times* (1865).

Some of the major business periodicals included *Thompson's Bank Note Reporter* (1836; published today as *American Banker,* ironically by the Thomson Corporation of Canada); the *Bankers' Weekly Circular and Statistical Record* (1845; issued today as the *Banking Law Journal*); and the short-lived *Wall Street Journal* (1852–1879; which proves that a good business magazine title has a certain enduring quality).

During the administration of Andrew Jackson, a distinct western presence was evident in this nation's capital, and the first business magazine was issued in what had been a "frontier" region.

The rapid geographical expansion of the United States was mirrored with the development of titles in Cincinnati, Ohio, and St. Louis, Missouri.

During the U.S. Civil War (1861–1865), Pittsburgh, Pennsylvania, emerged as one of the country's great industrial centers, a title this grand city of the Steelers held well into the 1970s. Business periodicals catering to the mercantile and oil industries emerged and enjoyed decades of success.

HISTORICAL MARKETS AND PURPOSES

Comparing these eighteenth- and nineteenth-century business magazine titles and market niches with the largest periodical categories in 1990 reveals an intriguing fact: there has been no significant change in business magazine market niches in over 180 years. The only exceptions are data systems, automotive, and radio and television; and even these groups are merely offshoots of the technology, transportation, and communications categories that were utilized in the nineteenth century. American business publishers have been servicing the same markets, albeit in a more sophisticated way, since the days when Thomas Jefferson was president and Albert Gallatin was the secretary of the treasury.

If this is the case, then has the purpose of America's business publications changed? Clearly, it has not changed. It was, and today still is, a "school of continuing education" for the nation's leaders in the fields of commerce, technology, science, and the professions. This goal of the business publishing industry was stated rather eloquently by Julius Elfenbein many years ago when he remarked that these specialized business or professional publications acted as an "extension school" for individuals unable to attend school or college but nonetheless keenly interested in keeping abreast of the latest developments in their industry or profession.[5]

Period of Rapid Expansion after 1865

Within the first 113 years of its history (1752–1865, including the colonial period), the United States of America witnessed the publication of a total of 124 business publications; yet only a mere forty-five of them were still functioning by the end of the Civil War. Within the next century (through 1964), business periodicals grew at a dramatic rate, reaching a staggering twenty-three hundred titles.[6] By 1990, the United States of America supported somewhere in the neighborhood of five thousand business publications, not including countless hundreds of electronic information systems and magazines issued irregularly, for example, annuals or trade meeting titles!

As opposed to the eighteenth and nineteenth centuries, it is exceptionally difficult to deal even briefly with the rapid expansion of business publishing in the United States since the end of the Civil War. Perhaps the most interesting way to address this dynamic period of business publishing history is to point out a *few* of the changes in the American landscape that afforded this industry the opportunity to experience such a rapid growth in business titles.

Improvements in the Graphic Arts and Business Administration

In the last century, the "systems" associated with publishing improved dramatically. Composition, printing, and binding equipment became standardized and readily available, as did a skilled labor force needed to operate this complicated equipment. The quality of letterpress and, later, offset lithography and gravure, and technological changes in paper, photography, and color reproduction systems materially changed the look and quality of the final product, making magazines more appealing to both advertisers and subscribers.

Effective circulation, auditing, fulfillment, and accounts payable and receivable systems were developed that made the publishing industry more "businesslike." The emergence of colleges of journalism and business administration also provided a source of critically needed editorial and managerial personnel.

Between 1920 and 1945, the U.S experienced an economic growth rate unrivaled in recent history. This business expansion created a dynamic market keenly interested in obtaining timely information about manufacturing products, processes, and procedures, along with data regarding the creation of better services for customers.

This nation's financial system provided publishers with needed capital to expand and satisfy the needs of the market.

In addition, the desire to succeed in business, an area keenly studied by historians, sociologists, and psychologists, created a pervasive business culture that emphasized quality and innovation. A sophisticated system of higher education provided an almost endless stream of research papers on both applied and theoretical science and technology developments, many of which were later adapted by the business community and turned into a series of major products, such as the transistor, the microchip, the personal computer, and a variety of items first developed for the U.S. space program.

Lastly, this country's premier graduate schools of business administration developed theoretical and practical systems in accounting, finance, management, marketing, and computer sciences that revolutionized the way business is conducted in the nation and especially within the publishing industry.

Add all of these technical and business developments to the emergence after 1920 of a group of highly sophisticated, creative editors (plus a great deal of hard work and a lot of luck), and you get an idea how the U.S. business publishing industry evolved into what it is today. For detailed statistical data on the rise of magazine publishing in the United States, see this researcher's book *Business Journalism: Management Notes and Cases*, published in 1988 by New York University Press.

Business Magazines and Changes in American Industry

Did business publications influence or change the industries they covered? No definitive answer can be presented since there are about five thousand different business publications issued annually in the United States. Yet after a review of the history of magazines in the United States, it is clear that an impressive number of these business periodicals have had a major impact on their industries and society. The following *brief* case studies of only a few specific business publications highlights this interesting phenomenon. The fact that only a few studies can be presented reveals clearly the need for systematic historical research in this area.

Railroad Periodicals. The railroad helped open up the great American West in the nineteenth century; yet few people know that the nation's numerous railroad publications played an instrumental role in the economic and social transformation of a key region in the United States. The *American Railroad Journal,* the preeminent title in the industry, was aided by the *American Railway Times* and the *Western Railroad Gazette,* among many others, in its attempts to lobby for the development of a transcontinental railroad. During the American Civil War (1861–1865), articles in these publications convinced the United States Congress of the military necessity for such an endeavor; and these publications were able to stimulate interest in the financial community to provide the vast amounts of capital desperately needed for this massive expansion of the nation's transportation system.

While railroad publications achieved a measure of success in the 1850s and 1860s unrivaled by many other industry publications, regrettably these railroad titles failed to lobby for effective safety regulations. This prompted blue-collar railroad employees to join the then-developing American labor unions in order to obtain much-needed protective legislation on the state and national level.[7]

The Book Trade. Since the late nineteenth century, one of United States's most influential business publications was, and remains, *Publishers Weekly,* today issued by Cahners (a unit of Reed International, a United Kingdom corporation). As the American book industry matured and no longer catered solely to readers in a few principal cities on the east coast of the nation, it became readily apparent that editors, bookstore owners, and other interested parties needed an effective national business publication devoted to its diverse needs. A number of titles surfaced, including the short-lived *Literary World: A Review of Current Literature.*

However, with the emergence of *Publishers Weekly* in 1873, the book industry was served with a superb business publication devoted to alerting industry leaders about national and international bestsellers, lobbying for effective copyright legislation, and providing an endless series of well-written articles that educated editors and storekeepers alike about the ever-changing business of the "accidental profession." Clearly *Publishers Weekly* became the distinguished, objective conscience of an entire industry.[8]

Medical Magazines. At times only a fine line separates the art of medicine from the "science" of quackery. In 1844 America's fledgling medical profession desperately needed to establish clearly defined standards regarding medical education and licensure. In that year a national convention of doctors met at New York University's medical school to address this problem. Because of the success of this meeting, the American Medical Association was created, and annual national meetings were held. While superb medical papers were read at the convention, it was exceptionally costly for the average doctor to attend these annual events. The nation's underdeveloped transportation system also hindered physicians since only a small percentage of the nation's doctors could navigate their way to the meetings.

Consequently, it was readily apparent to the leaders of this association that they needed an efficient way to get the latest information presented in these papers about anesthesia, medical botony, endemic and epidemic diseases, and hygiene and sanitation to practioners in small American communities.

On 14 July 1883, the *Journal of the American Medical Association* was launched. In the next century, this journal played a critically important role in keeping its members informed about the myriad of medical and scientific developments that changed the way Americans lived. The *Journal* lobbied effectively against quack "doctors" and alleged "cures" that in reality presented significant dangers to the American public. In addition the *Journal* was active in the critically important medical mobilizations during both World War I and World War II.[9] This business publication also played *the* major role in the creation of an effective medical profession in the United States, and, obviously, the world.

The Magazine Business. Yet which publication affected the development of the magazine industry in the United States? While this industry has its roots in colonial America, only recently has a major national publication emerged to serve the diverse needs of the magazine manager.

Less than twenty years ago, *Folio* was first issued. Since that time this publication, which describes itself as the "magazine for the magazine manager," has followed the honored dictate of Elfenbein and provided its readers with usable knowledge about this quickly changing industry.

Folio thoroughly covers the latest developments in editorial, advertising, sales, research, promotion, circulation, fulfillment, key business developments, and production areas. In addition it cosponsors (approximately) six regional and one national convention where hundreds of seminars and workshops are offered on matters of concern to both seasoned professionals and newly hired employees. Experienced magazine executives run these high quality educational seminars.

This magazine has "lobbied" for reasonable postal rates, called upon the industry to consolidate disparate, competing trade association functions, asked for better magazine auditing procedures, and demanded an emphasis on integrity in all phases of magazine research. In addition *Folio* created an educational foundation that administers the Publishing Hall of Fame and also provides financial grants to colleges with publishing programs.

Its publisher has become the industry's most eloquent spokesman and, to a substantial degree, overshadowed the efforts of the presidents of the two main trade associations representing business and consumer magazine publications in this nation.

Need for Historical Studies

Unfortunately, the list of influential business publications is endless, and, given the length of this chapter and the nature of this book, it is impossible to provide more examples. However, business publications have directly, and generally positively, affected the industries they serve and the nation as a whole.

What is needed, clearly, is a comprehensive history of the magazine industry in the United States. Mott's five-volume history ends abruptly early in the twentieth century because of his untimely death in 1938; Forsyth's superb book only covers the industry until 1865. The existing histories of magazine companies, although useful, do not match the narrative structure and richness of detail found in Mott's books, nor do they rival the detailed analysis of these industries found in Forsyth.[10]

The entire magazine industry and publishing scholars must be urged to address this shortage of historical studies on what is, unquestionably, one of the most interesting and influential forms of mass communications in the history of the United States.

CASE STUDIES OF MAJOR UNITED STATES AND FOREIGN BUSINESS PUBLISHERS

In order to provide some insight into the workings of America's eclectic, global business publishing industry, case studies of seven major U.S. and four foreign publishing companies (all doing business in the United States) will be presented.

Selecting only a few of the dozens of business publishers was not an easy task. Many sizable corporations had to be excluded, including such important American publishers as A/S/M/, Affiliated, Bill Communications, Commerce Clearing House, Cowles Media, Crain Communications, Hearst, the Nexis-Lexis unit of Mead, Pennwell, Penton, Whitney, Williams and Wilkins, and Ziff Communications. Many major foreign publishers also had to be excluded, for example, Maclean Hunter, Elsevier, Pearson PLC, and Axel Springer-Verlag AG.

This author decided to concentrate only on those concerns actively involved in the *entire* spectrum of business publishing, including the evolving and trend-setting electronic component. Most of the financial data covers the years 1987–1988.

Major U.S. Business Publishing Companies

Dow Jones. Dow Jones is America's premier business publisher and information services provider. In 1988 it was ranked number 238 on the *Fortune 500*, and it posted sales of $1.603 billion (up a strong 22 percent from 1987), operating profits of $228 million (+12 percent), and net income per share of $2.35. With total assets of $2.11 billion and a long-term debt of $290 million, down from over $408 million in 1987, it had a price-earnings ratio of 11. (This ratio is frequently called the "P-E". P-E is generally defined as the price of a single share of common stock divided by earnings per share for a twelve-month period. For example, a stock selling for one hundred dollars per share and generating earnings of ten dollars per share would have a P-E ratio of 10:1, normally called a P-E ratio of 10.)

In addition Dow Jones had a 14.2 percent profit as a percentage of sales, and its sterling reputation earned Dow Jones an A+ rating from Standard and Poor's.[11]

This large, global media corporation has three operating units.

Dow Jones

Business Publications	Community Newspapers	Information Services

Business publications clearly occupy the seat of honor at Dow Jones, led by its world-class daily newspaper the *Wall Street Journal* and its two international editions, the *Asian Wall Street Journal* and the *Wall Street Journal/Europe.*

Business periodicals generated $846.63 million in revenues and operating revenues of $174.18 million, which represented 47 percent of its revenues and 30 percent of its profits. Yet even the *Wall Street Journal* suffered through the same decline in advertising dollars that other business periodicals sustained since 1987.[12]

Circulation has been flat at the *Journal* since 1983, hovering at the 1.95 million mark. Advertising rates have increased each year since 1977 in spite of sharp decreases in advertising linage in the period 1985–1989.

Editors at the *Journal* have been told to curtail expenditures in order to compensate for a total decline in ad dollars. Yet everyone at the *Journal*, from editorial interns to top management, from its devoted coterie of readers to professors of publishing, are concerned that, sooner or later, these cutbacks will ultimately affect the quality of the paper.

In addition to the harsh impact of the October 1987 global stock market crash, and the resulting loss of advertising revenues, the *Journal* has also faced the specter of more direct, aggressive competition from a variety of publications, including the always-formidable *New York Times* (and its increased daily coverage of the business world), the popular *USA Today*, the interesting *Investor's Daily*, Reutters (a sophisticated corporation offering a plethora of impressive reporting services), and other business periodicals and electronic databases. In addition, many financial service companies, especially banks in the Pacific Rim region, have started to develop their own business reporting services for both in-house utilization and their customers' use. This business news niche has become a veritable battlefield; and shakeouts will become inevitable in the business publishing field in the early- to mid-1990s as corporations realize that they will not be able to provide the type of financial support needed to remain innovative and competitive in a highly charged technological-based business environment.

In 1988 many staffers at the *Journal* exhibited concern when rumors surfaced that one of the major global communications corporations indicated an "interest" in creating a national distribution system for an American version of the *Financial Times*. However, no concrete steps were undertaken on this project. Obviously this was a sign that even key managers are willing to admit that the *Wall Street Journal* no longer has a stranglehold over the national and, indeed, international dissemination of business information in the United States.

Dow Jones also issues two other important business publications. One of them is the well-known business weekly *Barron's*. Its 1988 circulation topped 246,500 (− 38,300; − 13.44 percent from

1987). Advertising lines were also soft in 1988, down a dramatic 11.6 percent one year after posting a sharp 8.9 percent increase over 1986.

Its other business title is the impressive statistical periodical *American Demographics*, one of the nation's fastest-growing business publications with a high subscription price.

Dow Jones's Information Services group is quite interesting. In 1987 it had sales of $252.15 million and operating revenues of $92.92 million, which represented 38 percent of total revenues and 58 percent of its profits. This unit is deeply involved in an impressive variety of national and global electronic information services, including News-Retrieval (+25 percent in revenues in 1987), a provider of global computerized business and financial news servicing upwards of 82 percent of the country's five hundred largest corporations and over 85 percent of the largest banks in America; the impressive Dow Jones News Service, often called the "Broadtape" (with 39,900 terminals in place); the Dow Jones Professional Investor Report; Text-Search Service (a database); the Capital Markets Report, an international newswire operating twenty-four hours a day for the fixed-income and financial-futures markets (revenues were up a strong 30 percent in 1987); the AP-Dow Jones, providing subscribers in more than fifty nations with timely news information and financial data; Dow Phone Audio Network; and Desktop Express, an electronic mail service.

Dow Jones also maintains a successful chain of twenty-three community newspapers. These papers had revenues in 1987 of $215.66 million and an operating income of $47.37 million; they generated 15 percent of the corporate revenues and 12 percent of Dow Jones's total profits.

Sources of operating income as a percentage of the corporation's annual revenues for 1987 were as follows: business publications, 20.6 percent; information services, 36.8 percent; and community newspapers, 22.0 percent.

In July 1987 Dow Jones purchased a 14 percent equity position in Groupe Expansion SA, France's leading business publisher. Two months later Dow Jones increased its ownership in Telerate (a major source of computerized financial information) from 45 to 55 percent. By 1988 its holding in Telerate increased to 66.5 percent, and in 1989 it purchased the rest of the company.

Telerate has exhibited great promise in the electronic publishing marketplace. In October 1987 Telerate and AT&T entered into a partnership to offer subscribers access to foreign exchange transaction services through desktop terminals or telephones. In March 1989 Dow Jones announced that Telerate and Intex Holdings. received a contract to supply the London International Financial Futures Exchange with a fully automated trading system, which is expected to become operational by 1990.

In February 1988 Dow Jones sold its high-visibility book-publishing unit, Richard D. Irwin, for $135 million in order to concentrate its efforts on print and electronic business information services.

In spite of the advertising linage problems at the *Wall Street Journal*, a problem that has plagued almost all U.S. business publishers since 1987, Dow Jones remains one of the world's major sources of business publications and information services. It has paid dividends continuously since 1906, and the Bancroft family owns or controls 55 percent of the Dow Jones common and Class B stock, providing a sense of stability for the corporation. Long-term debt has hovered near the $290 million mark.

In light of Dow Jones's immensely strong position as a global business publisher/information services company and its recent acquisition activity, Dow Jones should be able to increase its market share position in the 1990s in spite of intense competition within the United States and abroad.

Times-Mirror. The famed historian Jacques Barzun once wrote that "whoever wants to know the heart and mind of America better learn baseball, the rules and realities of the game." If Barzun is correct, then the Times-Mirror Company is ideally positioned to capitalize on the American and international communications market since they own the *Sporting News*, America's leading weekly baseball and general sports tabloid. In addition, this $3.333 billion company is also one of America's fastest-growing business publishing and information services entities, ranked number 138 on the 1988 *Fortune 500*. Profits tallied $332 million.[13]

In 1988 Times-Mirror had five operating units.

Times-Mirror

Newspapers	Books, Magazines, and Other Publications	Broadcast Television	Cable Television	Other Activities

Income for these divisions were as follows: newspapers generated revenues of $1.996 billion (60 percent of the corporation's total, 58 percent of its profits, and operating profits of $337.88 million); books, magazines, and other publications generated $648.4 million in revenues (26 percent of the total, 24 percent of the profits, and operating profits of $119.5 million); broadcast television's revenues topped $110.1 million (3 percent of the total, 8 percent of total profits, and $58.4 million in operating profits); cable television finished with over $239.8 million in total revenues (8 percent of the revenues and $48.8 million in operating profits); the "other" category accumulated $111.6 in revenues (3 percent of the profits and over $22.5 million [2 percent] in operating profits).

Times-Mirror publishes five daily newspapers, including the impressive Long Island, New York-based *Newsday* and the *Los Angeles Times*, one of the leading newspapers on the West Coast. It also owns four television stations and a large cable television system servicing fifteen states.

Its book, magazine, and other publishing division generated $648.4 million in 1987, up 10 percent over the previous year. Most of the revenues and profits came from the professional publishing component. This unit generated profits of $119.5 million in 1987 (up a staggering 26 percent over the prior year) on an impressive operations profit margin of 18.4 percent.

This large professional publishing group contained Matthew Bender, a leading loose-leaf supplement and book publisher servicing a variety of fields, including the legal and accounting professions; the Year Book Medical Publishing unit, with eighteen hundred titles; Jeppesen Sonderson, an intriguing firm specializing in providing published information for 240 firms in the airline industry; Richard D. Irwin, an impressive business book publisher with a backlist of over eleven hundred different titles; the *Sporting News* (this is *the* leading sports periodical in the United States; it also maintains a popular book publishing unit issuing some of the nation's premier statistical books on baseball, football, hockey, and basketball, plus an assortment of other sports titles); Dialog Information Services, one of the nation's leading computerized databases; and seven other publish ing units.

C. V. Mosby, a scholarly journal publisher with over two thousand titles, is an interesting operating unit. Mosby's titles in the highly important and lucrative medical-healthcare field is most impressive. It issues some of America's most important journals, including the *Journal of Allergy and Clinical Immunology* (released monthly with 8,576 paid subscribers), the famed *Journal of Pediatrics* (a monthly with 24,821 paid subscribers); and the *Journal of the American Academy of Dermatology* (another monthly with 12,776 paid subscribers).

Times-Mirror has total assets of $3.476 billion, generates a strong 14.5 percent return on assets, has a long-term debt of $876.9 million, and an impressive A- Standard and Poor's rating. In January 1988 it spent $167.5 million for four consumer magazines; the following month it purchased the Irwin unit for $135 million, which should be a good companion piece for the Times-Mirror professional and business publishing unit.

Clearly Times-Mirror is in the market for acquisitions. In January 1989 it acquired Zenger-Miller, a California firm that provides training programs and consulting services. In addition the PSG Publishing Company was obtained because of its strong list of titles in the health science area and a number of periodicals.

It is one of America's major business publishers/information systems companies; and, given its recent track record, it is likely that Times-Mirror will continue to evaluate possible acquisitions in order to increase its market share in the diverse business publications field.

Capital Cities/ ABC. Francis Bacon (1561–1626) once wrote that "a wise man will make more opportunities than he finds." Thomas

S. Murphy (Chairman) and Daniel B. Burke (President) of Capital Cities certainly personify what Bacon had in mind. They started out with a small television station in upstate New York. Now they lead one of the world's largest diversified communications companies.

Yet Capital Cities/ABC is no highly centralized company, reminiscent of IT&T under the famed Harold Geneen. The Capital Cities's motto is "decentralization." In their 1987 annual report, Murphy and Burke outlined this philosophy. "Our goal is to hire the best people we can possibly find and give them the responsibility and authority they need to perform their jobs."[14]

Capital Cities has a lean organizational chart. While income is reported for two groups, in reality they have three operating units.

Capital Cities/ ABC

ABC Television Network Group	Broadcast Group	Publishing

Does this system work? In 1988 Capital Cities had revenues of $4.773 billion, an operating income of $904 million, net income of $279.08 million, and produced a 13.4 percent return on average stockholders' equity. Capital Cities is the veritable cash machine that Bruce Henderson of the Boston Consulting Group described years ago, and its available cash flow in 1987 was $292.77 million, up 37 percent from the previous year.[15]

Obviously the ABC television-radio portion of Capital Cities is well known internationally. As of 3 January 1988 it operated the ABC Television Network of 222 primary affiliated stations and owned outright eight television stations (with five of them in the top five U.S. markets), twenty-one radio stations, and a cable television programming unit.

Broadcasting yielded $3.434 billion in 1987 revenues and $679.44 million in operating income. In 1977 all broadcasting and publishing units of Capital Cities generated only $306.15 million!

Publishing occupies a special niche at Capital Cities, which is involved in newspapers, shopping guides, specialty and business periodicals and books, consumer magazines, records, the world's largest religious publishing unit, and electronic databases. In 1987 specialized business publications had $312.51 million in advertising revenues, $62.23 million in circulation dollars, and another $184.24 million in "other" revenues, including $84.73 million from its important and growing electronic database operation.

Advertising inches at its business titles grew from 2.73 million lines in 1983 to over 3.77 million in 1987. Altogether these specialized business publications produced $558.97 million in total revenue for Capital Cities in 1987, up from only $166.64 million in 1983.

There are three specialized business publications components at Capital Cities/ABC: Fairchild, *Institutional Investor*, and the renowned ABC Publishing.

At Fairchild the key publications include *Women's Wear Daily*, *W*, *M*, and the *Daily News Record*. These titles hold the number one position in each market niche.

Institutional Investor, with domestic and international editions, is one of the world's leading publications in its field.

ABC Publishing produces some of America's major publications for the automobile, jewelry, food, machine, and manufacturing industries. Key titles include *Motor Age, Jewelers Circular Keystone* (an annual winner of the prestigious Neal Awards), *Hardware Age*, and *Manufacturing Systems*. Total revenues topped $1.006 billion in 1987.

Capital Cities owned publishing units before it became an international broadcasting giant. It is in publishing for the long haul. With an impressive A ranking from Standard and Poor's, a P-E of 18, $5.38 billion in assets, $1.7 billion in long-term debt, and an outstanding management team, it is able to achieve successes where other communications companies have failed. This company is, and will remain, one of America's major players in the hotly contested international business publications and information services field.

Edgell Communications. Edgell Communications was created in late 1987 in the $334.1 million leveraged buyout of Harcourt Brace Jovanovich's (HBJ) massive business publishing unit.[16] Partners in this purchase included Robert Edgell (one of America's most experienced and respected business publishing executives) and other key executives from the HBJ business publishing group; Wicks Communications (a New York City investment firm); the Labovitz Corporation; and the investment banking firm of Kidder, Peabody.

Edgell is one of America's largest publishers of specialized business magazines. It has carved out strong market niche positions in a wide variety of industries, including communications (four publications); education (four); energy (four); healthcare (twelve); manufacturing, distributing, and service (fourteen); merchandising (ten); paper (four); plastics (seven); processing and packaging (ten); recreation and leisure (seven); and travel, lodging, food, and beverage (six).

In addition Edgell manages eighteen trade shows (for example, Art Expo California and the Plastics Fair) and seventeen convention periodicals (including *Beverage Industry Show Daily* and *Hotel and Motel Management Show Daily*).

Edgell Communications is still in its nascent stage. To date Edgell has not developed an electronic information system for customers. Its international presence is somewhat limited and is substantially dependent on its existing business titles. However, it is conceivable that Robert Edgell could broaden the company's spheres of influence once the kinks are worked out of this new corporation.

These magazines generated $425 million in revenue for Harcourt Brace Jovanovich in 1987. Yet Edgell's overhead is significantly different from the one carried by HBJ prior to the sale. Interest payments on the leveraged buyout have placed a stiff financial burden on Edgell Communications for the foreseeable future, especially if keenly important advertising revenues continue to experience a peripatetic cycle in the United States.[17]

Edgell Communications has a strong collection of first-rate business publications. With recent takeover prices in the +$2 billion price range (for example, Macmillan), it appears that Edgell and his partners walked away with a superb collection of highly profitable titles at almost a "bargain-basement price." Edgell Communications is a force in America's business publishing industry; yet it is unlikely that this corporation can become very active in acquisitions, or even in the rapid development of an electronic information network, in the next few years, unless they merge or are acquired by a financially strong company (as Diamandis was by Hachette after it purchased the consumer magazine division from Columbia Broadcasting System). If that should take place, then a giant business publishing concern would be quickly created that could challenge some of the nation's other large business publishers.

What happened to Harcourt Brace Jovanovich? By the end of 1986, information publishing and services accounted for 28 percent of that corporation's revenues and 30 percent of its profits. Its highly successful educational publishing unit produced 47 percent of HBJ's revenues and 39 percent of its profits. Nonpublishing operations included theme parks and insurance companies, which accounted for the rest of the revenues (25 percent) and profits (31 percent).[18]

On 18 May 1987 HBJ's cozy world changed forever when Robert Maxwell offered to purchase all of HBJ for $1.7 billion in a very hostile takeover attempt. William Jovanovich and the other corporate directors decided to fight Maxwell, and HBJ's vulnerability quickly became apparent to everyone in the business publishing/information processing industry.

HBJ was compelled to undertake a series of exceptionally costly defensive measures in order to defeat the Maxwell offer. Certain assets had to be sold, and the business publishing was purchased by Edgell and his associates in a leveraged buyout for $334.1 million, which was significantly lower than HBJ hoped to generate in this dreaded but obviously necessary sale of assets.

In order to court the favor of concerned stockholders, HBJ provided stockholders with a special $40.00 per share dividend. The icing on the cake was the issuance of preferred shares to stockholders.

To cover the costs associated with these measures, plus the inevitable legal fees generated in any defense, HBJ borrowed +$2.5 billion. This saddled HBJ with (approximately) $375 million in annual interest payments plus the steep costs resulting from the gift of preferred stock (estimated cost, $675 million).

On 31 August 1988 Harcourt initiated a series of cost savings at the parks.[19] Yet these draconian measures proved to be too little, too late. In 1989 HBJ sold its park assets to raise additional capital to meet its stiff interest payment schedule; the sale price was below what HBJ originally expected, and Wall Street remained concerned about the fiscal viability of the remaining components.

HBJ's primary assets in late 1989 were its book publishing division and various insurance units. As long as HBJ holds onto its remaining business publishing unit, it will remain a small player in this industry. However, interest payments in the second quarter of 1988 topped $78.7 million, and HBJ posted a loss of $44.6 million in that quarter; additional losses were recorded in 1998. It remains to be seen whether HBJ will continue to survive as an independent company in light of the total costs associated with its "victory" over Maxwell. Additional shrinkage of HBJ is likely, and the valuable business titles might be for sale, thereby removing HBJ from this market niche.

Robert Edgell was a major corporate figure at HBJ prior to the sale of the business publishing unit. It is possible that Edgell Communications might be offered the remaining HBJ titles if they are put on the market. Edgell's own interest payment schedule, in addition to other obligations, may prevent it from taking advantage of this offer, leaving the door open for another business publishing company to capitalize on HBJ's weakness.

McGraw-Hill. Since 1985 McGraw-Hill has been a company under siege and, in the parlance of Wall Street arbitrageurs, "in play" (that is, the object of a possible merger or acquisition).[20]

In order to avoid the possibility of a hostile takeover, which had been the subject of New York's financial and publishing communities since 1986, McGraw-Hill announced on 30 June 1988 that it had reorganized its five operating units into three "super" divisions: publishing; financial services; and information services.[21] This sparked a plethora of openly negative responses from Wall Street financiers and other members of the financial service industry.[22]

Corporate earnings for 1987 topped $1.751 billions, up 11.1

percent over 1986.[23] *Fortune* placed it #211 on the *Fortune 500*. By 1988 it tallied $1.82 billion in sales, earned $186 million in profits, and fell to #223 on the *Fortune 500* list.

Operating revenues and profits from the five units were interesting. Broadcasting revenues reached $89.7 million (5 percent of the corporation's total) while profits were an impressive $26 million. The beleaguered book division generated $563.9 million in total revenues (32 percent of McGraw-Hill's total amount) yet yielded profits of only $46.2 million, which was significantly below book industry ratios. Standard and Poor's (one of America's major corporation rating services) shared in the business malaise that followed the October 1987 stock market crash and produced an $80.7 million profit on sales of $334.4 million (26 percent of the company's total). The glamorous information systems division provided the company with 33 percent of its total profits, with $103 million of $386.3 million in total sales.

The publications division had sales of $377 million (22 percent of McGraw-Hill's total), profits of $51.6 million (17 percent of the total), and an operating margin of 14 percent. In its 1987 annual report, McGraw-Hill stated that the publications division will continue to experience growth "through acquisitions and product development and the use of new information technologies in keeping with its commitment to provide value-added information to its customers through the most appropriate distribution channels."[24]

McGraw-Hill's crown jewel is the internationally respected *Business Week*. In 1989 *MagazineWeek* estimated that *Business Week* alone generated $255.566 million in total revenues and yielded a net profit of $114.49 million in 1987 on a net profit margin of 44.8 percent.[25] Other key publications in the impressive McGraw-Hill collection include the highly regarded *Aviation Week and Space Technology*, *Byte*, and the successful Black, Dodge, and Sweet's titles. In addition it produces a series of impressive and lucrative newsletters.

Clearly, McGraw-Hill is one of the leading diversified publishing-information corporations in the world. Yet this corporation remains an enigma. The McGraw family continues to play a dominant role in daily operations, but, how long will this continue? Why are so many of the McGraw-Hill units less profitable that industry averages? When and will customers abandon McGraw-Hill's printed journals and accept electronic versions, and at what cost? Will the company's stock remain seriously underpriced? Will McGraw-Hill remain an independent publishing company or will it be acquired, perhaps in a hostile takeover fight? Will the "peace in our time" agreement with Robert Maxwell prove to be a boon? Will its new, highly acclaimed "personalized" textbook process capture needed market share? Lastly, will this corporation remain a force, or become merely a foot note, in the history of the business publishing?

Many companies have shown an interest in, or have been mentioned in the business press as a possible suitor for, the McGraw-Hill company. If McGraw-Hill fails in its strategic reorganization, or if profits remain unimpressive (or dip), or if it begins to run out of operating divisions or titles that can be sold for a profit in order to generate quarterly earnings, a pattern rather evident to all industry analysts, then it might fall prey to outside forces and be acquired, thereby ending one of the most important chapters in the publishing history of the United States.

One thing is clear, however; this is a company under siege, selling off valuable assets to satisfy the insatiable demands of Wall Street analysts. In December 1989 McGraw-Hill again responded to the rumors circulating on Wall Street and within the advertising community. The company reorganized downward again from three to two operating units.[26] This is the second reorganization within a brief eighteen-month period, which is barely enough time to gauge the success of the last restructuring. McGraw-Hill announced the termination of one thousand employees, closed its book division (since no one wanted to purchase it), and promised even better days ahead for this company.

This type of "management by objectives" will result ultimately in failure; it is only a matter of time before the laws of physics, nature, and economics emerge triumphantly over this business publisher. The only way for McGraw-Hill to survive is to merge with or be acquired by a better-managed corporation.

The Paramount Corporation. The Paramount Corporation, re-named in 1989, achieved global fame as Gulf and Western; and it is by every type of measurement a publishing juggernaut.

It is of course better known as the owner of a string of highly successful and visible companies, including Paramount Pictures, the famed, internationally known Madison Square Garden, and two major teams (the exciting basketball Knicks and the traditionally inept hockey Rangers, who last won the coveted Stanley Cup in 1940).

However, at this company the balance sheet tells all, and Paramount's publishing division generated $1.074 billion of the corporation's total revenues of $2.904 billion.[27]

Paramount has two operating divisions.

Paramount

Entertainment	Publishing and Information Services

In 1987 its highly prized entertainment unit generated 38 percent of its profits (up from 23 percent in 1986). Everyone knows that the film and video industry is mercurial: it is not always easy to predict what the public will want to see in a movie theater; and video sales and rentals are even more difficult to estimate in advance. The countless number of multimillion-dollar film disasters has become part of the unstable Hollywood business tradition.

The consumer/commercial finance unit, sold in 1989, was active in an impressive array of activities, including real estate, revolving credit lending, real estate secured loans, the issuance of credit cards, and first mortgage loans. This was a major profit center, throwing off 41 percent of the old Gulf and Western's profits in 1987, down from 51 percent in 1986! Recently, the financial service sector has exhibited signs of instability, especially in light of the softening of the dollar, the rise in the prime rate of interest in the late 1980s, and the surge in 1989 in the Consumer Price Index. Clearly this has adversely affected the overall performance of this unit, which led to the rather dramatic reversal in total profits between 1986 and 1987. The unpredictable nature of this component of Paramount perhaps explains why this unit was sold.

To compensate for the consistently unpredictable financial nature of certain divisions of the corporation, the company's executives decided in 1984 to allow its highly respected book unit, Simon and Schuster, to launch a mammoth $1 billion acquisition spree in order to insulate the company from the perils of business cycles.[28]

Consequently, Paramount became one of the biggest players in the publishing business with the creation of its tremendously diversified publishing and information services division. As of 1987 this unit generated $1.074 billion in total revenues. Information services produced $240 million in revenues through the effective marketing of (1) a plethora of legal and loose-leaf supplements, services, and software ($65 million), (2) business newsletters and supporting books ($70 million), (3) and tax information (in a variety of printed and electronic formats, $105 million).

The educational publishing unit alone grossed $570 million in revenues in 1987. The consumer division produced $265 million.

Tallies for individual international sales were not recorded in each publishing division. The 1987 annual report merely stated that of the $1.074 billion in revenue, $76.2 million was generated through international sales. In light of Paramount's substantial international marketing expertise (with its Paramount film division, Prentice-Hall's strong global network, and other components), it is safe to assume that world-wide sales of publications will grow significantly in the future.[29]

The Information Services unit contains Prentice-Hall; Appleton and Lange; Globe Books; Allyn and Bacon; and Silver Burdett and Ginn.

Prentice-Hall is the gem among this collection of companies. Its legal, business, and accounting supplements, newsletters, two hundred new titles in 1987, including *Modern Job Safety and Health*, *Real Estate Investment Trusts*, and *Inside Litigation*. Also placed in the Prentice-Hall unit was the Bureau of Business Practice and the New York Institute of Finance.

Appleton and Lange published major journals in the growing

medical-healthcare field (for example, the *Journal of Family Practice* has a monthly controlled circulation of 74,111; the *Journal of the National Medical Association*, another controlled monthly publication, has a circulation of 24,999).

The professional publishing group is the nation's largest supplier of timely tax and legal information. This unit acquired five data services since 1986: INFO SEARCH (the leading American document search and filing service), Statewide Information Services (the country's only centralized database covering the bankruptcy, tax lien, and judgment areas), Search West (a document search and filing company handling California and other western states), Manac Systems International (a legal software concern),and Charles E. Simon and Company (which handles Securities and Exchange Commission searches).

In addition, they have been active in other electronic information areas. Prentice-Hall's PHINet is the market leader in the electronic retrieval of tax data for accountants, lawyers, etc. In 1987 Paramount announced the introduction of *Access-Plus* (tax and pension software). A PHINet CD-ROM version (which will contain up to two hundred thousand pages of information on each CD) is currently under development.

Paramount has a B+ rating from Standard and Poor's, a P-E ratio of 15, first quarter 1988 earnings of $705.6 million (versus $661.4 million for the first quarter 1986), expected 1988 earnings of $6.20 per share (up from $5.76 in 1986), 1987 assets of $1.87 billion, and a long-term debt of $1.35 billion.[30]

Its top management, especially in its publishing division, is well respected. With its current stable of printed and electronic products, and with many exciting and potentially highly lucrative ones currently under development or ready to be introduced, it is clear that this company will continue to grow and remain one of the world's most important international business publishing and information service corporations.

Knight-Ridder. While known primarily as one of the nation's preeminent newspaper companies, Knight-Ridder is a leading and growing force in the business publications field. Its organizational chart is lean, symbolic of its way of doing business.

Daily	Business	Television	Cable	Suburban	Foreign
Newspapers	Information	Stations	Operations	Newspapers	Bureau

In 1987 Knight-Ridder reported total operating revenues of slightly more than $2.07 billion, up a strong 8.5 percent over 1986's banner year. Expenditures topped $1.76 billion, producing $309 million in operating income (on a 14.9 percent profit margin). The company paid $1.03 per share in dividends in 1987 against $0.91 in the previous year, and it was listed as #188 on the *Fortune 500*.[31]

Second quarter 1988 earnings continued to shine. The company generated $544.6 million, up 3.4 percent over 1987.

Knight-Ridder's business information unit's revenues were a shade below the $100 million mark at $99.26 million, an increase of 11.6 percent over 1986 and 23.93 percent since 1985! Yet the costs associated with the diversification of this division have been heavy, and Knight-Ridder must be somewhat concerned about the $1 million loss posted by this unit in 1987.

Yet it appears that the corporation's executives believe that business information services will emerge as a major profit center in the years to come; so additional funding to purchase databases and publications should be available whenever capital is needed for a solid acquisition that fits in neatly with existing properties.

The business information services unit is rather diversified. The *Journal of Commerce*, based in New York City, is one of the nation's leading commercial publications; *PIERS* is the key reporting service covering the import and export fields; *RATES* is a well-respected rapid access tariff service. Other major operations include Vu/Text (another data service), two divisions providing information to the financial services and commodities industries, the highly acclaimed Dialog Information Systems unit (a superb on-line data retrieval system), Gulf Publishing Company, and a wide variety of news services, research bureaus, and financial quotation systems.[32]

Gulf Publishing issues nine specialized business publications servicing the economically depressed oil and gas industries. Some of its notable titles include *Hydrocarbon Processing, Ocean Industry, Oil, Gas, and Petrochemicals Abroad,* and *Petroleum, Production, and Processing.*

Knight-Ridder appears interested in obtaining strong business publishing/information units, and it has been mentioned over the years as a potential buyer of McGraw-Hill or other large, diversified publishing corporations.

Clearly Knight-Ridder is a company with solid publications and information services, a sterling reputation, and a sound profit/loss statement. It has $1.985 billion in assets and $508 million in long-term debt. Earnings in the second quarter of 1988 increased 4.6 percent.

This company is and is likely to remain one of the major players in the global business publications/information processing field in the years to come.

Five Foreign Business Publishing Corporations

Some Research Methodological Concerns. There are many foreign firms active in the United States's business publishing/information services field. However, any researcher involved in an analysis of a foreign firm realizes rather quickly that there are three significant problems to be encountered.

First, few of these corporations use generally accepted U.S. accounting procedures. Rupert Murdoch's News Corporation, for example, utilizes the Australian accounting system, which ultimately protects this company from certain problems associated with the reporting of intangible assets (such as a magazine title). In the United States, a company must charge off intangibles against earnings; under Australia's more liberal system, Murdoch is exempt from this rule. In addition, the News Corporation can periodically increase the value of a magazine's title, which also increases shareholders' equity and the borrowing power of the company. American firms are prohibited from doing this.

The *Wall Street Journal* estimates that shareholders' equity in the News Corporation would be (approximately) $2.3 billion if American accounting standards were followed. However, using Australia's methods, Murdoch was able to state legally that the News Corporation's shareholders' equity hovered at $4.5 billion!

A second and far more difficult problem concerns the dearth of acceptable financial data about certain firms. This researcher had to rely at times on published estimates that often bordered on thin guesses about certain corporations.

Lastly, the Bible states that "those who live by the sword will die by the sword." The same holds true for researchers who must rely on and use ever-changing foreign exchange rates to determine and convert foreign assets and liabilities into United States dollars. Nevertheless, in spite of these formidable problems, case studies of four major foreign business publishing companies doing business in the U.S. will be presented.

In the past few years, a good number of these companieshave been actively buying America's business publishers and information systems corporations and providing these firms with a supply of resources (both financial and human) along with needed ideas about new product development and the reformulation of old products. Consequently, these foreign publishing houses have become a major force in the industry.

Maxwell Communications. Maxwell Communications is a large, diversified corporation based in the United Kingdom with branches in sixteen countries. It employed (approximately) 16,992 people and generated in 1987 (approximately) $1.4 billion in total annual revenues.[33] It was ranked #436 on the 1987 *Fortune International 500*. Net income reached $216 million, and stockholders' equity was estimated by *Fortune* to be $1.89 billion. The company's founder and enigmatic chief executive officer is Robert Maxwell.

Recently Maxwell outlined his long-term strategic goal for Maxwell Communications: to become the world's leading totally integrated communications company with $9 billion in annual sales by 1993.[34]

He has maintained a highly visible profile in the United States, especially since his purchase of Macmillan.

Maxwell Communications

Publishing	Printing	Data Services
Pergamon Science Research Associates Macmillan	Eighteen various commercial printing companies	Ad/Sat Independent Network Services Orbit InfoLine Pub/Data

Macmillan was purchased in 1988 by Robert Maxwell for upwards of $2 billion.[35] Why would Maxwell pay such a high price for Macmillan when other corporations were also available?

Macmillan was unquestionably an attractive U.S. publishing property. Earnings had risen between 15 and 20 percent in the mid- to late-1980s. As of 1987 its information services division recorded annual pretax earnings in the 30 percent range and sales gains bordering at the 25 percent mark. Long-term debt hovered at the $225.5 million level in 1988. Earnings per common share (fully diluted) hit $2.69 in 1987; and 1988 earnings were predicted (at least prior to the hostile acquisition offers) to top easily the historic $955.8 million recorded in 1987 (up from $817.8 million in 1986). Macmillan reached a lofty #336 ranking on the 1987 *Fortune 500*. After Maxwell acquired Macmillan, he incorporated it directly into his global publishing operations, which meant that Macmillan as such would no longer be ranked by *Fortune*.

Macmillan had five operating units.

Macmillan

Publishing	Instruction	Information Services	Home Reference Materials	Retail

Business publishing occupied a special niche in Macmillan's diversified Information Services unit. Standard Rate and Data Service (SRDS) has been a proven money-maker for a number of years, as was the Health Care Information division. The internationally known directory division included the famous Marquis line of *Who's Who* publications; in addition Macmillan had three other operational groups. Information Services offered forty-seven business publications, and its on-line databases serviced the media and advertising industries. The professional journals were particularly strong in the high-tech, the engineering, and the always fast-growing medical-healthcare fields.

Standard Rate and Data totally dominated its market niche with nineteen publications for the advertising world. Its definitive *Business Publications Rates and Data*, Parts 1, 2, and 3 have become essential reading for anyone in this field; and it is, arguably, the single most important business publication in the United States in 1990!

In 1986 Information Services generated 22 percent of Macmillan's revenues and threw off 35 percent of its profits. Textbooks and educational publishing, long perceived as the central core of Macmillan, had 47 percent of the company's revenues and 45 percent of its profits, clearly not as impressive a ratio as Information Services in 1986.

By 1987 Information Services' revenues grew to $228.7 million and garnered 23.9 percent of sales and a significant $40 million in profits; Macmillan's total profits in 1987 totaled $99.9 million.

However, profits from text and educational publishing operations slipped to 41.4 percent of Macmillan's total. Clearly Information Services had emerged as the fastest-growing segment of Macmillan.[36]

Macmillan owned exceptionally strong product lines in a number of lucrative market niches; this is why Maxwell, ever vigilant for a good bargain, fought so aggressively for what was clearly one of the last "crown jewels" in the United States's publishing industry, and also one of the few remaining independent properties with strong publications.

Media diversification is costly, even for Robert Maxwell. Macmillan's second quarter 1988 earnings dipped; and the grand plans for Europe and the intense competition Maxwell faces in this nation and throughout the world are certainly draining off financial assets. So it appears likely that Maxwell and/or Macmillan will be forced to sell some additional assets, as it did with the Webb unit or the interesting Intertec publishing unit.

Of course cooperative endeavors with other global publishers might prove to be a useful tool allowing Maxwell an opportunity to expand while not overburdening the company with an unreasonable debt. A recent European venture with Rupert Murdoch and the cooperative textbook arrangement with McGraw-Hill might be a reasonable pattern to follow with other companies in the future. After all, Robert Maxwell has been known to do the unexpected!

Macmillan is a key player in the business publications/information services marketplace, and its cash flow makes it a valuable asset to Maxwell. Macmillan has a tough fight ahead because of the costs and competition associated with global publishing, but it will remain a powerful international force in the business publishing industry in the United States.

His British-based Pergamon Holding Corporation had global sales in 1986 of (approximately) $500 million. In the United States, Pergamon maintains an impressive list of scientific and technical titles that generated somewhere near $6 million in annual revenues in 1986.

In 1986 Maxwell tried unsuccessfully to purchase *Scientific American*. The following year he again failed with a hostile takeover attempt of Harcourt Brace Jovanovich. In 1988 he was unable to obtain control over Bell and Howell; yet his + $2 billion bid for Macmillan pushed Maxwell into the front ranks of international publishers.

His second biggest coup was the June 1988 $150 million acquisition of Science Research Associates, a technical publishing corporation, from the International Business Machine (IBM) Corporation.

In addition, since 1986 Maxwell has spent nearly $700 million to acquire eighteen commercial printing companies and has invested an additional $130 million in capital expenditures to upgrade and modernize these manufacturing facilities. It appears that an additional $50 million will be allocated for even more capital improvements, although rumors circulated in 1989 that Maxwell planned to sell the printing operations.[37] Maxwell is now the second largest commercial printing company in the United States with estimated 1987 sales revenues of $800 million, trailing only the internationally respected R. R. Donnelley and Sons' $2.48 billion. Printing market strengths exist in four distinct niches: magazine printing; catalog printing; free-standing inserts; and gravure.

It appears that commercial printing now accounts for a significant amount of Maxwell revenues; however, the company plans to diversify and generate no more than 50 percent of future revenues in this category. The major portion of revenues will be in publishing, at least if Maxwell has his say.

In 1987 the Maxwell Communications company sold $1.1 billion worth of stock to investors, thereby quickly providing this globally thinking leader with a sizable war chest to draw on. However, he has entered into a multiyear agreement with Mc-Graw-Hill, which means this vulnerable company will not be taken over by Maxwell. Others quickly come to mind, especially since Maxwell is quickly running out of new companies to go after in the United States. Of course he could look northward toward Canada, but he will face rather stiff competition from the Thomson Corporation and Maclean Hunter.

Maxwell is currently a major player in the American market. The next move is up to Maxwell, and it is likely that he will not wait very long if he plans to catchup to his old British rival Rupert Murdoch.

News Corporation. In July 1988 Rupert Murdoch's News Corporation was one of America's leading business publishing/information systems companies with exceptionally strong market positions in this industry.[38] Within one month Murdoch became one of *the* preeminent forces in the communications industry in the world, because of one major purchase and one small but significant diversification move. Murdoch's $3 billion very friendly offer to buy Triangle Publications, which includes *TV Guide* (one of America's largest consumer magazine), several other titles, and a printing plant placed Murdoch for a time in 1988 almost on the same level as Time, although Time's 1989 merger with Warner Communications unquestionably created the world's largest media corporation.[39]

His very quiet purchase of two major free-standing inserts companies (Quad Marketing and Product Movers; the number two and three companies in terms of market share) provided him with a 52 percent market share in the fast-growing $700 million American industry. Now the News Corporation can offer potential customers an attractive advertising package that few if any other companies can rival. This means that a client can arrange with the News Corporation to have an advertising campaign breaking on Fox television, which Murdoch owns, and supported with free-standing inserts, a print campaign in *TV Guide* and *Seventeen*, both Triangle properties, and additional coverage in a variety of other periodicals.

The News Corporation is a global Australian-based communications corporation with $3.527 billion in annual revenues. Net income in 1987 topped $548 million, and the company employed 26,700 people world-wide. The News Corporation, ranked #187 on the *Fortune International 500*, is controlled by Rupert Murdoch, who holds 49 percent of its stock. It has staked out major positions in newspapers (38 percent of the corporation's revenues and 45 percent of its profits), periodicals (11 percent of the revenues and 13 percent of its profits), film and entertainment (26 percent of the revenues and only 16 percent of profits), commercial printing (3 percent of revenues and 2 percent of profits), and other activities (9 percent of revenues and 10 percent of profits).

The bulk of the company's business activities were in the United States (54 percent of its 1987 revenues and 49 percent of the profits). European activities generated 25 percent of revenues and 42 percent of total profits; Australian and Pacific Rim endeavors were a tidy 21 percent of its revenues and 14 percent of profits.

Holdings in the United States are quite sizable and include *New York, New Woman, Mirabella*, Harper and Row, *European Travel and Life*, Twentieth Century Fox, and Fox Broadcasting.

Business publishing/information services are a very valuable part of the Harper and Row division, which the News Corporation purchased in 1987 for $300 million. Murdoch quickly sold 50 percent of Harper and Row for $156 million to Collins, a distinguished independent British publishing corporation. Murdoch later purchased Collins.

J. B. Lippincott, one of America's oldest publishers, begun in 1792 during the early days of the George Washington administration, is also one of Harper and Row's most successful and profitable. It holds a position of honor in the medical-healthcare field as a significant journal publisher with twenty-six titles. Eleven new ones were introduced in 1987. The other components of Harper and Row support Lippincott's business publishing/scholarly journal operation. Gower is also strong in the medical field. The loose-leaf unit has exhibited great strength.

The Triangle Publications acquisition brought a rich publishing tradition to Murdoch's company. *TV Guide, Seventeen* (a consumer magazine for young women), and the *Racing Form* (a daily tabloid for people interested in the "sport of kings") are highly successful publications. It is estimated that the *Racing Form* alone produced $40 million in profits on just $80 million in total revenues in 1987. Total profits for all of Triangle Publications topped $85 million in 1987 on $700 million in revenues.

As of 30 June 1987, the end of their fiscal year, the News Corporation had assets of $1.76 billion, liabilities of $2.056 billion, and a long-term debt of $2.92 billion.[40] The company has been active in electronic publishing, and they are working on a sophisticated electronic system for the hotel and tourism industry that just might revolutionize the way individuals plan their vacations.

It is difficult to say what is next on the Murdoch agenda; apparently he does not utilize strategic long-range plans, and he has rarely exhibited very much interest in the daily operations of a publication. One is tempted to say that there is not much left that he could purchase in light of the costs associated with the Triangle Publications acquisition. Yet only a fool would ever underestimate Rupert Murdoch, possibly *the* most important force in the international communications industry.

The Thomson Corporation. In August 1988 this researcher was discussing the American business publishing/information systems industry with representatives from one of the world's largest banks. Clearly the recent Murdoch offer of $3 billion to acquire Triangle Publications whetted their interest in increasing their position as an investment bank and international lending institution in the publishing industry.

Obviously the names Murdoch and Maxwell were discussed extensively, but it quickly became apparent that these bankers did not know very much about the Thomson Corporation. They were rather surprised to be told that Thomson is one of the world's largest communications companies, ranked on the 1988 *Fortune International 500* at #185, up from #221 in 1986 and a mere thirty-five slots behind Bertelsmann AG (#150).[41]

Thomson is a large Canadian conglomerate with $3.537 billion in total revenues, operating primarily in North America and the United Kingdom, although they do have holdings throughout Europe. In 1987 Thomson employed 23,200 people and had sizable positions in electronic information and publishing ($1.42 billion), leisure and travel ($1.69 billion; since sold), and oil and gas holdings ($423 million; also sold). Its operating profit was $329 million. The largest contributor to these profits were information and publishing, with $212 million. Leisure activities yielded $46 million, and oil and gas provided the remaining $71 million. Stockholders' equity reached $1.188 billion.

In the last ten years, Thomson's track record has been very impressive. Between 1977 and 1987, total sales grew from $756 million to $3.537 billion; operating profits increased from $183 million to $329 million. Over 75 percent of Thomson's common shares are held by the Thomson family.[42]

The strategic plan followed by Thomson has remained consistent for a number of years, indicative of the essentially meticulous nature of the Thomson family and top management:

To enhance our leading positions in specialized information and publishing . . . we place emphasis on quality, service, and market leadership. . . . In building for the future, we aim to avoid speculation, but we are prepared to take calculated risks. . . .[43]

The end result speaks for itself. Thomson's eclectic collection of decentralized business publications holds top market positions in many different niches, including financial (especially with *American Banker* and the *Bond Trader*) and the pivotal healthcare field (its *Medical Economics* dominates this niche).

Of special interest is its sophisticated electronic information network, which includes AutEx Trading Information Systems, Munifacts, InvestText, TRADEMARKSCAN, the Mortgage-Backed Securities Information Service, Spectrum, Cadence, Video Munifacts, Alert, Multi Port, and the Financial Software Series. Its directory unit boasts the internationally respected Jane's group (including *Jane's Fighting Ships*) and the Gale Research Company. Its collection of newspapers in North America is most impressive.

Thomson lacks the "glitz" of some of the Murdoch holdings and the global rumors often associated with Maxwell; all Thomson does is dominate market niches and make money. If only twelve companies come to control the global communications industry, it is a safe bet that Thomson will be one of them.

Reed International. Reed International is an important United Kingdom-based corporation with 34,600 employees throughout the world. It is always looking for significant business publishing/ information systems-based corporations. Ranked a disappointing #231 on the recent *Fortune International 500* after reaching #200 the previous year, Reed still generated $2.91 billion in revenues in 1987.[44] Net income hovered at the $190 million mark, and shareholders' equity was recorded at $1.116 billion. Reed's assets were $2.35 billion.

In the last five years, Reed has increased its level of activity in the United States. It purchased Technical Publications (from Dun and Bradstreet), the New York-based *Printing News* (the nation's principal weekly trade magazine servicing the printing and graphic communications industry), Miller-Freeman, and the impressive *Daily Variety* holdings.

Cahners is the single largest Reed publishing company in the United States, and it issues fifty-nine magazines. Reed Business Publications has twenty-five periodicals; and Miller-Freeman offers twenty specialized titles.

Reed's most interesting acquisition was *Daily Variety* (a specialized tabloid covering the entertainment industry) in October 1987 for $56.5 million. *Daily Variety's* principal rival is the *Hollywood Reporter,* a famous daily tabloid covering events in the motion picture, music, and television industries in Los Angeles.[45] The *Hollywood Reporter* was purchased by Affiliated Publications, owner of the internationally important *Billboard* for $26.7 million in April 1988.

The *Hollywood Reporter* generated $10.32 million in advertising revenues in 1987 and ended the year with between $15 and $20 million in total revenues. *Daily Variety* lagged behind the *Hollywood Reporter* in advertising dollars but had similar numbers for total revenues.

Affiliated (ranked #486 on the *Fortune 500*) made this acquisition because of two strategic goals: (1) to penetrate the Hollywood market left essentially untouched by *Billboard,* and (2) to absorb the information collected by the staff of the *Hollywood Reporter* into Affiliated's *Billboard* Information Network (BIN), a national electronic database monitoring music sales, radio airplay, and sheet-music sales.[46]

Known primarily as the owner of the *Boston Globe,* Affiliated has become an interesting competitor to Reed in the entertainment field. In the last eight months of 1987, business publications alone generated $44.17 million (out of Affiliated's $442.68 million) and $6.06 million in operating income (versus Affiliated's total operating income of $99.354 million from its other units). The *Billboard* titles had a cash flow of $8.394 million against $89.43 million for all of Affiliated, which posted a long-term debt of $95.24 million in 1987. It holds a superb A+ ranking from Standard and Poor's, a P-E ratio of 15, and a string of paid dividends dating back to 1882!

Cahners remains the heart and soul of Reed's American operations. The Cahners Magazine Network is a string of thirty-five impressive specialized publications with a combined circulation of more than three million. Some of the stars in this collection include *Publishers Weekly* (a world-class magazine and America's leading periodical covering the book industry, with a weekly paid circulation of 36,435), *Purchasing* (with a weekly readership of over one hundred thousand), *Plant Engineering* (the nation's leader in advertising and editorial pages with more than 128,000 readers), and *Datamation* (a major computer magazine with a "total reach" of 944,067).

Reed has carved out an impressive market position in America, and it is one of the dominant forces in the global business publishing industry.

NOTES

1. Frank Luther Mott, *A History of American Magazines, vol. 1, 1741–1850* (Cambridge, Mass.: Harvard University Press, 1966), 24; J. A. Leo Lemay, ed., *Benjamin Franklin: Writings* (New York: Library of America, 1987), 1476. Also see Allen Johnson and Dumas Malone, eds., *The Dictionary of American Biography* (New York: Scribner's, 1931), 60, 586–93; and Kenneth Silverman's chapter "From Cotton Mather to Benjamin Franklin," in the *Columbia Literary History of the United States,* ed. Emory Elliot (New York: Columbia University Press, 1988), 101–12.
2. Mott, *A History of American Magazines, vol. 1,* 13–17.
3. Ibid., 787–809; Frank Luther Mott, *A History of American Magazines, vol. 2, 1850–1865* (Cambridge, Mass.: Harvard University Press, 1957), 555–65; and Frank Luther Mott, *A History of American Magazines, vol. 3, 1865–1885* (Cambridge, Mass.: Harvard University Press, 1967), 563–69.
4. David Forsyth, *The Business Press in America: 1750–1865* (Philadelphia: Chilton, 1964), 20.
5. Julius Elfenbein, *Business Journalism* (New York: Harper & Row, 1960), 1–20.
6. Forsyth, *Business Press in America,* vii.
7. Mott, *A History of American Magazines, vol 2,* 81–83, 297–300.
8. Mott, *A History of American Magazines, vol. 3,* 454–56, 491–94.
9. Frank Luther Mott, *A History of American Magazines, vol. 4, 1885–1905* (Cambridge, Mass.: Harvard University Press, 1957), 524–35. For an interesting analysis of *Editor and Publisher,* the newspaper business publication, see Mott's *A History of American Magazines, vol. 5, 1905–1930* (Cambridge, Mass.: Harvard University Press, 1968), 59–71.
10. G. D. Crain, Jr., ed., *Teacher of Business: The Publishing Philosophy of James H. McGraw* (Chicago: Advertising Publications, 1944); Lyon N. Richard, *A History of Early American Magazines: 1741–1789* (New York: Thomas Nelson, 1931); Theodore Peterson, *Magazines in the Twentieth Century* (Urbana: University of Illinois Press, 1964).
11. Dow Jones & Company, *1987 Annual Report: 10–K.* Also see "The

Fortune 500," *Fortune*, 25 April 1988, D21. See Lloyd Wendt, *The Wall Street Journal: The Story of Dow Jones and the Nation's Business Newspaper* (New York: Rand McNally, 1982); and W. Parkman Rankin, *The Practice of Newspaper Management* (New York: Praeger, 1986), 17.

12. Alex S. Jones, "The Journal Gets a New Order," *New York Times*, 1 February 1988, D1, D3

13. Times-Mirror, *1987 Annual Report: 10–K;* and "The *Fortune* 500," *Fortune*, 25 April 1988, D15; Keith J. Kelly, "Times-Mirror Chiefs Mull Multi-Media Buy at N.Y. Pow Wow," *MagazineWeek*, 18 December 1989, 2.

14. Capital Cities/ABC, *1987 Annual Report and 10–K.*

15. Ibid. Also see Dennis Kneale, "Capital Cities Net Rose 14 Percent for Second Quarter," *The Wall Street Journal*, 25 July 1988, 22. Also see Laurence Shames, *The Big Time: The Harvard Business School's Most Successful Class and How It Shaped America* (New York: Harper & Row, 1986), 43–50, on Capital Cities' Thomas Murphy. Also see Bruce D. Henderson, *Henderson on Strategy* (New York: Mentor, 1979).

16. Edwin McDowell, "$1.7 Billion Bid Given Harcourt," *New York Times*, 19 May 1987, sec. 4, p. 6; "The *Fortune* 500," *Fortune*, 25 April 1988, D21; Geraldine Fabrikant, "Harcourt: A Vulnerable Giant," *New York Times*, 20 May 1987, sec. 4, p. 3; Geraldine Fabrikant, "Salomon Cites Stake in Harcourt," *Wall Street Journal*, 20 June 1987, sec. 1, p. 37; "Maxwell Plea on Harcourt," *New York Times*, 17 June 1987, sec. 4, p. 4; Geraldine Fabrikant, "Harcourt Gains in Debenture Fight," *New York Times*, 23 June 1987, sec. 4, p. 6; "Harcourt to Sell Magazine Unit," *New York Times*, 24 August 1987, sec. 4, p. 7; Alison Leigh Cowan, "Harcourt Considers Asset Sale," *New York Times*, 13 August 1987, sec. 4, p. 6; "Harcourt Sale of Units Near," *New York Times*, 9 October 1987, sec. 4, p. 4; Philip E. Ross, "Founder Regains Helm at HBJ Publications," *New York Times*, 19 November 1987, sec. 4, p. 2; Geraldine Fabrikant, "$334.1 Million Sale of Two Harcourt Units," *New York Times*, 19 November 1987, sec. 4, p. 4.

17. Patrick Reilly, "Trade Journals Riding Rebound of U.S. Industry," *Advertising Age*, 16 May 1988, 50.

18. Geraldine Fabrikant, "Harcourt's Loss Narrows, " *New York Times*, 12 August 1988, D16.

19. "Harcourt Sets Layoffs of 750 at Theme Parks," *New York Times*, 25 August 1988, D4.

20. Randall Smith, "McGraw-Hill Stock Rises on Takeover Rumor Despite Publisher's Steep $5 Billion Price Tag," *Wall Street Journal*, 16 February 1988, 71; "The *Fortune* 500," *Fortune*, 25 April 1988, D19; Kevin G. Salwen, "McGraw-Hill Once Again Attracts Rumors after More Than Two Years of Speculation," *Wall Street Journal*, 23 August 1988, 51; Leslie Wayne, "A Family Defends Its Dynasty," *New York*

Times, 24 July 1988, sec. 3, pp. 1 and 6; McGraw-Hill, *1987 Annual Report: 10–K.*

21. Edwin McDowell, "Major Reorganization Begun by McGraw-Hill," *New York Times*, 30 June 1988, D22; Johnnie L. Roberts, "McGraw-Hill Is Streamlining Its Organization," *Wall Street Journal*, 30 June 1988, 1.

22. Johnnie L. Roberts, "McGraw-Hill Stock Declines; Revamp Cited," *Wall Street Journal*, 1 July 1988, 22.

23. McGraw-Hill, *1987 Annual Report: 10–K.*

24. Ibid.

25. "Profit Profile: *Business Week*," *MagazineWeek*, 20 April 1988, 5; Jonathan P. Hicks, "McGraw-Hill", *New York Times*, 20 July 1988, D19; "Profits Jump 20 Percent at McGraw-Hill," *New York Times*, 20 April 1988, D22.

26. Erika Isler, "M-H [McGraw-Hill] Axes 1,000 Jobs," *MagazineWeek*, 18 December 1989, 1, 4.

27. Gulf & Western, *1987 Annual Report: 10–K.*

28. Laura Landro, "Simon & Schuster Becomes a Publishing 'Juggernaut': G & W Fuels Unit's Growth with Buying Spree, Focusing on Education," *Wall Street Journal*, 17 December 1987, 6.

29. Ibid.

30. Ibid.

31. Knight-Ridder, *1987 annual Report: 10–K;* and "The *Fortune* 500," *Fortune*, 25 April 1988, D17.

32. Ibid. Also see "Knight-Ridder," *Wall Street Journal*, 25 July 1988, 22.

33. Steve Lohr, "Britain's Maverick Mogul," *New York Times Magazine*, 1 May 1988, 52, 53, 80, 82, 107, 108; and "The International 500," *Fortune*, 1 August 1988, 436.

34. John Marcom, Jr., "Britain's Maxwell Is a Press Baron Who's Always on Deadline," *Wall Street Journal*, 19 November 1987; "Maxwell Signs Paper Deal," *Printing Impressions News Edition*, 1 July 1988, 18.

35. Cynthia Crossen and John Marcom, Jr., "Macmillan Receives $80–a-Share Offer from Maxwell, Topping Bass Group Bid," *Wall Street Journal*, 22 July 1988, 3; "The *Fortune* 500," *Fortune*, 25 April 1988, 336; Geraldine Fabrikant, "Maxwell Is Joining Fight for Macmillan," *New York Times*, 22 July 1988, D1; Geraldine Fabrikant, "Macmillan Profit Falls 10 Percent," *New York Times*, 12 August 1988, D16; Gregory A. Robb, "Macmillan Rejects Bid of Maxwell," *New York Times*, 27 August 1988, 31.

36. Macmillan, *1987 Annual Report: 10–K.* Also see Dennis Kneale, "Macmillan Board Rejects Maxwell Bid, Calling $2.34 Billion 'Inadequate,'" *Wall Street Journal*, 29 August 1988, 14.

37. Bill Esler, "Maxwell Measures Up," *Graphic Arts Monthly*, August 1988, 54, 60–61, 64.

38. Alex S. Jones, "Murdoch's *Post:* Futile Battle or Missed Opportunity?"

New York Times, 7 March 1988, B1, B2; William H. Meyers, "Murdoch's Global Power Play," *New York Times Magazine*, 12 June 1988, 18–19, 20–21, 36, 41, 42; and "The International 500," *Fortune*, 1 August 1988, D13.

39. Johnnie L. Roberts, "Murdoch's News Cor Will Buy Triangle Publications for $3 Billion," *Wall Street Journal*, 8 August 1988, 3; Kurt Eichenwald, "Murdoch Agrees to Buy *TV Guide* in a $3 Billion Sale by Annenberg," *New York Times*, 8 August 1988, 1, D3; Johnnie L. Roberts, Laura Landro, and John Marcom, Jr., "Rupert Murdoch Takes His Biggest Risk So Far in Purchasing Triangle," *Wall Street Journal*, 9 August 1988, 1, 16; Geraldine Fabrikant, "Industry Confident Murdoch Can Finance *TV Guide* Deal," *New York Times*, 9 August 1988, D1, D18.

40. Johnnie L. Roberts, "Murdoch To Sell off Reuters Stake, Land in Australia, U.K. to Pay for Triangle," *Wall Street Journal*, 10 August 1988, 3; Jeremy Gerard, *"TV Guide's* Power over the Air," *New York Times*, 11 August 1988, D1, 18; Steven Crist, *"Racing Form:* Trifecta for Murdoch?" *New York Times*, 11 August 1988, D1, D18; Albert Scardino, "How Murdoch Makes It Work," *New York Times*, 14 August 1988, sec. 3, pp. 1, 5; Patrick Reilly, "Murdoch Buy Stacks off the Racks," *Advertising Age*, 15 August 1988, 1, 62; "Murdoch the Amazing" [Viewpoint Editorial], *Advertising Age*, 15 August 1988, 16; Judann Dagnoli, "Murdoch's Reach Extends into FSIs," *Advertising Age*, 22 August 1988, 3; Linda Sandler, "Shares of Murdoch's News Cor Are Clouded by Australian Accounting, Critics Contend," *Wall Street Journal*, 16 August 1988, 53; Richard Thau, "Murdoch's *Premiere* Leads the Pack in Booming Movie Title Market," *MagazineWeek*, 18 December 1989, 5. In the Fall of 1989, the News Corporation reported that net operating profits before "extraordinary items" increased $356.1 million (+7 percent) for the year ending 30 June 1989. "Extraordinary items" is an accounting term referring to income generated through, for example, the sale of assets. In this case a number of publishing properties were sold, including the News Corp.'s share of *Elle* for $170 million. Overall revenues for the News Corp. were up a staggering 45.5 percent ($2 billion), jumping from $4.4 billion as of June 1988 to $6.4 billion in June 1989. Operating income in the United States grew +62 percent during the same time period. For additional details, see "News Corp.'s Operating Profits Rises 7 Percent for Year," *MagazineWeek*, 11 September 1989, 10.

41. International Thomson, *1987 Annual Report*. In June 1989 the Thomson Corporation was created because of the merger of the Thomson newspaper chain and the International Thomson Organisation.

42. Ibid. Also see "The International 500," *Fortune*, 1 August 1988, D13.

43. Ibid.

44. *"Fortune* International 500," *Fortune*, 1 August 1988, D15.

45. William M. Bulkeley and Daniel Akst, "Affiliated Publications' Billboard Unit Agrees to Acquire *Hollywood Reporter*," *Wall Street Journal*, 26 January 1988, 42; A. Donald Anderson, "Hollywood's Version of Trade Wars," *New York Times*, 7 August 1988, sec. 3, p. 4.
46. Affiliated, *1987 Annual Report*; "The *Fortune* 500," *Fortune*, 25 April 1988, D29.

THREE

The Advertising Industry in the United States

The advertising industry, unlike Gaul, can be divided neatly into ten highly competitive, and at times overlapping, market niches: (1) newspapers, (2) consumer magazines, (3) business magazines (which includes medical, scholarly, technical, and professional journals and publications, among many others), (4) farm magazines, (5) television, (6) radio, (7) yellow pages, (8) direct marketing (more frequently called direct mail), (9) outdoor (billboards), and (10) those ubiquitous miscellaneous publications (including annuals, directories, loose-leaf services, special supplements, special trade show papers, etc.).

The following table (3.1) outlines advertising spending in these varied markets in 1987 and 1988.[1] Clearly, not all niches posted strong gains during that two-year span of time. The outdoor segment, national newspapers, and network radio all reported unimpressive results. However, the fledgling cable industry, on both the national and local levels, national syndication television, and the national yellow pages reaped an impressive harvest of advertising dollars between 1987 and 1988, apparently a harbinger for the 1990s.

While the 7.7 percent increase in U.S. advertising expenditures

Table 3.1 / U.S. Advertising Volume: 1987–1988

Media	1987 Millions of Dollars	1987 Percent of Total	1988 Millions of Dollars	1988 Percent of Total	1987–1988 Percent Change
Newspapers					
National	$3,494	3.2	$3,586	3.0	+ 2.6
Local	25,918	23.6	27,611	23.4	+ 6.5
Total	29,412	26.8	31,197	26.4	+ 6.1
Consumer Magazines					
Weeklies	2,445	2.2	2,646	2.2	+ 8.2
Women's	1,417	1.3	1,504	1.3	+ 6.2
Monthlies	1,745	1.6	1,922	1.6	+10.1
Total	5,607	5.1	6,072	5.1	+ 8.3
Business					
Magazines	2,458	2.3	2,610	2.2	+ 6.0
Farm Magazines	196	0.2	196	0.2	0.0
Television					
Network	8,500	7.8	9,172	7.8	+ 7.9
Cable (National)	760	0.7	942	0.8	+23.9
Cable (Local)	203	0.2	254	0.2	+25.0
Syndication	762	0.7	901	0.8	+18.2
Spot (National)	6,846	6.2	7,147	6.0	+ 4.4
Spot (Local)	6,833	6.2	7,270	6.2	+ 6.4
Total	23,904	21.8	25,686	21.8	+ 7.5
Radio					
Network	413	0.4	425	0.4	+ 3.0
Spot (National)	1,330	1.2	1,418	1.2	+ 6.6
Spot (Local)	5,463	5.0	5,955	5.0	+ 9.0
Total	7,206	6.6	7,798	6.6	+ 8.2
Yellow Pages					
National	830	0.8	944	0.8	+13.7
Local	6,470	5.9	6,837	5.9	+ 5.7
Total	7,300	6.7	7,781	6.7	+ 6.6
Direct Mail	19,111	17.4	21,115	17.9	+10.5
Outdoor					
National	615	0.5	628	0.5	+ 2.2
Local	410	0.4	436	0.4	+ 6.3
Total	1,025	0.9	1,064	0.9	+ 3.8
Miscellaneous					
National	9,703	8.8	10,461	8.9	+ 7.8
Local	3,728	3.4	4,070	3.4	+ 9.2
Total	13,431	12.2	14,531	12.3	+ 8.2
Totals for Advertising Expenditures					
National	60,625	55.3	65,610	55.6	+ 8.2
Local	49,025	44.7	52,440	44.4	+ 7.0
Grand Total for all U.S. Advertising Expenditures	109,650	100.0	118,050	100.0	+ 7.7

Source: Robert J. Coen, "Ad Spending Outlook Brightens," *Advertising Age,* 15 May 1989, 24.

Table 3.2 / U.S. Advertising Spending: 1982–1989 (in billions of dollars)

Year	U.S. Spending	Percent Change	Overseas Spending	Percent Change
1982	$66.6	+ 10.2	$58.3	0.0
1983	75.8	+ 13.9	58.2	0.0
1984	87.8	+ 15.8	58.6	+ 0.7
1985	94.8	+ 7.9	63.3	+ 8.1
1986	102.1	+ 7.7	79.8	+26.1
1987	109.7	+ 7.4	102.9	+29.0
1988	118.1	+ 7.7	121.4	+18.0
1989*	126.2	+ 6.9	133.5	+10.0
Grand Total	781.1	—	676.0	—

*Estimated

Source: Joanne Lipman, "Ad Spending to Rise 6.9% in '89, Coen Says in a Warmer Forecast," *Wall Street Journal*, 15 June 1989, B4.

between 1987 and 1988 clearly outpaced the modest 4.08 percent growth in the Consumer Price Index (the CPI; the national measure of inflation in the United States), it barely exceeded the 1986–1987 advertising growth rate of 7.4 percent.

Advertising's lackluster performance was attributable to a number of disparate forces at work in the U.S. economy, including (1) the sharp reaction to the stock market crash of October 1987, which generated a corresponding decline in advertising space sold in business and consumer magazines and financial newspapers, (2) uneven and at times sagging retail sales, which directly and adversely affected a significant number of periodicals in a variety of market categories, (3) marked overall reductions in corporate expenditures due to declining quarterly and annual revenues and earnings, which brought about a curtailment of certain forms of corporate advertising, and (4) foolish rate card cutting and large-scale discounting of space rates by desperate magazine executives, an act of desperation that many clients appeared to take for granted by 1990.

The following table (3.2) outlines advertising spending within the United States and overseas between 1982 and 1989.[2] Clearly advertising revenues within this nation experienced a sharp, and at times a precipitous, decline beginning in 1985, a trend that many national media authorities expect to continue well into the 1990–1991 period.

Ironically, while domestic billings have sagged, overseas revenues have risen dramatically since 1986, a sign that many advertisers are indeed thinking globally. This phenomenon is in response to many complex events, including the exciting and expanding consumer and business market in Europe's Common Market, intriguing windows of opportunity in an expanding Pacific Rim market, and marketing possibilities in Latin America, Africa, and elsewhere.

By 1990 global marketing was a fact of life; yet far too many advertising managers in the United States failed to comprehend the true significance of this event, a situation that must be addressed effectively by publishers in the business publishing industry if they are to compete efficiently in this world arena.

While national and international data are important, an overview of where the top five hundred advertising agencies in the U.S. placed their eagerly sought advertising dollars provides the advertising manager with important insight into what media buyers perceive as the "hot" and "cool" market niches. The following table (3.3) outlines where these five hundred major agencies spent $34.951 billion, 29.64 percent of the total U.S. advertising expenditures in 1988.[3]

Yet do these five hundred major firms really represent the attitudes and feelings of the nation's media buyers and clients? Or is this data skewed because of its large size? Perhaps the only way to address these queries is to analyze the actual buying patterns of those elite firms who dominate the thinking on Madison Avenue.

The following table (3.4) contains comparative data on how the top twenty-five, the top one hundred, and the top five hundred agencies allocated their billings. This material provides an intriguing overview of how these media buyers, many of whom are in their mid- to late-twenties or early thirties, view the importance and significance of consumer, business, and farm periodicals and the broadcast media in the United States.[4]

A detailed analysis of this information reveals a significant fact.

*Table 3.3 / U.S. Media Billings by Category for the Five Hundred
Largest Agencies: 1988 (in billions of dollars)*

Media	Percent of 1988 Total Billings of $35 Billion	Dollar Amount
Print Media		
Newspapers	9.2	$3.22
Consumer Magazines	12.6	4.41
Sunday Magazines	0.2	0.07
Business Magazines	2.9	1.02
Medical Journals	1.3	0.45
Farm Publications	0.2	0.07
Outdoor	1.8	0.63
Broadcast Media		
Radio Television	6.4	2.24
Syndicated	0.8	0.03
Cable	1.8	0.63
Network	27.9	9.77
Spot TV	21.0	7.35
Other Media	13.9	4.87

Source: *Advertising Age*, 29 March 1989, 83.

The nation's top twenty-five agencies dominate significantly the advertising buying patterns for the entire county. These top twenty-five agencies billed $22.172 billion in 1988 whereas the top one hundred's billings hovered at the $29.366 billion mark, an increase of a mere $7.194 billion (+32.45 percent) even though an additional seventy-five firms were counted.

As for the top five hundred firms, they amassed billings of $34.951 billion, with the top twenty-five companies accounting for a staggering 63.43 percent of the total billings, with only 5 percent of the total number of agencies!

Yet a review of this data indicated another important trend. The following table (3.5), based on a statistical study of the material in Table 3.4, revealed the fact that the top twenty-five advertising firms purchased only 34.9 percent of all advertising space in business publications, a remarkably low figure when compared to the ratios for consumer magazines (63 percent) and newspapers (43.7 percent).

Table 3.4 / Percent of Media Billings by Top United States
Advertising Agencies: 1988

Media	Top Twenty-Five Agencies' Billings	Top One Hundred Agencies' Billings	Top Five Hundred Agencies' Billings
Print Media			
Newspapers	6.3	8.2	9.2
Consumer Magazines	12.6	12.6	12.6
Sunday Magazines	0.1	0.1	0.2
Business Magazines	1.6	2.1	2.9
Medical Journals	0.5	1.1	1.4
Farm Publications	—	0.1	0.2
Broadcast Media			
Television			
Spot	19.6	20.8	21.0
Network	36.9	31.8	27.9
Cable	1.7	1.9	1.8
Syndicated	1.0	0.9	0.8
Radio	5.5	5.9	6.4
Outdoor	1.7	1.8	1.8
Other	12.4	12.7	13.9

Source: R. Craig Endicott, "Y & R Stays on Top Despite Solid Run by Saatchi," *Advertising Age*, 29 March 1989, 1, 8, 70.

If the large agencies do not recommend strongly advertising in business publications, then which U.S. advertising agencies specialize in or at least promote advertising in business periodicals? This information can be of invaluable assistance to any advertising manager, since business magazines have faced intense competition from other media formats in recent years, most notably from selected consumer magazines in certain advertising niches.

However, the major agencies in the U.S. and the world must first be identified; then those agencies buying space in business magazines can be listed. The following table (3.6) ranks the top twenty-five U.S. agencies in 1988, the last year comparative data was available.[5]

If all of the major international advertising agencies were listed in one table, an interesting phenomenon would occur.

Table 3.5 / Purchasing Ratios: Percentage of Total Billings, 1988

Media	Top Twenty-Five Agencies' Billings	Top One Hundred Agencies' Billings	Top Five Hundred Agencies' Billings
Print Media			
Newspapers	43.7%	74.8%	100%
Consumer Magazines	63.0	83.4	100
Sunday Magazines	27.0	66.7	100
Business Magazines	34.9	62.1	100
Medical Journals	25.0	65.7	100
Farm Publications	1.6	54.8	100
Broadcast Media			
Television			
Spot	59.4	83.2	100
Network	84.1	95.9	100
Cable	61.4	90.4	100
Syndicated	77.6	91.9	100
Radio	54.4	77.6	100
Outdoor	61.3	82.8	100
Other	56.3	76.8	100

Source: R. Craig Endicott, "Y & R Stays on Top Despite Solid Run by Saatchi," *Advertising Age*, 29 March 1989, 1, 8, 70.

Dentsu, a Japanese firm, would replace Young and Rubicam in the first position, and Grey Advertising would neatly fall out of the top ten. Dentsu's worldwide gross income exceeded $1.23 billion in 1988, up a strong 38.9 percent over 1987, and a staggering $471 million (+62.1 percent) ahead of Young and Rubicam.

The following table (3.7) lists the top twenty-five agencies with the largest dollar billings in 1988 in business magazines.[6] Ten agencies on this list reduced their business magazine advertising placements between 1987 and 1988. Even more interesting was the fact that three agencies posted unusually large increases in 1988, including Levine, Huntley, Schmidt, and Beaver, the leading agency in this classification in 1988, with a staggering +2,514.8 percent jump in billing dollars!

These firms accounted for over $538.4 million in total billings,

Table 3.6 / Top Twenty-Five Advertising Agencies in the United States: 1988 (in millions of dollars)

Rank	Agency	Worldwide Gross Income	Percentage Change, 1987–1988
1	Young & Rubicam	$758.6	+ 3.0
2	Saatchi & Saatchi	740.5	+ 8.1
3	Backer Spielvogel Bates Worldwide	689.8	+14.8
4	McCann-Erickson Worldwide	656.8	+28.2
5	FCB-Publicis	653.3	+26.0
6	Ogilvy & Mather Worldwide	635.2	+12.6
7	BBDO Worldwide	585.9	+ 6.6
8	J. Walter Thompson	559.3	+14.7
9	Lintas: Worldwide	537.6	+28.6
10	Grey Advertising	432.8	+17.2
11	D'Arcy Masius Benton & Bowles	428.7	+15.5
12	Leo Burnett Co.	428.4	+16.0
13	DDB Needham Worldwide	399.9	+ 8.5
14	HMD	279.0	+36.7
15	N. W. Ayer	185.2	+11.5
16	Bozell, Jacobs, Kenyon & Eckhardt	179.2	− 3.2
17	Wells, Rich, Greene	117.3	+ 9.6
18	Scali McCabe Sloves	107.0	+14.9
19	Ketchum Communications	105.9	+20.2
20	Campbell-Mitchum-Esty	105.6	+ 5.7
21	TBWA Advertising	97.4	+30.6
22	Ogilvy & Mather Direct Response	97.0	+15.4
23	Ross Roy Group	85.2	+19.5
24	Della Femina, McNamee WCSR	84.4	+ 7.0
25	Wunderman Worldwide	68.6	+10.5
Grand Total		9,018.6	—

Source: "Top 100 Agencies by Gross Income," *Advertising Age*, 30 March 1988, 6–14.

an impressive 20.63 percent of all revenues spent in this business periodical market niche in 1988.

Medical journals were serviced by a different group of advertising agencies that apparently concentrated in and heavily pro-

Table 3.7 / Top Twenty-Five U.S. Agencies in Percent of Business Magazine Advertising Billings: 1988 (in millions of dollars)

Rank	Agency	Media Billings		Percent Change, 1987–1988	Percent of Business Magazines in Total Billings
		1988	*1987*		
1	Levine, Huntley, Schmidt, & Beaver	$53.8	2.2	+2,514.8	32.1
2	Young & Rubicam	57.9	55.1	+5.0	3.0
3	J. Walter Thompson Co.	52.7	51.1	+3.1	3.3
4	Della Femina, McNamee WCRS	44.7	42.6	+5.0	7.6
5	Doremus & Co.	43.0	54.0	−20.4	22.1
6	FCB-Publicis	37.3	15.6	+139.3	2.6
7	Ketchum Communications	36.9	27.9	+32.0	6.0
8	Ogilvy & Mather Worldwide	35.0	12.0	+191.7	2.4
9	McCann-Erickson Worldwide	33.1	27.2	+21.7	3.1
10	HMD	16.1	16.4	−1.8	7.8
11	Campbell Mitchell-Esty	15.9	18.2	−18.2	n/a
12	LGFE	15.6	10.8	+44.0	n/a
13	Albert, Frank, Guenther, Law	15.5	15.6	−0.2	n/a
14	Fallon McElligott	13.7	8.7	+58.1	n/a
15	Lewis, Gilman, & Kynett	12.5	13.9	−10.1	n/a
16	Hammond Farrell	12.4	12.2	−2.1	n/a
17	Hoffman York & Compton	10.8	7.5	+43.1	n/a
18	Al, Paul, Lefton	9.8	10.4	−5.8	n/a
19	Christopher Thomas/ Muller, Jordan Weiss	9.0	n/a	n/a	n/a
20	Fahlgren & Swink	8.9	10.4	−14.3	n/a
21	Chiat/Day	8.9	18.9	−53.1	n/a
22	N.W. Ayer	8.7	15.4	−43.6	n/a
23	Meldrum & Fewsmith	8.6	8.1	+5.0	n/a
24	McKinney & Silver	7.5	7.0	+7.1	n/a
25	Rumrill-Hoyt	7.4	7.8	−4.7	n/a
	Grand Total	575.7	469.0	+22.8	

Source: "Top Ten by Print Media," *Advertising Age,* 29 March 1989, 83; "Tops in the Trades," *Advertising Age,* 12 June 1989, S2.

Table 3.8 / Top Ten U.S. Agencies in Medical Journals Advertising Billings: 1988 (in millions of dollars)

Rank	Agency	Media Billings		Percent Change, 1987–1988	Percent of Total Billings
		1988	1987		
1	McCann-Erickson Worldwide	$60.0	$49.2	+22.0%	5.6%
2	Klemtner Advertising	46.8	33.4	+40.1	66.9
3	William Douglas McAdams	43.0	45.5	−5.5	42.6
4	Lavey/ Wolff/Swift	42.0	36.0	+16.7	58.2
5	Young & Rubicam	35.1	29.5	+19.0	1.8
6	Dorritie & Lyons	29.4	24.5	+20.0	65.3
7	FCB- Publicis	22.9	32.2	−28.7	1.6
8	Kallir, Philips, Ross	22.1	16.8	+31.0	17.8
9	William R. Biggs/ Gilmore Associates	20.6	14.6	+41.1	51.2
10	Barnum Communications	18.7	20.0	−6.7	49.4
	Grand Total	340.6	301.7	+12.9	—

Source: "Top Ten by Print Media," *Advertising Age,* 29 March 1989, 83.

moted these publications; in fact, four of the top ten agencies allocated over half of all of their billings in this healthcare niche. The following table (3.8) lists those firms specializing in the medical field.[7]

The following table (3.9) lists the twenty-five largest advertisers in the United States.[8]

Since the vast majority of these corporations were active in a plethora of business categories (for example, Coca-Cola manufactured a significant number of different soft drinks and also owned Columbia Pictures, a major motion picture firm), it is necessary to

Table 3.9 / Top Twenty-Five Advertisers in the United States: 1988 (in millions of dollars)

Rank	Advertiser	Advertising Spending	Percent Change, 1987–1988
1	Philip Morris	$1,558	+ 7.4%
2	Proctor & Gamble	1,387	− 7.6
3	General Motors Corp.	1,025	+ 22.2
4	Sears, Roebuck & Co.	887	− 19.8
5	RJR Nabisco	840	− 6.1
6	PepsiCo	704	+ 9.7
7	Eastman Kodak Co.	658	+ 7.9
8	McDonald's Corp.	649	+ 9.7
9	Ford Motor Corp.	640	− 1.7
10	Anheuser-Busch Co.	635	− 1.4
11	K Mart Corp.	632	+ 10.1
12	Unilever NV/PLC	581	+ 6.9
13	General Mills	572	+ 4.0
14	Chrysler Corp.	569	+ 12.9
15	Warner-Lambert Co.	558	+ 0.9
16	AT&T	531	+ 1.6
17	Kellogg Co.	525	+ 41.3
18	J. C. Penney Co.	513	+ 3.5
19	Pillsbury Co.	474	− 4.3
20	Johnson & Johnson	459	+ 11.8
21	Ralston Purina Co.	437	− 8.7
22	Kraft	401	− 14.4
23	American Home Products	390	− 0.5
24	Mars	379	+ 19.3
25	Coca-Cola Co.	365	− 1.5
	Grand Total	16,369	—

Source: "Advertising Power Charts," *Advertising Age,* 26 December 1988, 10–13.

ascertain the major advertising categories represented by these and similar companies in the United States.

The following table (3.10) outlines these categories.[9] Unfortunately, specific data regarding business periodicals was not available; so data pertaining to advertising information for the entire spectrum of the magazine industry was listed.

How did global corporations allocate their advertising dollars

Table 3.10 / Top Thirty-One Advertising Categories: 1987–1988 (in millions of dollars)

1988 Rank	Category	Total Advertising Spending		Percent Change, 1987–1988	Magazine Percent		Percent Change, 1987–1988
		1987	1988		1987	1988	
1	Retail	$5,584	$5,715	+2.3%	$140	$173	+23.6
2	Automotive	4,318	4,931	+14.2	678	800	+18.0
3	Business, Consumer Services	3,508	3,726	+6.2	494	464	−6.1
4	Food	3,559	3,656	+2.7	377	376	−0.2
5	Entertainment	2,315	2,483	+7.3	30	28	−3.3
6	Toiletries and Cosmetics	1,936	2,086	+7.7	468	565	+20.7
7	Travel and Hotels	1,835	1,955	+6.5	273	303	+11.0
8	Drugs and Remedies	1,464	1,535	+4.8	142	144	+1.4
9	Beer, Wine, and Liquor	1,342	1,299	−3.2	208	213	+2.4
10	Snacks and Soft Drinks	1,149	1,176	+2.3	23	51	+18.6
11	Direct Response	960	1,047	+9.1	405	446	+10.1
12	Insurance and Real Estate	832	860	+3.4	122	127	+4.1
13	Apparel and Footwear	644	760	+18.0	310	351	+13.2

14	Publishing and Media	694	—	186	191	+2.7
15	Cigarettes and Tobacco	600	+9.3	334	352	+5.4
16	Household Equipment	647	−5.3	98	101	+3.1
17	Computers and Office Equipment	561	+7.3	241	251	+4.1
18	Soaps and Cleansers	570	+0.4	51	51	—
19	Sporting Goods and Toys	552	+1.3	90	117	+30.0
20	Building Materials	363	+8.3	77	87	+13.0
21	Jewelry and Cameras	364	+3.3	117	137	+17.1
22	Electronic Entertainment	254	+22.8	78	88	+12.8
23	Household Furnishings	273	+12.1	111	114	+2.7
24	Miscellaneous	289	+5.9	154	157	+1.9
25	Gasoline and Lubricants	279	+4.7	16	23	+43.8
26	Pets and Pet Food	281	−12.1	24	31	+29.2
27	Horticulture and Farming	230	−4.8	21	24	+14.3
28	Freight, Industrial	82	+76.8	34	41	+20.6
29	Industrial Materials	80	+36.3	41	54	+31.7
30	Business Propositions	28	+7.1	14	13	−7.1
31	Airplanes and Aviation	14	+14.3	12	13	+8.3

Source: "National Ad Spending by Category," *Advertising Age*, 27 September 1989, 8.

among all of the various media formats available to them in this nation? The following three tables outline the print spending patterns of the top twenty-five advertisers in the United States.

Unfortunately, specific business magazine advertising data for 1988 was not made available. On 6 December 1989, this author reviewed this situation with Rance Crain, president of Crain Communications and president and editor-in-chief of *Advertising Age.* He outlined the data collection formats and sources utilized by *Advertising Age,* and he said that detailed business periodicals data could no longer be tracked as a separate niche. Consequently, business press statistics contained in *Advertising Age* in 1987, plus additional calculations and analyses by the author, had to be utilized and can be found in the following table (3.11).[10] An asterisk indicates that total print expenditures for a specific corporation was under $1 million for that year.

Did these firms allocate more advertising dollars, or even a higher percentage of their total expenditures, for consumer rather than business publications? Did any of these major firms spend more dollars, or a larger percentage of their total advertising allocations, on purchasing space in business titles rather than consumer periodicals?

The following table (3.12) outlines buying patterns of advertising space in consumer magazines; all figures were rounded off by the author during the various statistical analyses.

A radically different picture emerges when business periodicals are studied. The next table (3.13) indicates quite clearly that many of these major national advertisers do not allocate significant amounts of money to purchase advertising space in these publications.

AT&T was the only one of the top twenty-five firms to allocate at least 3 percent of its total advertising budget for space in business books. Either this pool of affluent companies eschews business advertising (in spite of the obvious ability of business publications to target potential or actual purchasers of goods and services) or else it underestimates the impact of business publishing advertising.

In any case, if a clear majority of these top firms fail to take advantage of this media, what companies do utilize America's vast

Table 3.11 / Newspaper Spending Patterns of the Top Twenty-Five Advertisers in the United States: 1987 (in millions of dollars)

Rank	Advertiser	Advertising Spending Totals	Newspapers Spending	Percent of Total Spending	Newspaper Supplements Spending	Percent of Total Spending
1	Philip Morris	$1,558	$49	3.1%	$9	0.6%
2	Proctor & Gamble	1,387	5	0.4	2	0.1
3	General Motors Corp.	1,025	174	17.0	7	0.7
4	Sears, Roebuck & Co.	887	n/a	—	6	0.7
5	RJR Nabisco	840	20	2.4	12	1.4
6	PepsiCo	704	8	1.1	*	—
7	Eastman Kodak Co.	658	2	0.3	1	0.2
8	McDonald's Corp.	649	n/a	—	1	0.2
9	Ford Motor Corp.	640	100	15.6	*	—
10	Anheuser-Busch Co.	635	11	1.7	*	—
11	K Mart Corp.	632	n/a	—	2	0.3
12	Unilever NV/PLC	581	1	0.2	*	—
13	General Mills	572	*	—	*	—
14	Chrysler Corp.	569	70	12.3	4	0.7
15	Warner-Lambert	558	1	0.2	1	0.2
16	AT&T	531	35	6.6	6	1.1
17	Kellogg Co.	525	*	—	*	—
18	J.C. Penney Co.	513	n/a	—	1	0.2
19	Pillsbury Co.	474	*	—	*	—
20	Johnson & Johnson	459	*	—	*	—
21	Ralston Purina Co.	437	2	0.5	*	—
22	Kraft	401	2	0.5	2	0.5
23	American Home Products	390	*	—	*	—
24	Mars	379	*	—	*	—
25	Coca-Cola Co.	365	5	1.4	*	—

Source: "Print Spending by 100 Leaders," Advertising Age, 28 September 1988, 10.

Table 3.12 / Consumer Magazine Spending Patterns of the Top Twenty-Five Advertisers in the United States: 1987 (in millions of dollars)

Rank	Advertiser	Advertising Spending	Consumer Magazines Spending	Percent of Consumer Magazines of Advertising
1	Philip Morris	$1,558	$243	15.6%
2	Proctor & Gamble	1,387	79	5.7
3	General Motors Corp.	1,025	153	14.9
4	Sears, Roebuck & Co.	887	21	2.4
5	RJR Nabisco	840	105	12.5
6	PepsiCo	704	*	n/a
7	Eastman Kodak Co.	658	32	4.8
8	McDonald's Corp.	649	7	1.1
9	Ford Motor Corp.	640	125	19.5
10	Anheuser-Busch Co.	635	11	1.7
11	K Mart Corp.	632	23	3.6
12	Unilever NV/PLC	581	58	10.0
13	General Mills	572	19	3.3
14	Chrysler Corp.	569	100	17.6
15	Warner-Lambert	558	14	2.5
16	AT&T	531	76	14.3
17	Kellogg Co.	525	3	0.6
18	J.C. Penney Co.	513	9	1.7
19	Pillsbury Co.	474	5	1.1
20	Johnson & Johnson	459	32	6.9
21	Ralston Purina	437	18	4.1
22	Kraft	401	29	7.2
23	American Home Products	390	13	3.3
24	Mars	379	11	2.9
25	Coca-Cola Co.	365	5	1.4

Source: "Print Spending by 100 Leaders," *Advertising Age*, 28 September 1988, 10.

Table 3.13 / Business Magazine Spending Patterns of the Top Twenty-Five Advertisers in the United States: 1987 (in millions of dollars)

Rank	Advertiser	Advertising Spending Totals	Business Magazines Total	Percent of Business Magazines of Total Advertising
1	Philip Morris	$1,558	$3	0.2%
2	Proctor & Gamble	1,387	3	0.2
3	General Motors Corp.	1,025	10	1.0
4	Sears, Roebuck & Co.	887	*	n/a
5	RJR Nabisco	840	4	0.5
6	PepsiCo	704	*	n/a
7	Eastman Kodak Co.	658	6	1.0
8	McDonald's Corp.	649	*	n/a
9	Ford Motor Corp.	640	5	0.8
10	Anheuser-Busch	635	1	0.2
11	K Mart Corp.	632	*	n/a
12	Unilever NV/PLC	581	2	0.3
13	General Mills	572	1	0.2
14	Chrysler Corp.	569	2	0.4
15	Warner-Lambert	558	2	0.4
16	AT&T	531	16	3.0
17	Kellogg Co.	525	*	n/a
18	J.C. Penney Co.	513	*	n/a
19	Pillsbury Co.	474	*	n/a
20	Johnson & Johnson	459	*	n/a
21	Ralston Purina	437	*	n/a
22	Kraft	401	1	0.3
23	American Home Products	390	1	0.3
24	Mars	379	4	1.1
25	Coca-Cola Co.	365	*	n/a

Source: "Print Spending by 100 Leaders," *Advertising Age*, 28 September 1988, 10.

network of business periodicals? The following table (3.14) lists the largest advertisers in this category.[11]

Farm publications have traditionally comprised a major segment of the business magazine market. The top advertisers in this niche are listed in the following table (3.15).[12]

Rank	Advertiser	Expenditures		Percent Change, 1986–1987	Percent of Total 1987 Advertising Budget
		1987	1986		
1	AT&T	$16.5	19.9	− 16.8%	3.1%
2	du Pont	12.5	9.7	+ 28.9	8.4
3	Hewlett-Packard	11.6	8.0	+ 44.3	25.6
4	General Electric	10.9	13.7	− 20.4	4.0
5	General Motors	9.7	10.3	− 5.8	0.9
6	NEC Corp.	9.5	8.9	+ 6.0	17.3
7	IBM	8.9	13.3	− 32.9	3.7
8	3M	8.9	8.7	+ 1.9	15.7
9	Tektronix	7.8	n/a	n/a	n/a
10	Motorola	7.1	n/a	n/a	n/a
11	Compaq Computer	7.0	n/a	n/a	n/a
12	ITT Corp.	6.9	6.1	+ 12.5	4.6
13	Honeywell	6.5	n/a	n/a	n/a
14	Eastman Kodak	6.1	5.7	+ 5.9	0.9
15	Caterpillar Tractor Co.	5.7	n/a	n/a	n/a
16	NCR Corp.	5.5	n/a	n/a	n/a
17	Ford Motor Corp.	5.5	5.3	+ 3.7	0.9
18	Toshiba Corp.	5.3	5.1	+ 3.8	12.1
19	Emerson Electric Co.	5.3	n/a	n/a	n/a
20	McGraw-Hill Publications Co.	5.2	n/a	n/a	n/a
21	Tyson Foods	5.1	3.5	+ 45.9	12.2
22	Parker Hannifin Corp.	4.9	n/a	n/a	n/a
23	Time	4.9	5.6	− 12.4	2.5
24	Texas Instruments	4.7	n/a	n/a	n/a
25	Premark International	4.7	n/a	n/a	n/a

Source: "Top 25 Business Publication Advertisers," *Advertising Age*, 28 September 1988, 20.

Table 3.15 / Top Twenty-Five Farm Publication Advertisers: 1987 (in millions of dollars)

Rank	Advertiser	Advertising Expenditures		Percent Change, 1986–1987	Percent of Total Advertising Expenditures
		1987	*1986*		
1	Imperial Chemical Industries PLC	$8,299	$7,726	+7.4%	17.2%
2	Ciba-Geigy	7,159	6,622	+8.1	12.0
3	Monsanto Co.	5,997	5,501	+9.0	7.1
4	Bayer AG	5,647	5,341	+5.7	3.9
5	American Cyanamid	5,423	5,376	+0.9	2.2
6	du Pont	4,978	3,832	+29.9	3.3
7	Deere & Co.	4,366	5,904	−26.1	n/a
8	Rhone-Poulenc	4,284	1,874	+128.6	n/a
9	Ford Motor Co.	4,267	4,475	−4.6	0.7
10	Elanco Products Co.	4,233	5,251	−19.4	n/a
11	Tenneco	3,378	2,715	+24.4	n/a
12	General Motors Corp.	3,355	2,263	+48.3	0.3
13	FMC Corp.	2,448	2,783	−12.0	n/a
14	Sandoz	2,094	1,519	+37.9	3.6
15	MSD Agvet Merck & Co.	1,891	1,530	+23.6	n/a
16	Pioneer Hi-Bred International	1,881	2,146	−12.3	n/a
17	BASF Corp.	1,845	1,600	+15.3	n/a
18	IMC International	1,739	826	+110.5	n/a
19	Hoechst-Roussel	1,603	1,671	−4.1	n/a
20	Upjohn	1,575	1,909	−17.5	n/a
21	Pfizer	1,558	1,067	+46.0	0.9
22	Dow Chemical Co.	1,448	1,388	+7.2	1.1
23	Ralston Purina Co.	1,143	1,229	−7.0	0.3
24	Farnam Co.	1,122	716	+56.7	n/a
25	Deutz/Allis Corp.	1,101	1,006	+9.4	n/a

Source: "Top 25 Farm Publication Advertisers," *Advertising Age,* 28 September 1988, 24.

Table 3.16 / Major Media Corporations in the United States: 1988 (in millions of dollars)

Rank 1988	Company	Total Media Revenues		Total Magazine Revenues		Percent of Total Media Revenue	
		1988	1987	1988	1987	1988	1987
1	Capital Cities/ABC	$4,589	$4,256	$379	$375	8.3	8.8
2	Time Inc.	3,686	3,306	1,752	1,621	47.5	49.0
3	General Electric	3,638	3,241	n/a	n/a	—	—
4	Gannett Co.	3,211	2,991	n/a	n/a	—	—
5	CBS Inc.	2,777	2,762	n/a	n/a	—	—
6	Times Mirror	2,678	2,549	299	203	11.1	8.0
7	Advance Publications	2,656	2,482	745	678	28.0	27.3
8	Knight-Ridder	2,077	1,944	n/a	n/a	—	—
9	Hearst Corp.	1,986	1,886	919	873	46.3	46.3
10	Tribune Co.	1,985	1,877	n/a	n/a	—	—
11	TCI	1,705	1,225	n/a	n/a	—	—
12	New York Times Co.	1,700	1,642	249	246	14.6	15.0
13	News Corp.	1,683	1,250	510	333	30.3	26.6
14	Cox Enterprises	1,578	1,464	n/a	n/a	—	—
15	Washington Post Co.	1,306	1,240	328	322	25.1	26.0
16	Scripps Howard	1,203	1,129	n/a	n/a	—	—
17	Thomson Corp.	1,126	973	596	528	52.9	54.3
18	Viacom International	1,114	939	n/a	n/a	—	—
19	Dow Jones & Co.	973	988	36	39	3.7	3.9
20	Ingersoll Publications Co.	645	609	n/a	n/a	—	—
23	Reader's Digest Assoc.	600	522	600	522	100.0	100.0
28	McGraw-Hill	510	468	414	377	81.2	80.6
29	Affiliated Publications	507	473	62	31	12.2	6.6
30	Warner Communications	494	425	40	38	8.1	8.9

32	Meredith Corp.	475	449	365	329	76.8	73.3
37	Cahners Publishing Co.	420	340	420	340	100.0	100.0
48	Hachette Publications	366	321	366	321	100.0	100.0
52	International Data Group	352	300	352	300	100.0	100.0
53	Reuters Holdings PLC	351	294	n/a	n/a	—	—
54	Cowles Media Co.	315	295	42	28	13.3	9.5
60	National Geographic Society	245	223	245	223	100.0	100.0
67	Macfadden Holdings	209	n/a	45	n/a	21.5	—
70	Ziff Communications	200	145	200	145	100.0	100.0
72	Times Publishing Co.	194	183	25	23	12.9	12.6
74	Petersen Publishing	187	162	187	162	100.0	100.0
76	Forbes Inc.	181	166	175	160	96.7	96.4
77	Maclean Hunter	181	163	70	68	36.7	41.7
84	LIN Broadcasting	158	156	21	19	13.3	12.2
87	Whittle Communications	152	106	97	67	63.8	63.2
89	General Media International	150	140	150	140	100.0	100.0
91	Edgell Communications	148	144	148	144	100.0	100.0
92	Playboy Enterprises	144	145	120	115	83.3	79.3
93	U.S. News & World Report	142	124	142	124	100.0	100.0
95	Crain Communications	137	128	137	128	100.0	100.0
98	CMP Publications	133	111	20	16	15.0	14.4

Source: "100 Leading Media Companies by Revenue," *Advertising Age*, 26 June 1989, S2.

While major advertising agencies and corporations have been identified, what firms make up the major media corporations operating in the United States? The following table (3.16) lists and ranks the top twenty "media" firms in this nation.

Information from *Advertising Age* was utilized to create this list of corporations, and this definitive business periodical defined the term media as including the following advertising revenue generating formats: (1) newspapers, (2) magazines, (3) commercial radio and television, (4) cable television, and (5) other media. However, in order to provide an overview of the magazine component among these media firms, leading companies with magazine operating units outside the top twenty were also listed and ranked, using the *Advertising Age* rankings.[13]

What media firms dominate the European market? Bertelsmann AG (the giant West German communications company that owns Bantam, Doubleday, Dell, *Parents* magazine, and other major properties in the United States) had a small lead over Reed International (the parent of the important Cahners group in the U.S.). In fact, most of the top ten foreign corporations have a highly visible presence in the North American market.

The top fifty European media companies, operating in seventeen different nations, generated over $31 billion in media revenues in 1988, with the top ten firms accounting for slightly more than $13.497 (43.54 percent) of the total. Ironically no single company accounted for more than 4 percent of the total + $50 billion in total revenues, a clear barometer of the intense competitive nature of the industry in Europe, which might explain why so many of these firms have been eager to enter the large U.S. market.

The United Kingdom had the largest number of firms in the top fifty (sixteen companies; 32 percent of the total). Germany was ranked second with ten corporations (20 percent).

The following table (3.17) lists the ten largest European media companies.[14] *Media* refers to radio, television, magazines, newspapers, cable television, and other media; nonadvertising revenue media properties (for example books, book clubs, etc.) were excluded in the "media revenue" category but included in the "total revenue" column.

Table 3.17 / Ten Largest European Media Companies: 1988 (in billions of dollars)

Rank	Company	Total Media Revenues	Total Revenues	Percent of Total Revenues
1	Bertelsmann AG	$1.665	$6.453	25.8
2	Reed International	1.649	2.225	74.1
3	Fininvest	1.468	9.685	15.2
4	Axel Springer-Verlag	1.425	1.620	87.9
5	Hachette	1.382	4.100	33.7
6	Havas	1.286	2.654	48.5
7	United Newspapers PLC	1.212	1.341	90.4
8	Hersant	1.176	1.176	100.0
9	Heinrich Bauer Verlag	1.142	1.142	100.0
10	RCS	1.092	1.092	100.0
	Grand Total	13.497	31.488	42.9

Source: David Murrow, "Bertelsmann Tops in Euro Media," Advertising Age, 27 November 1989, 102.

NOTES

1. Robert J. Coen, "Ad Spending Outlook Brightens," Advertising Age, 15 May 1989, 24. Also see Joanne Lipman, "Meager Rise Forecast for '89 Ad Spending," Wall Street Journal, 13 December 1989, B6; Joanne Lipman and Thomas R. King, "Ad Spending Expectations Turn out to Be Too Great," Wall Street Journal, 21 August 1989, B1; Robert J. Coen, "TV Forms Hot; Print, Outdoor Waver," Advertising Age, 30 November 1987, S2–S4; and Robert J. Coen, "Rate Hikes Fall off Pace as Poor Year Hits Pricing," Advertising Age, 28 November 1988, S1–S18. Also see Laurie Weaver, "Rates Bending, but Will They Break?" Advertising Age, 28 November 1988, S1–S2. Generally, the best impartial source of information about the U.S. economy is the definitive work published by the National Bureau of Economic Research (NBER). For example, see three major and highly useful articles by Victor Zarnowitz: "Economic Outlook Survey: Third Quarter 1988," NBER Reporter, Fall 1988, 11–12; "Economic Outlook Survey: First Quarter 1989," NBER Reporter, Spring 1989, 11–12; and "Economic Outlook Survey: Second Quarter 1989," NBER Reporter, Summer 1989, 12–13. For more detailed information about the U.S. economy, see Robert E. Hall, "Economic Fluctuations," NBER Reporter, Summer 1989, 1–7; Business Conditions Digest 28 (February 1988):

6–9, 40–47; and the *Survey of Current Business* 67 (July 1987): 20–29. Also see "The Next Recession: Just Around the Bend?" *Wall Street Journal*, 6 March 1989, A1; "Quarterly Review of Corporate Earnings: Second Quarter 1989," *Wall Street Journal*, 7 August 1989, A5–A14; "Corporate Profits Fell 18 Percent in Third Quarter, for First Drop since '87," *Wall Street Journal*, 6 November 1989, A1; Joanne Lipman, "Gap Between Ad-Revenue Figures and Reality Grows," *Wall Street Journal*, 20 November 1989, B6; and Richard Edel, "Growth Robust for Promo Shops," *Advertising Age*, 4 April 1988, S1–S2.

2. Joanne Lipman, "Ad Spending to Rise 6.9 Percent in '89, Coen Says in a Warmer Forecast," *Wall Street Journal*, 15 June 1989, B4. Also see Randall Rothenberg, "Shifts in Marketing Strategy Jolting Advertising Industry," *New York Times*, 3 October 1989, A1, D23; "Ad rates Climb at *TV Guide* and *People* Weekly Magazines," *MagazineWeek*, 9 October 1989, 3; and Joanne Y. Cleaver, "Magazine Rate Card More of a Wild Card," *Advertising Age*, 30 November 1987, S22–S23.

3. *Advertising Age*, 29 March 1989, 83; and calculations by author. Dollar figures were rounded off. Also see "Total U.S. Advertising Dollars by Media," *Advertising Age*, 28 September 1988, 158. Also see Randall Rothenberg, "Job Shuffle at Industry Publications," *New York Times*, 2 August 1989, D18.

4. R. Craig Endicott, "Y & R Stays on Top Despite Solid Run by Saatchi," *Advertising Age*, 29 March 1989, 1, 8, 70; plus additional calculations (which were rounded off) by the author. Also see R. Craig Endicott, "Y & R Maintains Its Lead," *Advertising Age*, 20 March 1989, 3. For historical data on agencies, see Dennis Chase, "Y & R Group Holds on to Top Spot," *Advertising Age*, 21 April 1986, 63;

5. "Top 100 Agencies by Gross Income," *Advertising Age*, 30 March 1988, 6–14 (also includes data on the top five hundred agencies with U.S. and worldwide billings income and related rankings, number of employees, etc.; and "Agency Billings by Media," *Advertising Age*, 30 March 1988, 18–25. For material on the geographical distribution of advertising agencies, see "U.S. Billings by Region," *Advertising Age*, 30 March 1988, 88.

6. "Top Ten by Print Media," *Advertising Age*, 29 March 1989, 83; and "Tops in the Trades," *Advertising Age*, 12 June 1989, S2.

7. "Top Ten by Print Media," 83.

8. "Advertising Power Charts," *Advertising Age*, 26 December 1988, 10–13.

9. "National Ad Spending by Category," *Advertising Age*, 27 September 1989, 8. Also see "Ads-to-Sales Ratio Study Uncovers Big Hikes," *Advertising Age*, 24 October 1988, 49. For historical data on advertising categories covering the years 1985–1986, see "Advertising as Percent of Sales," *Advertising Age*, 23 November 1987, S4. Also see "Ad-

vertising-to-Sales Ratios, 1989," *Advertising Age,* 13 November 1989, 32.

10. "Print Spending by 100 Leaders," *Advertising Age,* 28 September 1988, 10. Additional calculations by the author. Also see R. Craig Endicott, "'86 Ad Spending Soars," *Advertising Age,* 23 November 1987, S2; "Second 100 Leading National Advertisers," *Advertising Age,* 23 November 1987, S2–S12; and "Ad Spending by Leaders Ranked 101 to 200," *Advertising Age,* 21 November 1988, S2–S34.

11. "Top 25 Business Pub Advertisers," *Advertising Age,* 28 September 1988, 20.

12. "Top 25 Farm Publication Advertisers," *Advertising Age,* 28 September 1988, 24. Also see "National Measured Ad Spending," *Advertising Age,* 28 September 1988, 156; and for historical data about U.S. and Canadian farm periodicals, see "Ad Pages in Farm Publications for 9 Months, 1987–1986," *Advertising Age,* 12 October 1987, 94.

13. "100 Leading Media Companies by Revenue," *Advertising Age,* 26 June 1989, S2. For historical data see R. Craig Endicott, "Media Companies Post Robust Growth," *Advertising Age,* 27 June 1988, S2–S3; "100 Leading Media Companies by Revenue," *Advertising Age,* 27 June 1988, S6; R. Craig Endicott, "Sales Surge 11 Percent for Media Giants," *Advertising Age,* 29 June 1987, S2; "100 Leading Media Companies," *Advertising Age,* 29 June 1987, S3.

14. David Murrow, "Bertelsmann Tops in Euro Media," *Advertising Age,* 27 November 1989, 102. For a useful article about the European market, see Kevin Cote, "Uncertain Future Plagues Marketers Planning for 1992," *Advertising Age,* 5 June 1989, 1, 42. Also see "Global Media and Marketing," *Advertising Age,* 14 December 1987, 53–65; Keith Kelly, "Rizzoli Plans Push into U.S. Market," *MagazineWeek,* 30 October 1989, 1, 3; Ron Schneiderman, "A New Industry Springs Up: Europe 1992," *New York Times,* 26 November 1989, F16; and Steven Greenhouse, "Europe's Buyout Bulge," *Wall Street Journal,* 5 November 1989, 1, 6. For two interesting articles about a U.S. publications's attempts to penetrate the European market, see Scott Donaton, "*Forbes* Readies Push into Europe," *Advertising Age,* 16 October 1989, 36; and "*Playboy* Beats *Penthouse* With Hungary Launch," *MagazineWeek,* 20 November 1989, 7.

FOUR

Mergers, Acquisitions, and Business Publishing: 1984–1988

INTRODUCTION

Recently there has been a sizable increase in the number of mergers and acquisitions in the United States, especially by foreign corporations. Robert Hamrin, formerly an economist with the U.S. Congressional Joint Economic Committee, reported that between 1968 and 1973 there were 4,900 mergers and acquisitions in the United States with an average value of $30 million. By 1975 the total value of mergers and acquisitions exceeded $11.8 billion for 981 acquisitions.

In the 1980s this pattern accelerated, reaching 3,336 corporate acquisitions in 1986, worth $173 billion. In 1987 this increased to 3,565 acquisitions, valued at over $219.5 billion. Another dramatic surge in 1988 generated a phenomenal $311.4 billion in sales covering 3,637 deals. Wall Street firms specializing in acquisitions earned an impressive $1.28 billion in various consulting fees for arranging and managing these transactions in 1988. Goldman,

Sachs, and Company alone worked on 158 mergers and acquisitions in 1988 (worth $93.4 billion in sales).[1]

The publishing industry participated in this frenzy of activity. Rupert Murdoch's $3 billion purchase of Triangle Publications and Robert Maxwell's $2.6 billion acquisition of Macmillan set the pace for the entire industry in 1988.[2]

Why was there a surge in mergers and acquisitions? What impact will this period of consolidation have on American society? Could the burden of debt associated with these megadeals force some corporations into bankruptcy? Is it wise for American firms to sell off their valuable publishing assets and possibly lose control over their editorial independence? Should foreign-owned firms oversee the planning and writing of textbooks used in America's elementary, junior, and high schools?

To address these issues, *some* of the major publishing mergers and acquisitions covering the years 1984–1988 will be analyzed. These data came from the *Wall Street Journal*, the *New York Times*, *Mergers and Acquisitions* magazine, financial reporting services (Moody's, Standard and Poor's, and Value Line), annual reports, 10–Ks, "tombstones" (display advertisements placed by investment banking firms in financial service publications), and quarterly reports pertaining to the major publishing corporations operating in this nation. In addition some theories will be presented explaining why there was an unprecedented growth in the number of mergers and acquisitions. Finally, some key public policy issues directly associated with these mergers and acquisitions will be discussed.

RECENT MERGERS IN PUBLISHING

Between 1984 and 1988, publishing mergers and acquisitions involved dozens of major U.S. firms that spent a *reported* $23.1 billion on corporate takeovers. The actual costs associated with these acquisitions were probably closer to $40 billion. During these years, total revenues generated by the entire publishing industry topped the $177.354 billion mark. Periodicals reached $79.822 billion; and miscellaneous publishing (directories, annuals, newsletters, etc.) set records with an impressive $23.9 billion total; the book industry alone generated $59.9 billion. The following table (4.1), based on data published in *Book Industry Trends 1988*, outlines total book sales between 1984 and 1988.[3]

Until quite recently, U.S. publishing houses emphasized single-market niches, for example books, magazines, or scholarly journals. Product diversification was limited. As Walter W. Powell points out in *Getting into Print*, the amount of acquisition activity in the 1960s was "only a fraction of the rate of formation of new publishing companies. . . . The industry's overall concentration rate [did] not increase. . . . "[4]

The following table (4.2) is based upon an intensive review of the financial documents and databases listed earlier. It is a *partial* but representative list of the major U.S. mergers and acquisitions in the publishing and mass communications industry since 1984. "N/A" indicates that price information is not available to the public. Estimated prices are indicated with an asterisk.

The following table (4.3) is a *partial* but representative list of the major mergers and acquisitions of U.S. publishing corporations by *foreign* publishing firms since 1984, and it indicates clearly an intense level of activity. "N/A" indicated that price information is not available to the public. Estimated figures are marked with an asterisk.

SOME THEORIES CONCERNING THE GROWTH OF MERGERS AND ACQUISITIONS

International and United States corporations participated in this merger and acquisition process for many different, complex reasons. Although no Rosetta stone can decipher the myriad of forces and issues that created this phenomenon, some observations can be made about this situation.[5]

For several years the U.S. dollar has been quite weak. This economic malaise attracted the attention of a plethora of chief executive officers and investment bankers in Western Europe and elsewhere because foreign corporations were able to purchase U.S. companies at what they perceived to be "below market" prices.[6] So the United States's problem became an opportunity for indi-

Table 4.1 / Total Book Sales: 1984–1988 (in millions of U.S. dollars)

Category	1984	1985	1986	1987	1988	Percent Change 1984–1988
Trade	$2,281.4	$2,710.1	$2,978.7	$3,537.3	$4,044.0	+77.3%
Religious	660.1	657.3	684.9	720.3	765.1	+15.9
Professional	2,080.3	2,270.4	2,533.0	2,720.6	2,951.1	+41.9
Book Clubs	533.6	560.0	573.3	645.7	729.1	+36.6
Mail Order	552.6	578.4	580.4	587.4	598.5	+8.3
Mass Market	916.5	947.9	936.6	1,014.1	1,098.4	+19.9
Scholarly	98.4	104.5	112.6	120.5	129.0	+31.1
El-Hi Texts	1,307.9	1,478.8	1,582.4	1,684.7	1,812.9	+38.6
College Texts	1,415.5	1,472.3	1,551.2	1,679.3	1,803.7	+27.4
Subscription Reference	221.4	218.5	215.8	216.3	217.5	−1.8
Total	$10,067.7	10,996.9	11,748.9	12,926.2	14,149.3	+40.5

Source: The Center for Book Research, University of Scranton, *Book Industry Trends 1988* (New York: Book Industry Study Group, 1988), 111–12, 115–16, 120.

Table 4.2 / Mergers and Acquisitions by U.S. Firms: 1984–1988 (in U.S. dollars)

Company	Acquired	Price	Year
Advance Publications	Vanguard Press	n/a	1988
	Details Magazine	$2 million*	1988
	New Yorker	$167.6 million	1985
Affiliated Publications	Billboard	$100 million	1987
	Photo Design	n/a	1987
	Back Stage	n/a	n/a
	American Film	n/a	1988
	Hollywood Reporter	$26.7 million	1988
	McCaw Cellular (Additional 8% Share)	$264 million	1988
American Express Publishing Co.	Auburn House Publishing	n/a	1987
	East Woods Press	n/a	1987
Ballantine/Del Ray Fawcett Books	L.A. Style	n/a	1988
Robert M. Bass Group, (BHW Acquisition Corp.)	House of Collectibles	n/a	1985
	Bell & Howell Co.	$678.4 million	1988
Bell & Howell Co.	University Microfilms International	$100 million	1985
Berkshire Hathaway	Scott Fetzer Co.	n/a	1985
Boston Properties	U.S. News & World Report	$100 million	1984
Boston Ventures Management	Billboard, Watson-Guptill Publications, and Other Publications	$40 million	1985
Capital Cities/ ABC	Bill Communications	$90 million*	1989
	NILS Publishing	n/a	1988
	Institutional Investor	$72 million	1984
CBS	Ziff-Davis's Consumer Magazines	$362.5 million	1985
Conde Nast	Woman Magazine	n/a	1988
	Gourmet	$24 million	1984

Company	Subsidiary/Acquisition	Value	Year
Cowles Media Co.	Hanson Publishing	$25 million*	1987
	Empire Press	n/a	1988
	Historical Times	n/a	1986
Crossroad/Continuum	Frederick Ungar Publishing Co.	n/a	1985
Diamandis Communications	CBS Magazines	$650 million	1987
Dun & Bradstreet Corp.	IMS International	$1.6 billion	1988
	A.C. Nielsen Co.	$1.339 billion	1981
Forbes	American Heritage Publishing Co.	$8-10 million	1986
Grolier	*Academic American Encyclopedia*	n/a	1985
Gulf & Western	Prentice-Hall	$710 million	1984
	Maxwell Communications' Macdonald Children's Books	n/a	1989
	Home Health Care Nurse	$2.5 million	1988
	Stratemeyer Syndicate	n/a	1984
	Ginn & Co.	$500 million	1985
	Silver Burdett Co.	$125 million	1986
	Regents Publishing Co.	$12 million	1987
	Law & Business	n/a	1986
Harcourt Brace Jovanovich	CBS Educational and Professional Publishing	$500 million	1987
	Davis Publishing	n/a	1984
Harper & Row	Addison-Wesley's Children's Book List	n/a	1984
	Winston-Seabury Press	n/a	1986
	W. B. Saunders	n/a	1987
	Holt, Rinehart & Winston	n/a	1987
	New American Library	n/a	1983
Ira J. Hechler & Odyssey Partners (see Mezzanine Capital)			
Kampmann & Co.	Beaufort Books	n/a	1984
K-Mart	Waldenbooks	n/a	1984
Knight-Ritter Publishing Co.	Dialog Information Service	$353 million	1988
MCA Inc. (Putnam Publishing Group)	American Publishing Corp.	n/a	1986
McGraw-Hill	Random House's School and College Book Divisions	$200 million	1988

Table 4.2 (Continued)

Company	Acquired	Price	Year
	Macmillan's Science and Technical Publishing	n/a	1987
	News America's Aerospace and Defense Publications	$50 million*	1987
	Educational Management Services	n/a	1984
	Telecommunications Information Co.	n/a	1984
Mead Corp.	Maxwell Communication's Michie Co.	$226.5 million	1988
Mezzanine Capital	Odyssey Partner's Share of New American Library	n/a	1984
Macmillan	Zehring Co.	n/a	1984
	Four Winds Press	n/a	1984
	Collamore Press	n/a	1985
	Dellen Publishing Corp.	n/a	1984
	Harper & Row's School Division	n/a	1984
	ITT Business Publishing	$75 million	1985
	Scribner Book Co.	$14.9 million	1984
	Que Corp.	n/a	1986
	Walker-Davis Publications	n/a	1986
	Book Division of Hayden Publishing Co.	n/a	1986
	Texas Instruments Book Division	n/a	1987
	Laidlaw Educational Publishers	n/a	1987
	Octopus and Pan Books	n/a	1987
	Pennwell Book Division	n/a	1982
National Textbook Co.	Institute of Modern Languages	n/a	1984
	Advertising Age Library	n/a	1985
New American Library	E.P. Dutton	n/a	1985
New Century Communication (Kidder, Peabody, Group and	110 Harcourt, Brace, Jovanovich Business Publications	$337 million	1987

Acquirer	Acquisition	Price	Year
Members of HBJ Management; Edgell Communications) New SFN Corp. (E. M. Warburg Pincus & Co. and an investor group)	Scott Foresman & Co., South-Western Publishing, Silver Burdett Co., and Other Properties	$424 million	1985
New York Times	*Sailing World*	n/a	1988
MCP	Seven Regional Business Newspapers	$46.3 million	1988
Penton Publishing	Two McGraw-Hill Business Titles	n/a	1988
Petersen Publishing Co.	*Sport*	$8-10 million	1988
Price/Stern/Sloan Publishing	HB Books	$14 million	1987
R.A.B. Holdings (Western Management and Richard A. Bernstein)	Western Publishing	$71 million	1984
Random House	Times Books	n/a	1984
	Schocken Books	n/a	1987
Reader's Digest Assoc.	*50 Plus*	n/a	1988
	Family Handyman	$30 million	1988
Time, Inc.	Scott Foresman	$520 million	1986
	Whittle Communications (50% share)	$185 million	1988
	Hippocrates (50% interest)	$9 million	1988
	Children's Book Division of Atlantic Monthly	n/a	1987
	Southern Progress Corp.	$480 million	1985
Scholastic	*Child Care Center*	$1.5 million	1988
SI Holding	Scholastic	$88.5 million	1987
Times Mirror Co.	Richard D. Irwin (from Dow Jones & Co.)	$135 million	1988
John Wiley & Sons	Four Titles from Diamandis Co.	$167 million	1987
	Scripta Technica	n/a	1984
	Harwal Publishing Co.	n/a	1986
	Media Medica	n/a	1986
Zebra Books	Pinnacle Books	n/a	1987
Ziff-Davis Publishing Co.	*MacWeek*	n/a	1988
Mortimer B. Zuckerman	*U.S. News + World Report*	$152 million	1984

Table 4.3 / Mergers and Acquisitions of U.S. Publishing Firms by Foreign Corporations (in U.S. dollars)

Company	Acquired	Price	Year
Argus Press (U.K.)	70 U.S. Titles	$351 million*	1988
	Cardiff Publishing	$7.3 million	1984
Associated Newspapers Holdings PLC (U.K.)	Whittle Communications (Partial Ownership)	n/a	n/a
	American Lawyer	n/a	n/a
Bertelsmann AG (West Germany)	Bantam, Doubleday, and Dell	$500 million*	1986
Bonnier Magazine Group (Sweden)	Parents Magazine	n/a	n/a
	Cook's Magazine	n/a	n/a
William Collins PLC	One-half of Harper & Row	$156 million	1987
Economist Newspapers (U.K.)	Business International Corp.	$7.68 million	1986
Elsevier-NDU NV (Holland)	Springhouse Corp.	$100 million*	1988
	Real Estate Data	n/a	1988
	Damar Corp.	n/a	1988
	University Publications of America	n/a	1988
	Laser and Optronics and Fiberoptics News	n/a	1987
	Three Titles from Machalek Publishing	$3.5 million	1987
	Orthopedic Review and Anesthesiology Review	n/a	1987
	Three Publications from Scott Periodicals	n/a	1987
	Packaging Digest	n/a	1985
	Gordon	$38 million	1985
	Computer Reseller	$4.5 million	1988
	Praeger Publishers	n/a	1986
Fairfax (Australia)	Ms.	$10 million*	1987
Hachette (France)	Grolier	$462.2 million	1988
	Diamandis Communications	$712 million	1988
	Elle Magazine (U.S.A.) (Remaining 50% Share from News Corp.)	n/a	1988

Acquirer	Acquisition	Value	Year
Longman Group (UK)	Farnsworth Publishing	n/a	1984
	Independent School Press	n/a	1987
Maclean Hunter (Canada)	Two McGraw-Hill Business Titles	n/a	1987
	Two McGraw-Hill Titles, Directories, and Newsletters	n/a	1988
	Frozen Food Age	n/a	1987
	Six Business Magazines from Lakewood Publications	n/a	1986
	National Mall and *Monitor*	n/a	1985
	Guitar Player, *Frets*, and *Keyboard*	n/a	1985
	Comprint	$10.2 million	1988
Matilda Publications (Australia)	*Ms.* and *Sassy*	n/a	1988
Maxwell Communications (U.K.; Luxembourg)	Twelve Farm Titles	n/a	1986
	Science Research Associates	$150 million	1988
	Dun & Bradstreet's Official Airline Guides	$750 million	1988
	Macmillan	$2.6 billion	1988
News Corporation PLC (Australia)	Williams Collins PLC (Remaining 54%)	$717 Million	1989
	Harper & Row	$300 million	1987
	TV Guide, *Racing Form*, *Seventeen*, and *Good Food*	$3 billion	1988
	Twelve Business Magazines	$350 million	1985
	European Travel and Life	n/a	1985
	New Woman	$20 million	1984
	In Fashion	n/a	1988
	Salem House	n/a	1985
	Zondervan Corp.	$56.9 million	1988
Nihon Keizai Shimbun (Japan)	Nikkei-McGraw-Hill (Remaining 49% Share Held by McGraw-Hill of This *Japanese* Publishing Corporation)	$283 million	1988

Table 4.3 (Continued)

Company	Acquired	Price	Year
Pearson PLC (U.K.)	Addison-Wesley Publishing Co.	$284 million	1988
	New American Library and E.P. Dutton	n/a	1986
Reed International PLC (U.K.)	Variety	$56.5 million	1987
	Technical Publishing	$250 million	1986
	Eight Titles from Communications/Today	$35 million*	1988
	Modern Bride	$63.7 million	1987
	American Baby	n/a	1986
	VA Practitioner	n/a	1986
	R.R. Bowker Co. (including Publishers Weekly)	$90 million	1985
	Whitney Communications	n/a	1984
	Physicians Travel & Meeting Guide	n/a	1985
	Interior Design and Corporate Design	$25 million	1984
	Chemical Purchasing	n/a	1983
	Journal of Cardiovascular Medicine	n/a	n/a
	Emergency Medicine	n/a	1983
	Printing News	n/a	1988
	PC Telemart		1984
Southam (Canada)	Sixteen Regional Trucking Magazines	$11 million	1987
Thomson Corp. (Canada)	Securities Data Corp.	n/a	1988
	CPAid	n/a	1986
	UTLAS	n/a	1985
	South-Western Publishing	$270 million	1986
	Six Titles from U.S. Business Press	$15.0 million	1986
	Clark Boardman Co.	n/a	1980
	Practioners Pub. Co.	n/a	1986
	Warren, Gorham, & Lamont	n/a	1980
	Medical Economics Co.	n/a	1980
	Gale Research Co.	$66 million	1985

Company	Property/Publication	Amount	Year
	Van Nostrand Reinhold	n/a	1981
	American Banker	n/a	1983
	Bond Buyer	$58 million	1983
	Wadsworth Publishing	n/a	1978
	Callahan & Co.	n/a	1979
	Sheshunoff Information Service	n/a	1988
	Mitchell International	n/a	1986
	Carswell Publishing	n/a	1987
Torstar Corp. (Canada)	Silhouette Books	n/a	1984
United Newspapers PLC (U.K.)	Television Broadcast	n/a	1988
	Computer Language Videography	n/a	1988
	Corporate Television	n/a	1988
	AI Expert	$5 million	1987
	Paper Trade Journal	n/a	1987
	Medical World News	$4.6 million	1987
	Pro Sound News	n/a	1986
	Miller Freeman Pub.	$9.4 million	1985
	Four Optometry Titles	$8.5 million	1985
	Sew Business	n/a	1984
	Gralla Publications	$44 million	1983
	Dealers' Digest	n/a	n/a
	Diversified Communications	$15 million*	1988
VNU (Verenigde Nederlandse Uitgeversbedrijven) (Holland)	Hayden Publishing (Non-book Division)	$44 million*	1987
	McGraw-Hill's Electronics	$17 million	1988
Verlagsgruppe Georg von Holtzbrinck Group (W. Germany)	General Book Division of Holt, Rinehart & Winston (renamed unit Henry Holt & Co.)	n/a	1985
	Scientific American	$52.6 million	1986
Wheatland Corp. (George Weidenfeld of Weidenfeld and Ann Getty) (U.K.)	Grove Press	n/a	1985
Woltors Sampson Group (West Germany)	Raven Press of New York	n/a	1985

viduals willing and able to invest in America's factories, real estate, and corporations.

The U.S. system of capitalism and free enterprise traditionally has placed few limitations on such purchases, as long as antitrust laws were followed. In the communications industry, the only significant restrictions pertain to the foreign ownership of radio and television stations.

The first such federal law was the 1927 Radio Act, which created the Federal Radio Commission. This law was augmented by the 1934 Communications Act (which was crafted to regulate the newly emerging telecommunications industry) and other key pieces of Congressional legislation and a plethora of U.S. Supreme Court and Federal Court decisions, including *Joseph Burstyn, Inc.* v. *Wilson, 343 U.S. 495, 503* (1952) (in which the Supreme Court ruled that federal law or regulatory agency decisions can indeed differentiate between print and electronic media).

Print publishing operations, on the other hand, are essentially available to the highest bidder regardless of national origin because of the freedom of speech provision of the First Amendment to the United States Constitution. Congress stated that it

shall make no law respecting an establishment of religion, or prohibiting the free exercise thereof; or abridging the freedom of speech, or of the press; or the right of the people peaceably to assemble, and to petition the government for a redress of grievances . . . .

This right has been upheld in numerous U.S. Supreme Court and Federal Court decisions, including *Martin* v. *Struthers, 319 U.S. 141, 143* (1943), *Lovell* v. *Griffin, 303 U.S. 444* (1938), and *Speiser v. Maryland, 357 U.S. 513, 526* (1958).

This "free enterprise" situation clearly acted as a stimulus to foreign corporations eager to buy into the world's largest, richest, and most stable business and consumer economy, one that sustains over fifteen thousand magazines and a book industry that produces over fifty-two thousand *new* titles each year.

Another reason for specific interest in publishing was that U.S. firms with successful magazines (and, in some instances, electronic database information services) throw off vast amount of cash because they collect their subscription fees up front and maintain small inventories, if any. A publishing firm outgrowing its traditional niches could take advantage of an expanding U.S. publishing industry without allocating large amounts of cash. Leveraging the purchase of U.S. publishing companies has become an art practiced by deft U.S. and international money managers.

Of course a recently purchased publishing firm blessed with an influx of new financial and/or managerial expertise might yield larger profit ratios than past managers were able to produce. This profit potential also acts as a motive to acquire a publishing firm with unrealized potential; these extra revenues, which enrich the coffers of the mother company, may be relatively inexpensive to generate.[7]

According to Peter Drucker, America's premier management consultant and author, a company exists to satisfy the needs of a customer; a second reason is to make a profit.[8] Publishing in the United States certainly affords foreign executives an opportunity to make money. According to the 1989 *Fortune 500* ranking of industries, publishing and printing (and printing clearly plays a secondary role) were ranked second among all industries for return on sales (+8.4 percent), sixth for total return to investors between 1978 and 1988 (+22.1 percent), third for return on assets (+8.5 percent), and fourth for return on stockholders' equity (+18.9 percent).[9]

The following table (4.4) is based on data contained in the 1989 *Fortune 500* ranking of U.S. publishing corporations.

Because of this laudable performance record, publishing concerns of all types were attractive and lucrative acquisition properties. The following tables (4.5 and 4.6), based upon data generated by the United States Department of Commerce, outlines recent business trends in this industry.[10]

Another key reason for this merger and acquisition activity was the fact that it was cheaper and certainly easier for a firm to enter a new market niche by purchasing a company (or a title) with an existing leadership position rather than undergoing the usually lengthy, complex, and not always successful procedures associated with the start-up of a new publication, a new line of books, or, for that matter, a new corporation. Market share, image, and a certain amount of "good will" could be obtained overnight. This

Table 4.4 / Publishing Firms Listed in the 1989 Fortune 500 (in millions of dollars)

Rank	Company	Sales	Percent of Total Sales of Top Firms	Percent Change 1987–1988	Profits	Percent of Total Profits of Top Firms	Percent Change 1987–1988	Employees
102	Time Inc.	$4,507	17.7%	+7%	$289	12.9%	+16%	21,000
134	Gannett	3,314	13.0	+8	364	16.3	+14	37,000
138	Times Mirror	3,259	12.4	+3	332	14.8	+25	27,963
181	Tribune	2,335	9.1	+8	210	9.4	+49	24,500
192	Knight Ridder	2,194	8.6	+6	156	7.0	+1	22,200
223	McGraw-Hill	1,818	7.1	+4	186	8.3	+13	16,255
228	New York Times	1,755	6.9	+4	168	7.5	+5	10,700
238	Dow Jones	1,603	6.3	+22	228	10.2	+12	9,080
269	Washington Post	1,368	5.4	+4	269	12.0	+44	6,300
293	Scripps	1,214	4.8	+6	70	3.1	+18	11,400
331	Macmillan	1,019	4.0	+7	n/a	—	n/a	n/a
437	Commerce Clearing House	612	2.4	+11	49	2.2	−6	7,207
477	Affiliated Publications	534	2.1	+9	−81	—	−140	3,020
	Total	25,532		—	2,240		—	196,625

Source: "The Fortune 500," Fortune, 24 April 1989, 352–399.

Table 4.5 / Total Value of Shipments (in billions of U.S. dollars)

Time Period	Periodicals	Book Publishing	Miscellaneous Publishing	Electronic Database Publishing	Total
1984	$14.053	$9.459	$3.223	n/a	26.735
1985	15.246	10.196	4.437	n/a	29.879
1986	15.719	10.732	4.887	n/a	31.338
1987	16.758	11.675	5.425	n/a	33.858
1988	18.046	12.775	5.96	6.2	42.981
1989	19.478	14.000	6.525	7.5	47.503
Total	99.300	68.837	30.457	13.700	212.294

Source: U.S. Department of Commerce, International Trade Administration, *1989 U.S. Industrial Outlook* (Washington, D.C.: USGPO, 1989), 37–1–37–12, 45–1–45–5.

explains why McGraw-Hill purchased Random House's college text-book division; why Time was willing to spend $520 million in 1986 for Scott Foresman; and why the News Corporation acquired Harper and Row in 1987 for $300 million and William Collins **PLC** in 1989 for $717 million.

Another reason centers on the fact that a publishing company with mature properties or flat or declining profit margins must diversify in order to survive in turbulent times and withstand the ravages of economic uncertainty.

Admittedly some firms entered the acquisition phase in order

Table 4.6 / Annual Market Share Percentage

Year	Periodicals	Book Publishing	Miscellaneous Publishing	Electronic Database Publishing
1984	52.56%	35.38%	12.06%	n/a
1985	51.02	34.12	14.85	n/a
1986	50.16	34.25	15.59	n/a
1987	49.49	34.48	16.02	n/a
1988	41.98	29.72	13.87	14.42
1989	41.00	29.47	13.74	15.79

Source: U.S. Department of Commerce, International Trade Administration, *1989 U.S. Industrial Outlook* (Washington, D.C.: USGPO, 1989), 37–1–37–12, 45–1–45–5.

to buyout, and therefore eliminate, pesky competitors or would-be rivals.

One theory deals not with the economic environment but with Europe's. On 31 December 1992 trade restrictions in the twelve European Common Market nations will end. This means that there will be a free exchange of capital, goods, and services among these countries, making the Common Market the largest single consumer market in the world, with 324 million inhabitants. Trade "guidelines" will be created for non-Common Market states.

According to the Association of American Publishers, in 1988 U.S. exports to the European market (including key sales in the important business, technical, scientific, and scholarly fields) tallied $400 million. Of this sum $250 million was purchased by Common Market nations, with the United Kingdom alone accounting for over one-half of all sales. The balance was shared by the rest of Western Europe ($75 million) and the Soviet Union and Eastern Bloc countries (also $75 million).[11] This is unquestionably a significant market for U.S. publishing corporations.

In order to compete successfully in this deregulated Common Market, U.S. publishing firms must have access as of 31 December 1992 to effective global marketing and advertising expertise and an attractive collection of English-language publications. Consequently, purchasing a United States publishing corporation with a strong marketing department, an active position in the international marketplace, or a strong product mix of scientific, technological, copyright, or patent databases or serials would enable the acquiring corporation to obtain a much-needed business foundation in order to maximize its market share in this new Common Market business environment.

The last but perhaps the most interesting theory is the "dinosaur" theory. Most astute international publishers believe that in the near future only about ten large, global, diversified corporations will control most forms of communications (that is, publishing, information systems, electronic databases, television, films, etc.) in the world. In order to avoid extinction, aggressive companies planning to survive, if not dominate, in this Darwinian environment must purchase the right types of publishing and communications companies.

One event in early March 1989 illustrates graphically the "dinosaur" theory. On 3 March 1989 the boards of Time and Warner Communications agreed to merge, creating a global corporation with total revenues in excess of $10 billion. This merged corporation would be significantly larger than the West German firm of Bertelsmann, which, prior to this announcement, was the world's largest media company. Consequently, Time Warner would be "able to compete with any of the major foreign companies, such as Bertelsmann, Murdoch, or Maxwell." Floyd Norris reported that "the new Time Warner Inc. will expand to become a communications powerhouse in Europe and the Pacific Rim countries." Gordon Crawford of Capital Research in Los Angeles said that "there's a compelling logic if you want to be [a] major player [in the communications industry] to be vertically integrated and global in breadth." The *Wall Street Journal* maintained that this merger will help Time Warner "beat down, or at least survive, the competition from other global media giants."[12]

As far as international managers are concerned, publishing companies do not sell books or magazines; they sell information, whether it is printed in a scholarly journal, appears on a computer monitor, or is packaged in a microfiche or microfilm format.

Critics of the "dinosaur" theory could quickly point to the fact that even if ten firms were able to "control" (or seek "control" of) the international communications-information industry, stringent antitrust laws in the U.S. would be triggered. Gordon B. Spivack, a partner at Coudert Brothers, remarked during the early Time Warner merger discussions that

there is nothing under the [U.S.] antitrust laws that will arise [from the proposed Time-Warner merger] that cannot be taken care of by a negotiated settlement. . . . The market is defined as the media, all the media, and, if you look at all the media, Time-Warner has a very small share of the overall market.

Obviously the proposed Time Warner merger sparked a public debate in 1989 about these very issues. Yet legal events in 1989 indicated clearly that such a merger was not a "restraint of free trade."[13]

Other skeptics argued that such market dominance could never take place in light of the current technological metamorphosis. In the old days, high economic barriers prevented small companies from entering the publishing industry (for example, the high start-up costs associated with developing a strong line of titles and effective distribution channels, marketing and production expenditures, etc.). How will these industrial leaders prevent small companies from penetrating existing or new markets?

In short they cannot; and, probably, they will not. The ironclad laws of economics dictate that no company can achieve total control over a market; and, sometimes, corporations decide to deemphasize their role in a niche that they deem to be marginally profitable. A good example of this phenomenon was the decision some years ago by large book companies to cease publishing mid-list books.[14]

In accordance with the "dinosaur" theory, these ten corporations will try to obtain legal hegemony over most of the market; the remaining portion, covering marginally profitable or newly emerging areas, can be serviced more effectively by small publishing companies closer to the market. However, such operations can and probably will be acquired when revenues or market penetration reach a certain level.

The following table (4.7), utilizing data from the 1989 "International *Fortune 500*," provides a brief overview of the comparable size of a few of the major foreign publishing firms active in the United States.[15] The Thomson Corporation was not listed on the "International *Fortune 500*" (and, consequently, in the following table) because it sold its oil holdings in the United Kingdom in late 1988, thereby reducing its total revenues below the minimum level required to make the list of top performers. However, in June 1989 the International Thomson Organisation merged with the formidable Thomson Newspaper Corporation, thereby created a unified Thomson Corporation with total sales placing it fifth among all communications corporations in the world. The 1990 "International *Fortune 500*" will list this new company.

How do these publishing firms compare with other industries listed on this "International *Fortune 500*"? Publishing placed third among all industries for changes in sales (+25%) and nineteenth for changes in profits (+19.4%).

Table 4.7 / Major Foreign Publishing Firms: 1989 (in millions of U.S. dollars)

Rank	Company	Sales	Profits	Profits as Percent of Sales	Stock-Holders Equity	Number of Employees
121	Bertelsmann	$6,538.9	$127.8	2.0%	$641.5	41,961
182	News Corporation	4,383.9	340.6	7.8	4,022.8	28,305
195	Hachette	4,098.0	55.0	1.3	365.5	28,500
240	Reed International	3,424.0	492.4	14.4	1,867.1	31,300
362	Pearson	2,127.9	313.0	14.7	849.1	26,017
381	Maxwell Communication	2,010.2	241.5	12.0	1,808.5	30,000
454	Axel Springer Verlag	1,617.4	53.2	3.3	240.4	11,594
	Total	24,200.3	1,623.5	6.7	9,794.9	197,677

Source: "The International Fortune 500," Fortune, 31 July 1989, 291–310.

PUBLIC POLICY ISSUES

The acquisition of U.S. publishing firms by foreign corporations has had a number of positive effects. These companies were (1) provided with better access to the global communications market; (2) allowed to utilize the financial and human resources of the parent company in order to diversify, develop new products, and become more competitive; and (3) positioned to withstand the onslaught of fierce international competition. However, some downside results are directly attributable to this reformulation of the publishing industry in the United States.

First, mergers and acquisitions per se are not detrimental to America's economy. Yet the apparently mindless acquisition of some properties has displaced hundreds, if not thousands, of employees and contributed little if anything to the Gross National Product. Only Wall Street financiers have really benefited from what has become a paper exchange of assets.

Second, the already-strained U.S. educational system is totally dependent upon a constant supply of textbooks for use in classrooms. Traditionally these books have been one of the major sources of information about the American democratic system. If these books are planned and written by foreign-owned companies, will they continue to help educate the youth of America (which is after all the hope of the future) about our history and way of life?

Third, most of the profits generated by foreign-owned corporations in the United States ultimately leave America, thereby depriving this nation of needed capital. Should we accept America's new status as an economic "province" of foreign nations?

Another critically significant issue deals with the loss of editorial independence that book, periodical, or database publishers need in order to maintain a sense of objectivity. Obviously, a small number of publishing companies specialize in "liberal" or "conservative" causes. However, for the most part, U.S. publishing enterprises remain neutral in the political arena. Will this continue? Or will a foreign-owned publishing company refuse to publish, for example, a "liberal" or a "conservative" author just because this individual's viewpoint does not agree with the stated position of the "mother country" or "mother company"? Is it in the best interests of this country to have a small handful of corporations deciding what we read, see, or hear? Professor Ben H. Bagdikian remarked that

the [Time Warner] merger means there will be a further concentration of power over programming and an enormous increase in private power as well. . . . This merger also means more uniformity of content in the media because the big companies all have the same goal. . . .[16]

Is it possible that the next generation of Woodwards and Bernsteins, the heirs of Ida Tarbell and Lincoln Stephens, will be unable to get into print? Answers to these questions are needed.

The United States has become far too dependent on foreign nations for capital. Between 20 and 35 percent of all U.S. treasury bill sales are made to foreign banks. Our Government relies on cash generated through these treasury bill sales to pay its bills; so a foreign nation (or nations) might be able to influence directly the political decision-making process on the federal and state level. After all, these nations have invested over $1.5 trillion in the U.S., and it is safe to assume that they are keenly interested in making sure that their investments are duly protected.[17]

Last, many firms involved in mergers and acquisitions have leveraged their money; they are carrying a significant amount of debt that is repayable at high interest rates. These corporations are vulnerable to any fluctuation, even minor ones, in the U.S. and international economies. The specter of an increased number of bankruptcies exists, which could seriously weaken the underpinnings of our economy.[18]

Harcourt Brace Jovanovich is an interesting example of a company that was directly and adversely affected by this merger and acquisition process. In 1987 Robert Maxwell initiated a hostile takeover of Harcourt. In order to remain independent and thwart Maxwell's plans, Harcourt completed a recapitalization plan in July 1987 whereby $1.67 billion was paid out in a special one-time-only cash dividend of $40.00 per share; in addition $1.3 billion in debt was assumed. As of November 1988, Harcourt Brace Jovanovich had a long-term debt of $2.6 billion.

While Harcourt Brace's sales were up a strong 16 percent in the first half of 1988, so were its interest payments directly associated with this recapitalization plan. Standard and Poor's estimated that, in spite of its sales increases, Harcourt sustained losses of $84.77 million in 1988; losses were projected for 1989, and Harcourt will be unable to issue any cash dividend before 1993. On 18 December 1988, William Jovanovich resigned as Harcourt's chief executive officer, reportedly because "the bankers have been getting tougher and tougher, and finally they have told Jovanovich, 'that's it'."[19]

SUMMATION

As long as this merger and acquisition process is proceeding at its current fast pace (and events in 1989, including the Cahners/Reed purchase of the News Corporation's travel magazines for $825 million and Thomson's decision to acquire Lawyers' Cooperative for $810 million, indicate clearly that there are no signs of any abatement), it is exceptionally difficult to develop a detached opinion about the acquisition process and the results.

However, certain observations can be made at this time. First, the frenetic surge in mergers and acquisitions has prompted far too many firms to assume a heavy debt burden that some beleaguered companies might not be able to service, thereby creating a potential financial nightmare that will adversely affect countless thousands of individuals. Second, corporations in the United States have been far too eager to sell off valuable assets that cannot be replaced. A major side effect of this malady is the undeniable fact that the editorial integrity of certain publishing firms has been placed in jeopardy, a situation that will weaken seriously the transmission of information in the years to come. Finally, Americans should not be placed in the unreasonable position of utilizing textbooks in our elementary, middle school, and high school classrooms that have been written and edited by publishing firms owned by foreign corporations. This is not xenophobia; this is common sense.

In addition many key questions remain unanswered. Will the press runs of books be shortened? Will the price of the typical college textbook really become astronomical? Will books go out of print faster than they currently do just in order to generate enough cash to service this debt?

This merger and acquisition process is far from complete. Additional detailed analysis is needed, especially by academics and other individuals keenly interested in and concerned about the future of the communications industry and the dissemination of knowledge in the United States and the world. The situation clearly warrants serious attention in the years to come.

NOTES

1. Robert Hamrin, *America's New Economy: The Basic Guide* (New York: Franklin Watts, 1988), 254–58; "Mergers and Acquisitions Set Record in '88," *New York Times*, 31 January 1989, D19.
2. "88: The Year of the Mega-Sale," *Folio*, February 1988, 111–12, 115–16, 120.
3. The Center for Book Research, University of Scranton, *Book Industry Trends 1988* (New York: Book Industry Study Group, 1988), 42–95.
4. Walter W. Powell, *Getting into Print* (Chicago: University of Chicago Press, 1985), 17. Other historical works include Frank Luther Mott, *A History of American Magazines, vol. 1, 1741–1850* (Cambridge, Mass.: Harvard University Press, 1966), 24; David Forsyth, *The Business Press in America: 1750–1865* (Philadelphia: Chilton, 1964), 20; Julius Elfenbein, *Business Journalism* (New York: Harper & Row, 1960), 1–20; Frank Luther Mott, *A History of American Magazines, Vol. 2, 1850–1865* (Cambridge, Mass.: Harvard University Press, 1957), 81–83, 297–300; Frank Luther Mott, *A History of American Magazines, Vol. 3, 1865–1885* (Cambridge, Mass.: Harvard University Press, 1967), 454–56, 491–94; Frank Luther Mott, *A History of American Magazines, Vol. 4, 1885–1905* (Cambridge, Mass.: Harvard University Press, 1957), 524–35; Frank Luther Mott, *A History of American Magazines, Vol. 5, 1905–1930* (Cambridge, Mass.: Harvard University Press, 1968), 59–71. Also see G.D. Crain, Jr., ed. *Teacher of Business: The Publishing Philosophy of James H. McGraw* (Chicago: Advertising Publications, 1944); Lyon N. Richard, *A History of Early American Magazines: 1741–1789* (New York: Thomas Nelson, 1931); Theodore Peterson, *Magazines in the Twentieth Century* (Urbana: University of Illinois Press, 1964). Also see John Tebbel, *Between Covers: The Rise and Transformation of Book Publishing in America* (New York: Oxford University Press, 1987); or Tebbel's *A History of Book Publishing in the United States, Vol. 1, The Creation of an Industry, 1630–65* (New York: R.R. Bowker, 1972); *A History of Book Publishing in the United States, Vol.*

3, *The Golden Age between Two Wars, 1920–1940* (New York: R.R. Bowker, 1978); Kenneth C. Davis, *Two-Bit Culture: The Paperbacking of America* (Boston: Houghton Mifflin, 1984); Lewis A. Coser, Charles Kadushin, and Walter W. Powell, *Books: The Culture and Commerce of Publishing* (Chicago: University of Chicago Press, 1985). For a statistical analysis of the American business publishing industry, see two studies by Albert N. Greco: *Business Journalism: Management Notes and Cases* (New York: New York University Press, 1988), 8–35; and "The Business Publishing Industry in the United States," chapter 4 in *The Handbook of Business Publications*, ed. Iwao Obe (Toyko, Japan: Nikkei Business Publications and Nihon Keizai Shimbun, 1989; in Japanese). For additional data about publishing and information markets, see Martin Greenberger, ed., *Electronic Publishing Plus* (White Plains, N.Y.: Knowledge Industry Publications, 1985); Joost Kist, *Electronic Publishing* (London: Croom Helm, 1987); Judith S. Duke, *The Technical, Scientific, and Medical Publishing Market* (White Plains, N.Y.: Knowledge Industry Publications, 1985); "Legal Publications: A New Growth Industry," *New York Times*, 19 August 1988, B5; Gary Levin, "Industry Back on the Right Track," *Advertising Age*, 15 June 1987, S1.

5. Linda Sandler, "Shares of Murdoch's News Corporation Are Clouded by Australian Accounting, Critics Contend," *Wall Street Journal*, 16 August 1988, 53.

6. Neal Weinstock, "Leaner Times Bedevil Business Magazines," *Advertising Age*, 20 June 1988, S24–S25; Joanne Lipman, "Estimate for '88 U.S. Ad Spending Is Sliced by Prominent Forecaster," *Wall Street Journal*, 16 June 1988, 28; Philip H. Dougherty, "Smaller Gain for Ads in '88 Is Predicted," *New York Times*, 16 June 1988, D23; Johnnie L. Roberts, "Forecast Lowered for '88 Spending on Newspaper Ads," *Wall Street Journal*, 3 August 1988, 24g; "Bank Magazines Still Bear Scars from October 19," *Publishing News*, Pilot Issue (July 1988), 13; Tom Herman, "Economists Expect Expansion to Continue for at Least a Year Despite a Faster Inflation Pace and Increase in Interest Rates," *Wall Street Journal*, 5 July 1988, 3; "A Sampling of Interest-Rate and Economic Forecasts," *Wall Street Journal*, 6 July 1988, 37; Pamela Sebastian, "Robust Economy Raises Inflation Fears," *Wall Street Journal*, 11 July 1988, 22; Alan Murray, "Greenspan Signals Higher Interest Rates," *Wall Street Journal*, 14 July 1988, 2; Lindley H. Clark, Jr., and Alfred Malabre, Jr., "Economists Fret over Consumer Outlays," *Wall Street Journal*, 3 August 1988, 6; and Victor Zarnowitz, "Economic Outlook Survey: Second Quarter 1988," *NBER* [National Bureau of Economic Research] Reporter, Summer 1988, 11–14.

7. Patrick Reilly, "Trade Journals Riding Rebound of U.S. Industry," *Advertising Age*, 16 May 1988, 50; Gary Levin, "Industries Back on Track," *Advertising Age*, 15 June 1987, S1; Van Wallace, "Turnabout

Fair Play for Some Publishers," *Advertising Age*, 15 June 1987, S10; and Christopher J. H. M. Shaw, "Buying and Selling Magazines: Innovation and Expansion," *Folio*, June 1988, 192; U.S. Department of Commerce, International Trade Administration, *1988 U.S. Industrial Outlook* (Washington, D.C.: GPO, 1988), 29–5–29–7; Gale Research, *The Gale Directory of Publications* (Detroit, Mich.: Gale Research, 1987); U.S. Department of Commerce, Bureau of the Census, *1982 Census of Manufacturers: Newspapers, Periodicals, Books, and Miscellaneous Publishing* (Washington, D.C.: GPO, 1985), 27A-6–27A-11, and *1977 Census of Manufacturers: Newspapers, Periodicals, Books, and Miscellaneous Publishing* (Washington, D.C.: GPO, 1980), 27A-6–27A-11; Martin Feldstein, ed., *The U.S. in the World Economy* (Cambridge, Mass.: National Bureau of Economic Research, 1987), 49–53.

8. Peter Drucker, *Management: Tasks, Responsibilities, Practices* (New York: Harper & Row, 1974), 79.

9. "The *Fortune 500*," *Fortune*, 24 April 1989, 352–99.

10. U.S. Department of the Commerce, International Trade Administration, *1989 U.S. Industrial Outlook* (Washington, D.C.: GPO, 1989), 37–1–37–12, 45–1–45–5. Also see James P. Moore, Jr., "Highlights of the 1989 U.S. Industrial Outlook," in *1989 U.S. Industrial Outlook*, 16–23.

11. "1992 and All That," *Publishers Weekly*, 3 February 1989, 21–24. Also see W. Gordon Graham, "The Shadow of 1992," *Publishers Weekly*, 23 December 1988, 24–26; Vivienne Menkes, "London '89: A Growing Internationalism," *Publishers Weekly*, 5 May 1989, 33–36; Adrian Higham, "Selling Abroad? Are We Doing Enough?" *Book Research Quarterly* 4 (Winter 1988–1989): 45–51; Robert Bolick, "A European Beachhead: MIT Press's Oxford Editorial Office," *Scholarly Publishing* 19 (April 1988): 130–35; "Europe's Houdini Market," *The Economist*, 6 May 1989, 9–10; John F. Magee, "1992: Moves Americans Must Make," *Harvard Business Review* 67 (May-June 1989): 78–84. (Interview with William Lofquist, of the United States Department of Commerce, 15 February 1989); Steven Greenhouse, "The Growing Fear of Fortress Europe," *New York Times*, 23 October 1988, 3–1, 3–24.

12. Floyd Norris, "Time Inc. and Warner to Merge, Creating Largest Media Company," *New York Times*, 5 March 1989, A1, A39; Albert Scardino, "Companies Hope to Avoid Turmoil with Merger," *New York Times*, 5 March 1989, A38; Laura Landro, "Time-Warner Merger Will Help Fend off Tough Global Rivals," *Wall Street Journal*, 6 March 1989, A1, A5; Edwin McDowell, "Time-Warner Combination Joins Giants in Publishing," *New York Times*, 6 March 1989, D8; Geraldine Fabrikant, "Time-Warner Merger Raises Concerns on Power of a Giant," *New York Times*, 6 March 1989, A1, D9; Randall Rothenberg, "Time-Warner Bid for Global Marketing," *New York Times*, 6 March 1989, D11; Floyd Norris, "In Media Merger, Tandem Control," *New York Times*, 6 March 1989, D6; Linda Sandler, "Time-Warner Deal Fuels

Run-Ups in Other Media Issues: But Terms Disappoint Some Time Holders," *Wall Street Journal*, 7 March 1989, C1, C2; David B. Hilder and Randall Smith, "Time-Warner Deal Fuels Run-Ups in Other Media Issues: Proposed Stock Swap Could Be Vulnerable," *Wall Street Journal*, 7 March 1989, C1, C18; Geraldine Fabrikant, "Time Deal Worrying Competitors," *New York Times*, 7 March 1989, D1, D22; Floyd Norris, "Time and Warner Look to Europe and Pacific," *New York Times*, 7 March 1989, D22; "Plenty of Fish in Pond Time Warner Wants to Swim In," *Wall Street Journal*, 7 March 1989, B1, B8; Laura Landro, "Time's Nicholas Must Fuse Two Cultures," *Wall Street Journal*, 7 March 1989, B9; Joanne Lipman, "Time-Warner Deal May Yield One-Stop Shopping Possibility," *Wall Street Journal*, 7 March 1989, B7; Sarah Bartlett, "Time Soars $9.25 amid Rumors," *New York Times*, 8 March 1989, D1, D17; Dennis Kneale, "Time-Warner Pact May Be Fodder for Program Talks," *Wall Street Journal*, 8 March 1989, B1; Randall Smith and Laura Landro, "Time Inc. Shares Soar on Rumors That a Hostile Bidder May Emerge," *Wall Street Journal*, 8 March 1989, C1. For an outstanding analysis of the major strategic planning issues, see Michael E. Porter, *Competitive Strategy* (New York: Free Press, 1980), 237–53. Also see Kenichi Ohmae, *The Mind of the Strategist* (New York: Penguin, 1988), 11–35.

13. Joel Kurtzman, "Prospects: Two Giants Become One," *New York Times*, 12 March 1989, Sec. 3, p. 25.

14. Albert N. Greco, "University Presses and the Trade Book Market: Managing in Turbulent Times," *Book Research Quarterly* 3 (Winter 1987–1988): 34–53.

15. "The International *Fortune 500*," *Fortune*, 31 July 1989, 291–310. Other useful sources include Steve Lohr, "Britain's Maverick Mogul," *New York Times Magazine*, 1 May 1988, 52–53, 80, 82, 107, 108; Edwin McDowell, "$1.7 Billion Bid Given Harcourt," *New York Times*, 19 May 1987, sec. 4, p. 6; Geraldine Fabrikant, "Harcourt: A Vulnerable Giant," *New York Times*, 20 May 1987, sec.4, p. 3; Geraldine Fabrikant, "Salomon Cites Stake in Harcourt," *Wall Street Journal*, 20 June 1987, sec. 1, p. 37; "Maxwell Plea on Harcourt," *New York Times*, 17 June 1987, sec. 4, p. 4; Geraldine Fabrikant, "Harcourt Gains in Debenture Fight," *New York Times*, 23 June 1987, sec. 4, p. 6; "Harcourt to Sell Magazine Unit," *New York Times*, 24 August 1987, sec. 4, p. 7; Alison Leigh Cowan, "Harcourt Considers Asset Sale," *New York Times*, 13 August 1987, sec. 4, p. 6; "Harcourt Sale of Units Near," 9 October 1987, sec. 4, p. 4; Philip E. Ross, "Founder Regains Helm at HBJ Publications," *New York Times*, 19 November 1987, sec. 4, p. 2; Geraldine Fabrikant, "$334.1 Million Sale of Two Harcourt Units," *New York Times*, 19 November 1987, sec. 4, p. 4; Geraldine Fabrikant, "Harcourt's Loss Narrows," *New York Times*, 12 August 1988, D16. Laurie P. Cohen, "Maxwell to Buy for $750 Million Dun & Bradstreet

Airline Guides," *Wall Street Journal*, 31 October 1988, B4; "Maxwell Seeking Stake in IDG Communications?" *MagazineWeek*, 31 October 1988, 1. Bill Esler, "Maxwell Measures Up," *Graphic Arts Monthly*, August 1988, 54, 60–61, 64. Randall Smith, "McGraw-Hill Stock Rises on Takeover Rumor Despite Publisher's Steep $5 Billion Price Tag," *Wall Street Journal*, 16 February 1988, 71; Kevin G. Salwen, "McGraw-Hill Once Again Attracts Rumors after More Than Two Years of Speculation," *Wall Street Journal*, 23 August 1988, 51; Leslie Wayne, "A Family Defends Its Dynasty," *New York Times*, 24 July 1988, sec. 3, 1, 6; McGraw-Hill, *1987 Annual Report: 10–K*; Edwin McDowell, "Major Reorganization Begun by McGraw-Hill," *New York Times*, 30 June 1988, D22; Johnnie L. Roberts, "McGraw-Hill Is Streamlining Its Organization," *Wall Street Journal*, 30 June 1988, 1; Johnnie L. Roberts, "McGraw-Hill Stock Declines; Revamp Cited," *Wall Street Journal*, 1 July 1988, 22; "Profit Profile: Business Week," *MagazineWeek*, 20 April 1988, 5; Jonathan P. Hicks, "McGraw-Hill," *New York Times*, 20 July 1988, D19; "Profits Jump 20 Percent at McGraw-Hill," *New York Times*, 20 April 1988, D22; Gulf & Western, *1987 Annual Report: 10–K*; Laura Landro, "Simon & Schuster Becomes a Publishing 'Juggernaut': G & W Fuels Unit's Growth with Buying Spree, Focusing on Education," *Wall Street Journal*, 17 December 1987, 6; Cynthia Crossen and John Marcom, Jr., "Macmillan Receives $80–a-Share Offer from Maxwell, Topping Bass Group Bid," *Wall Street Journal*, 22 July 1988, 3; Geraldine Fabrikant, "Maxwell Is Joining Fight for Macmillan," *New York Times*, 22 July 1988, D1; Geraldine Fabrikant, "Macmillan Profit Falls 10 Percent," *New York Times*, 12 August 1988, D16; Gregory A. Robb, "Macmillan Rejects Bid of Maxwell," *New York Times*, 27 August 1988, 31; Macmillan, *1987 Annual Report: 10–K*. Also see Dennis Kneale, "Macmillan Board Rejects Maxwell Bid, Calling $2.34 Billion 'Inadequate,'" *Wall Street Journal*, 29 August 1988, 14; Knight-Ridder, *1987 Annual Report: 10–K;* "Knight-Ridder," *Wall Street Journal*, 25 July 1988, 22; John Marcom, Jr., "Britain's Maxwell Is a Press Baron Who's Always on Deadline," *Wall Street Journal*, 19 November 1987; "Maxwell Signs Paper Deal," *Printing Impressions News Edition*, 1 July 1988, 18. Also see Alex S. Jones, "Murdoch's *Post:* Futile Battle or Missed Opportunity?" *New York Times*, 7 March 1988, B1, B2; William H. Meyers, "Murdoch's Global Power Play," *New York Times Magazine*, 12 June 1988, 18–19, 20–21, 36, 41, 42; Johnnie L. Roberts, "Murdoch's News Corp. Will Buy Triangle Publications for $3 Billion," *Wall Street Journal*, 8 August 1988, 3; Kurt Eichenwald, "Murdoch Agrees to Buy *TV Guide* in a $3 Billion Sale by Annenberg," *New York Times*, 8 August 1988, 1, D3; Johnnie L. Roberts, Laura Landro, and John Marcom, Jr., "Rupert Murdoch Takes His Biggest Risk So Far in Purchasing Triangle," *Wall Street Journal*, 9 August 1988, 1, 16; Geraldine Fabrikant, "Industry

Confident Murdoch Can Finance *TV Guide* Deal," *New York Times*, 9 August 1988, D1, D18; Johnnie L. Roberts, "Murdoch to Sell off Reuters Stake, Land in Australia, U.K. to Pay for Triangle," *Wall Street Journal*, 10 August 1988, 3; Jeremy Gerard, *"TV Guide's* Power over the Air," *New York Times*, 11 August 1988, D1, 18; Steven Crist, *"Racing Form:* Trifecta for Murdoch?" *New York Times*, 11 August 1988, D1, D18; Albert Scardino, "How Murdoch Makes It Work," *New York Times*, 14 August 1988, sec. 3, pp. 1, 5; Patrick Reilly, "Murdoch Buy Stacks off the Racks," *Advertising Age*, 15 August 1988, 1, 62; "Murdoch the Amazing" (Viewpoint Editorial), *Advertising Age*, 15 August 1988, 16; Judann Dagnoli, "Murdoch's Reach Extends into FSIs," *Advertising Age*, 22 August 1988, 3. "The International *Fortune 500*," *Fortune*, 24 April 1989, D13; Standard & Poors, "News Corp.," *Standard NYSE Stock Reports*, 21 October 1988, 1314–15. Paul Hemp, "News International's Collins Bid Advances as Opponent Withdraws," *Wall Street Journal*, 5 January 1989, B4. Also see Lloyd Norris, "Behind the Wave of Leveraged Buyouts, High Profit Potential," *New York Times*, 21 October 1988, D13; Randall Smith and George Anders, "Year of the Megadeals Is upon Us," *Wall Street Journal*, 21 October 1988, C1, C22; Anise C. Wallace, "Behind the Boom in Takeovers: Enormous Capital Is Available to Buy Undervalued Assets," *New York Times*, 9 September 1988; John R. Dorfman, "When a Stock Is in Play, Patience and a Little Study Can Pay," *Wall Street Journal*, 21 October 1988, C1, C23. Also see "The International *Fortune 500*," *Fortune*, 24 April 1989, D15. International Thomson, *1987 Annual Report*.

16. Kurtzman, "Prospects . . . ," 25. (See note 13.)
17. Martin and Susan Tolchin, *Buying into America: How Foreign Money is Changing the Face of Our Nation* (New York: Times Books, 1988), 6. Also see Milton Moskowitz, *The Global Marketplace: 102 of the Most Influential Companies outside America* (New York: Macmillan, 1987); Jeffrey S. Arpan, Edward B. Flowers, and David A. Ricks, "Foreign Direct Investment in the United States: The State of Knowledge in Research," *Journal of International Business Studies* (Spring/Summer 1981): 137–54; Jane Sneddon Little, "Foreign Direct Investment in New England," *New England Economic Review* (March-April 1981): 51–56. Also see "The Financial Health of U.S. Manufacturing Firms Acquired by Foreigners," *New England Economic Review* (July-August 1981): 5–18; and "Foreign Direct Investment in the United States," *New England Economic Journal* (November-December 1980): 5–22.
18. George Anders, "Study by KKR Outlines Virtues of Buy-Outs," *Wall Street Journal*, 23 January 1989, C1, C9; Robert D. Hershey, Jr., "Greenspan Shuns Curb on Buyouts," *New York Times*, 27 January 1989, D1–D2; Alan Murray, "Brady Suggests LBOs Could Be Curbed by Shifting Tax Deductions to Dividends," *Wall Street Journal*, 25

January 1989, A4. Also see Edson W. Spencer, "Capital-Gains Shift Could Curb LBO Break-Up," *Wall Street Journal*, 27 January 1989, A14; Irving Kristol, "The War against the Corporation," *Wall Street Journal*, 24 January 1989, A20. Also see John Brooks, *The Takeover Game* (New York: Dutton, 1987); Peter T. Kilborn, "Brady Voices Concern over Takeover Debts," *New York Times*, 25 January 1989, D1; Randall Smith, James A. White, and Thomas E. Ricks, "Wall Street Fears Grow That Congress Will Out Brake on LBOs," *Wall Street Journal*, 16 January 1989, C1, C15; Alison Leigh Cowan, "For Business, the Thrills and Chills of Life with Debt," *New York Times*, 27 November 1988, sec. 3, p. 5; "Why Fight Leveraged Buyouts?" *New York Times*, 28 November 1988, A24; Wayne E. Green and Sonya Steptoe, "Metropolitan Life Joins Backlash against Leveraged Buy-Outs," *Wall Street Journal*, 18 November 1988, C1, C21; Jack J. Honomichel, "Buyout Aftershocks among Lows of 1988," *Advertising Age*, 23 January 1989, 12.

19. Standard & Poor's, "Harcourt Brace Jovanovich," *Standard NYSE Stock Reports*, 21 October 1989, 1096K-97K; Peter Weldman, "Jovanovich of Harcourt Brace to Resign as Chief Executive, Names Caulo to Post," *Wall Street Journal*, 19 December 1988, B6.

FIVE

Global Publishing: Europe in 1992, the Pacific Rim, and the U.S. Business Publishing Industry, with Cases

INTRODUCTION

A dramatic change in the composition and structure of the international publishing industry will take place on 31 December 1992, and this metamorphosis will have a direct and critically important impact on the entire business publishing industry in the United States.

First, on that day in 1992 all trade restrictions will be terminated in the Common Market (European Economic Community; EEC) nations, thereby creating a single, multibillion-dollar business unit with over 320 million inhabitants. This new consolidated market, stretching from the United Kingdom and Spain in the West to Greece in the East and from the northern corridor of

Denmark and West Germany to the southern tip of Italy, will become the largest consumer and industrial market in the world. Clearly, such a massive, almost Kafkaesque economic metamorphosis will require access to an abundance of publishing and information products.[1]

Second, the Pacific Rim region, comprised of dynamic economic units including Japan, South Korea, Taiwan, Singapore, Hong Kong, Australia, China, Indonesia, etc., will continue to experience the greatest period of prosperity in its history, or at least in this century. While per capita income for the entire Rim lags significantly behind both the United States and the Common Market nations, this region has become the third largest export market for U.S. publishing products, trailing only Canada and the Common Market countries.[2]

In the 1980s diplomats, economists, and business leaders from the Pacific Rim region have discussed the possibility of creating an East Asian version of the Common Market, including the need to establish "trade guidelines" (in essence, trade restrictions) to stimulate economic growth within this proposed Asian economic bloc at the direct expense of nonmember nations.

What are the business implications of a consolidated European Common Market as of 1992 and a Pacific Rim version of the Common Market to business publishers in the United States (or Canada) who are interested in establishing or maintaining effective marketing relationships in Europe or the Pacific Rim?

WORKABLE ECONOMIC BLOCS

Can workable economic blocs in Western Europe and in the Pacific Rim be created? What powerful forces can be utilized by the political and economic leaders of these countries that will galvanize nations that have fought each other since the days of Charlemagne or countries that were occupied during World War II? Can people in these states put aside their deep-seated concerns and agree to create a unified economic entity? Can such an economic relationship last?

While crafting workable, realistic economic units will not be an easy task, a significant number of academic and business observers believe that these problems can be addressed effectively, leading ultimately to the establishment of workable "Common Market" economic units in both Western Europe and East Asia.

One such scholar is Theodore Levitt, formerly editor of the *Harvard Business Review* and author of the highly acclaimed article "Marketing Myopia." Levitt, writing in *The Marketing Imagination*, maintains that "a powerful new force now drives the world toward a single converging commonality, and that force is technology."[3]

A number of highly visible members of the international business community agree with Levitt's position. W. Michael Blumenthal, a former Cabinet official in Washington, D.C., and currently chairman of Unisys, analyzes this issue in a perceptive 1988 article entitled "The World Economy and Technological Change," which appeared in *Foreign Affairs*. Blumenthal wrote that "world industry and commerce are being reshaped by technological change. . . . There is now one capital market"; to Blumenthal the global market is now a reality that must be confronted directly.[4]

Roger B. Smith, president of the General Motors Corporation (GM), points out in "Global Competition: A Strategy for Success" that Americans must eschew adversarial relations with foreign nations and accept the fact that one global market now exists. Donald B. Marron, president of Paine Webber, describes in some detail in "The Globalization of Capital" how successfully the financial services market currently operates, utilizing advanced telecommunications systems, in a global capital market dominated by a New York-London-Tokyo triad. James E. Olson, the late chairman of AT&T, outlines in "Toward a Global Information Age" that the creation and implementation of this advanced information network provides corporations with the requisite electronic technology necessary to operate successfully in the global arena. Olson's use of statistics paints a broad, intriguing picture of the complex global information, management, and financial markets, which generated over $500 billion in 1987 and is expected to hover near the $880 billion mark in 1990.[5]

Walter B. Wriston, the former chairman of Citicorp and Citibank and the author of *Risk and Other Four-Letter Words*, publicly joined Blumenthal's ranks. In the January-February 1990 issue of the *Harvard Business Review,* Wriston tackles the thorny theme of globalization in a perceptive article entitled "The State of American Management." As far as Wriston is concerned, globalization is "a large part of this new age, not only in terms of products but also in the range of decisions that managers must make." However, Wriston is concerned about the apparent misconceptions about globalization that permeate far too many levels of management in the United States. "Today a lot of people talk about global markets, but only a small group understand what it really is. It is not a transnational corporation. It is a horizontal integration of production across many different countries." Will global managers need new skills? Wriston believes they will. "Leaders must have a wide enough span, a broad enough vision to understand that world and operate in it. . . . It means that they must understand the law of comparative advantage."[6]

As the chief executive officer at one of the world's preeminent corporations, manager Wriston operated within the confines of a global company with ready access to vast financial resources and a rich pool of talented managers. Can small companies really participate in this highly charged global marketplace? Wriston maintains that they can. "This is not just a managerial issue for large corporations. In fact what fascinates me are the little companies that are far ahead in making global decisions."[7]

In "Technology and Sovereignty," which appeared in *Foreign Affairs,* Wriston stresses the idea that technology has had a profound impact on the transfer of knowledge and business information in the world's global marketplace—trend, Wriston emphasizes, that is not to be a short-term one.[8]

While eschewing a dependence on technology alone as the determining factor in the creation of global markets, M. Panic in *National Management of the International Economy* maintains that the growing global economic interdependence has transformed national markets and problems into global markets and concerns that affect all of the developed countries and many of the developing nations of the world. Panic adroitly emphasizes the point that nations still clinging to the concept of "national" markets will experience severe difficulties adjusting to the reality of the new complex global marketplace.[9]

Felix Rohatyn, an investment banker at Lazard Freres, addresses this issue in "America's Economic Dependence." To Rohatyn "all of these [Western] European countries seek higher standards of living, better education and lower unemployment. . . ."[10] Sir Michael Butler in *Europe: More Than a Continent* writes eloquently about the need to create a clearly defined, focused, and workable Common Market.[11]

The end result of all of this, as far as these authors are concerned, is the "death" of purely "national" markets, tainted by xenophobia, and the creation of a truly global marketing environment. "Corporations geared to this new reality [will] generate enormous economies of scale in production, distribution, marketing, and management."[12] Companies unable to think and market on such an international plane will perish. "The global corporation looks to the nations of the world not for how they are *different* but for how they are *alike*."[13]

However, some analysts doubt whether certain "structural" economic and political concerns can indeed be corrected in time to forge a workable European organizational structure by 1992 or an Asian version of the EEC.

John Palmer in *Europe Without America? The Crisis in Atlantic Relations* maintains that Europe can indeed develop an economically viable Common Market without the United States. Yet Palmer is deeply concerned about the composition, viability, and direction of such an entity if America fails to play a critical role in its creation and development.[14]

Robert A. Scalapino, a leading scholar on Asian economic and political events, addresses this key issue in a perceptive article entitled "Asia's Future." Scalapino stresses the fact that Japan's recent growth rate has hovered near the 2.5 percent rate; unemployment held at a steady 3 percent pace, far too high for most Japanese governmental and business leaders. Competition from South Korea, Taiwan, and other Pacific Rim nations has intensified to the point that Japan's prices are no longer as competitive as they were in the early 1980s. Scalapino maintains that bold, creative policies must be initiated by the Japanese if these trends are to be reversed by what is a "greying," homogeneous work force.[15] Clearly Professor Scalapino wonders about the viability of crafting a workable "Asian EEC" in light of Japan's economic troubles.

Peter Drucker, professor emeritus of management at New York University, is equally concerned about Japan's economic stability. "The export boom of the last few years cannot possible go on. . . [and] the Japanese economy has become increasingly dependent on the export boom"; consequently, the Japanese are compelled to develop effective policies regarding the increased level of competition from Pacific Rim countries.[16]

If Professor Drucker's advice is followed by the Japanese, then it is obvious that their attempts to play a significant role, or possibly *the* major one, in the formulation of an "Asian EEC" will not be an easy task.

R. Taggart Murphy, managing director of Japanese Private Placements at Chase Manhattan Area Limited in Tokyo, also surveys this theme in "Power without Purpose: The Crisis of Japan's Global Financial Dominance." Japan's wealth now rivals that of the legendary Croesus, the last king of Lydia, and Japan's role in the capital market of the U.S. is significant. Yet Murphy questions Japan's ability to operate in this global capital market. "Japan lacks certain qualities necessary to be the kind of financial leader that can maintain stability and openness in the world's financial and trading system."[17]

Why? To Murphy Japan does not have the "ideology and political commitment necessary to fulfill the obligations that go with financial power. To turn sheer financial strength into leadership, a country must be able to think in global terms, to view itself as a world central banker, to sacrifice certain short-term gains to maintain stable financial and trading systems. Japan does not have this world view."[18] As for Marron's triad, "policymakers, business people, and even bankers still think of New York and London as the financial centers of gravity, of the dollar as the ultimate standard of value, and of the venerable firms of Wall Street and 'The City' in London as dominant."[19]

Events in early 1990 appeared to support many of these concerns about Japan. Roger Lowenstein, writing in the *Wall Street Journal*, reports that "Japan's stock market is declining almost daily, and its bond market is in turmoil as long-term interest rates surge toward seven percent."[20] Michael R. Sesit, also with the *Wall Street Journal*, commented on the dismay felt in Japan with the financial collapse of the Campeau retail store empire in the United States in January 1990. "Japan's big banks, which have supplied up to sixty percent of the loans for some U.S. leveraged buy-outs [LBOs], are likely to cut back on LBO lending in the wake of bankruptcy filings by two Campeau Corpora tion subsidiaries."[21]

Kamran Kashani, a professor of marketing at the International Management Development Institute (IMEDE) in Switzerland, critically surveys this phenomenon in "Beware the Pitfalls of Global Marketing" in the *Harvard Business Review*. "For every victory in globalization, there are probably several failures that are not broadcast. It is not fashionable to talk about failure."[22]

Kashani studied seventeen globalization endeavors conducted by nine different corporations in the United States and Europe, and he identified five reasons why these companies were unable to execute successfully their campaigns: (1) insufficient research, (2) overstandardization, (3) poor managerial follow-up, (4) narrow vision, and (5) rigid implementation.

Michael Schrage, in "A Japanese Giant Rethinks Globalization: An Interview with Yoshihisa Tabuchi," also addresses this area of concern. Tabuchi, president and chief executive officer of Nomura Securities Company (the largest and most profitable financial institution in the world), admitted that "some businesses are inherently domestic. So why try to make them global? Retail brokerage is a good example. The style and structure we use to sell securities in Japan cannot work in America; so we would be foolish to try."[23]

Michael E. Porter, Kenichi Ohmae, and Theodore Geiger, among many others, have written detailed and impressive studies on the significance of and the need to address effectively the ever-evolving nature of the global marketplace.[24]

A NEW ENVIRONMENT FOR BUSINESS PUBLISHERS

Since no clear consensus exists regarding the viability of creating and maintaining regional economic blocs, then what must a business publisher in the United States or Canada know about these potentially significant new business environments in order to compete effectively in this diverse, global publishing marketplace?

Answering this conundrum requires that two critically important questions be addressed. First, what are the key marketing questions that must be analyzed, for example, by a U.S. publisher of business periodicals or electronic databases or CD-ROM products interested in either entering into or expanding upon existing product niches in Europe in 1992 and the Pacific Rim region? Second, what real marketing opportunities exist for a business publisher in these two disparate business regions?

THE NEED FOR REALISTIC MARKETING RESEARCH

Many firms in Canada, Europe, and the United States have entered foreign publishing markets and lived to regret it. Their list of problems included experiences with bureaucratic and convoluted governmental regulatory agencies, inadequate distribution or financial service systems, poor understanding of local cultural patterns, or inability to understand the sometimes subtle configurations of the unique business publishing market in a nation (or a specific market niche). These problems caused many firms, including some of the world's most famous and established ones, to sustain dramatic financial or market reversals when they entered the global business publishing marketplace. Generally speaking, these firms failed to follow universally accepted marketing procedures, including setting clear marketing objectives, choosing target markets, analyzing the local legal framework of business, developing defined market positions, and carrying out effective marketing controls.

An interesting example is Verenigde Nederlandse Uitgeversbedrijven (generally known in the United States and Canada as VNU Amvest), a respected Dutch business publishing corporation that generated worldwide (estimated) sales of $1.5 billion in 1988.

Apparently after some detailed analysis, VNU decided in 1987 to enter the specialized business magazine and book market in the United States. They targeted the lucrative and fast-paced computer and electronics industries, and they purchased the respected

Table 5.1 / VNU Publications (in U.S. dollars).

Category	Electronics	Percent of Total Revenues	Microwaves and RF	Percent of Total Revenues	Personal Computing	Percent of Total Revenues
Total Revenues	$10,343		6,484		31,042	
Advertising	$8,261	79.9	6,483	100.0	26,607	85.7
Subscription	$2,082	20.1	0	0.0	5,435	17.5
Total Advertising Pages	1,506		1,729		2,224	
Yield Per Page	$5,484		3,750		11,965	
Average CPM	$80.00		61.75		24.25	

Source: Standard Rate and Data Service, Business Publications Rates and Data, part 1 (Wilmette, Ill.: Standard Rate and Data Service, 24 January 1988), 1784.

Table 5.2 / VNU's Competition in the Electronics Publications Market: 1989 (in U.S. dollars)

Title	U.S. Ranking Top 500 Magazines	Total Revenues	Percent Market Share	Total Advertising Pages	Percent Market Share	Circulation	Percent Market Share	Average CPM
EDN	92	$34,300	28.4%	6,082	31.9%	137,189	18.3%	$41.11
Electronic Engineering Times	104	29,937	24.8	3,742	19.6	121,537	16.2	65.82
Electronic Design	175	17,378	14.4	3,165	16.6	137,191	18.3	40.03
Electronic Buyers Design	191	15,934	13.2	2,993	15.6	60,121	8.0	88.55
Electronic News	242	12,802	10.6	1,588	8.3	88,481	11.8	76.84
Electronics	289	10,343	8.6	1,506	7.9	68,551	9.1	80.00

Source: 1988 MagazineWeek 500 (Natick, Mass.: Magazineweek Partners, 1988), 1–12, 65.

Hayden Publishing Company in New Jersey for an estimated $44 million. At that time Hayden issued a number of important computer and electronics technology periodicals and books, and they had also developed an interesting software unit. VNU hoped to build a viable business publishing unit around Hayden's existing titles and reputation, which were significant.

According to the definitive *Business Publication Rates and Data* and the *1988 MagazineWeek 500*, as of 24 January 1989, the VNU Business Publications corporation issued the following titles, as outlined in Table 5.1.

In 1988 VNU launched a new periodical, *Macintosh Business Review*. *Business Publication Rates and Data* reported that it was a monthly, nonpaid title with a "controlled" base of sixty thousand readers. Additional information on this magazine was not available.[25]

VNU unsuccessfully reorganized the corporate and marketing staffs of its business publications while, ironically, the computer and electronics industries underwent an economic slowdown. Advertising revenues and, ultimately, market share declined. VNU faced incredibly stiff competition from a number of successful titles.

The following table (5.2), which utilizes material cited in the above footnote, outlines the position of VNU's publication *Electronics* and its top six competitors in the electronics field as of January 1989.

On 8 February 1989, VNU decided to sell its troubled business publishing unit because of "disappointing sales" in the business magazine unit.[26]

Apparently VNU was either (1) "pushed" into this American market because of declining business opportunities in Holland or in its other markets, or (2) "pulled" in because of what VNU perceived incorrectly to be a burgeoning market in 1987 for computer magazines. In any case, VNU failed.

MARKET ANALYSIS TECHNIQUES

How can a business publisher analyze an international publishing market or niche if this publisher does not have a strategic planning staff and is concerned about trusting the judgment of outside business consultants in what is unquestionably a complex decision? This is not a simple task; if it were, VNU would not have experienced its recent reversal.

Fortunately, Susan Douglas, C. Samuel Craig, and Warren J. Keegan have written an excellent article on market analysis, which appeared in the Fall 1982 issue of the *Columbia Journal of World Business.*[27] In this important article, these three marketing professors present a series of suggestions that most business publishers should find quite useful. The following material is based on their approach to global marketing.

Initially, the business publisher must obtain concrete data on the following three items.

First, undertake a market entry analysis by reviewing the published literature *and* if necessary draw upon the work of experienced consultants active in the field. Second, determine the actual and projected market size for the company's periodical(s) or electronic databases or CD-ROM products by using standard mathematical analysis, that is, "lead-lag" analysis, surrogate indicators, market potential indicators, macrosurveys, aggregate barometric analysis, segment extrapolation, and econometric forecasting models, including regression techniques. Lastly, the publisher must monitor all business environmental changes in the geographical area(s) under consideration.

Using the Douglas-Craig-Keegan framework as a model, this author developed a series of questions that a business publisher in the United States or Canada could use to ascertain the viability of establishing a sales or marketing operating unit in another country, for example, Korea.

1. Does Korea have any existing (or planned) trade barriers (for example tariffs, quotas, or an embargo system) that will or could impede sales to or from that nation?
2. What is the basic economic environment in Korea? Is it an undeveloped nation (that is, on the subsist ence or raw-material level)? Is it a newly indus trialized country (NIC) or a developing nation caught in the painful economic and cultural throes of industrializing? Or does it have an industrial econ-

omy where people have discretionary income to purchase business publications? What are the income distribution patterns in Korea's urban, rural, and agricultural regions?

3. What are Korea's major manufacturing and service industries? What is Korea's Gross National Product (GNP) and per capita income? What are the latest five-year projections for Korea's overall economy? Who are Korea's primary and secondary trading partners for exports and imports?

4. What are the inflation rate, the prime interest rate, and short-term interest rate? What is the nature of the Korean accounting system? In what ways is it similar and dissimilar to the generally accepted accounting principles utilized in the United States? What is the state of Korea's transportation system?

5. What is the political and legal environment in Korea? Does this country have a "democratic" tradition? Are there any political restrictions? What is the attitude of the central government and the people toward the foreign ownership of publishing, information, and communications corporations? Are the existing regulatory agencies "pro" or "anti" business, especially foreign business?

6. What is Korea's existing publishing, television, radio, and communications network? Are there any existing or proposed laws that would limit or restrict "freedom of speech" and "freedom of the press"? Is Korea a signatory to the Berne (copyright) Convention? Has Korea had any problems with copyright violations in the last five years?

7. What is this country's cultural and educational tradition? How much money is allocated by the central government in these areas? Do local governmental units support the nation's cultural, educational, and library systems? How many libraries are there? How many business publications exist and how many are purchased each year by businesses, consumers, college students, and libraries? What is the per capita expenditure for these publications? What business publication niches are doing well or are expected to grow or decline in the next few years? Is this nation dominated by small, independent business publication distributors or does Korea have large, centralized distribution companies? Can business publications be purchased in

"non-traditional" magazine establishments, i.e., specialty stores, etc.?

After reviewing Korea's political, social, and economic environment, a publisher must ascertain the marketing goals and objectives of the proposed operating unit in Korea *and* in its home and other markets.

What percentage of sales income and profits should be generated in Korea? What is the expected and desired return on the company's investment in the first year, the second year, and the first five years? What are the short-run and long-run markets for this firm's product in Korea? What will the start-up costs be for the first year and the first five years? What is the break-even point? Should this firm establish an operating unit only in Korea *or* should such units be created in a few or all of the other Pacific Rim countries?

While professional advice is needed from bankers, lawyers, international business executives, trade association leaders, reliable governmental sources, and business publishing experts, the marketing framework briefly outlined above can be rather useful, especially in verifying the opinions and recommendations of these outside individuals.[28]

Candor, objectivity, *and* determination are needed in order to address these critically important questions. If this analysis does not generate a critical mass of *positive* economic data, then it might be prudent to place any expansion into Korea (or any new market for that matter) "on hold" in order to prevent the loss of scarce resources.

Of course, business publishing firms can draw upon an interesting variety of tested business procedures once the decision has been made to enter a foreign market. These include (1) direct and indirect exports, including the traditional use of an overseas sales force and traveling sales agents, (2) the joint venture, including various licensing and manufacturing arrangements, and (3) the direct investment in an existing publishing corpora tion, with its abundantly clear advantages of lower labor and manufacturing expenditures and its concomitant lower exposure to financial or political risks.

A BUSINESS MODEL

Since 1980 business books have posted an exceptionally impressive sales record in the United States. *In Search of Excellence, Iacocca, Theory Z,* to name only a few titles, were all bestsellers, with *Iacocca* remaining the number one bestseller for two straight years. Many observers have noticed the fascinating symbiotic relationship that has developed and indeed matured in the United States between these business titles and related business periodicals, newsletters, and various software products.

If business books help "prime the pump" for these other business publications, is it possible, therefore, to use the business book industry's varied experiences as a *model* to determine the existing or anticipated potential for business periodicals, electronic databases, or CD-ROM products in Europe and the Pacific Rim?

In order adequately to address this query, it is nescessary to analyze a number of significant issues affecting the book industry, an industry in which a significant number of business periodical companies became actively involved during the mid- to late-1980s.

First, what is the current percentage of exports and the real growth potential for books? Second, will the creation of a revamped EEC in 1992 adversely affect the market for U.S. books in Europe? Third, will nations in the Pacific Rim region create an Asian "Common Market" with trade policies similar to those that will be introduced in Europe in 1992?

A detailed analysis of data contained in the *1989 U.S. Industrial Outlook* reveals that book exports constitute a small percentage of *total* U.S. book shipments, reaching only a modest 7.2 percent in 1988.[29] The following table (5.3), based upon U.S. Department of Commerce data and calculations by this researcher, outlines this trend.

What are the key market categories for U.S. book exports? The following two tables (5.4 and 5.5) are based on material in an article by Chandler B. Grannis and additional calculations by this researcher.[30]

Where did U.S. book publishers export their products?

The following table (5.5), also based on the invaluable research

Table 5.3 / U.S. Book Exports: 1972–1989 (in millions of U.S. dollars)

Year	Total Book Exports	Percent Change from Prior Year	Percent of Exports of Total Book Shipments
1972	$174	—	6.0
1973	196	+ 12.60	6.2
1974	246	+ 25.50	7.2
1975	273	+ 10.98	7.2
1976	203	− 5.60	7.2
1977	320	+ 57.60	6.4
1978	377	+ 17.80	6.7
1979	446	+ 18.30	7.7
1980	519	+ 16.36	8.1
1981	612	+ 17.90	8.7
1982	650	+ 6.20	8.3
1983	616	− 5.20	7.3
1984	649	+ 5.36	7.2
1985	591	− 8.94	5.8
1986	604	+ 2.20	5.7
1987	739	+ 22.35	6.4
1988	915	+ 23.82	7.2
1989	1,075	+ 23.82	7.7
Grand Total	9,205	—	—

Source: U.S. Department of Commerce, International Trade Administration, 1989 U.S. Industrial Outlook (Washington, D.C.: USGPO, 1989),37–1–37–12.

of Chandler B. Grannis and additional analysis by this researcher, outlines shipments to the Common Market, other European nations, and the Pacific Rim.[31] As for the next five years, the U.S. government and the Book Industry Study Group are both optimistic that book (and indeed all) publishers in the United States will be able to increase the total dollar revenues generated through exports. According to the U.S. Department of Commerce, books are expected to average a solid 5 percent growth rate through 1993, which, based on the experiences evident during the 1980s, should help increase the sales of related publishing products, especially periodicals and software.[32]

Table 5.4 / U.S. Book Exports by Category: 1988 (in millions of U.S. dollars)

Book Category	Value of Exports	% of Total Exports	Number of Units Exported (in millions)
Religious	$42.700	4.62	44.48
Dictionaries and Thesauruses	5.054	0.55	0.87
Encyclopedias	33.659	3.63	6.69
Textbooks	162.078	17.52	18.33
Technical, Scientific, and Professional	242.619	26.22	54.22
Mass Market Paperbacks	106.960	11.56	99.04
Books Not Specifically Provided For	314.990	34.04	138.10
Children's Picture and Coloring	8.847	9.56	n/a
Total	925.224	—	n/a

Source: Chandler B. Grannis, "Balancing the Books: U.S. Export Ratios; World Figures Reported," Publishers Weekly, 2 June 1989, 42–45.

THE EUROPEAN ECONOMY

While many publishers in the United States (and Canada) look inward to their own major consumer and industrial markets for increased sales, Europe as of 1992 will be the largest single market in both of these critically important categories in the world. The following two tables are based on a detailed review of statistical data culled from various issues of the *Wall Street Journal* and *The Statesman's Yearbook: 1988–1989*. These tables provide some interesting comparative data on the size and significance of the Common Market and the United States; Russian economic statistics are found in Table 5.7.[33]

While Russia has the *potential* to become a major market for many U.S. or Canadian business publishing products, especially scientific and technical journals, it lags significantly behind the Common Market and the United States in many key economic

Table 5.5 / U.S. Book Exports: 1988 By Geographical Region (in millions of 1988 U.S. dollars)

Region	Total Receipts	Percent of Total U.S. Exports	Units (in millions)	Percent of Total World Units Exported
Common Market				
Belgium	$4.780	0.571%	1.336	0.419%
Denmark	1.880	0.225	0.700	0.022
France	19.076	2.278	5.851	1.837
West Germany	28.395	3.391	10.150	3.186
Greece	0.362	0.043	0.110	0.035
Ireland	7.027	0.839	1.360	0.427
Italy	7.147	0.854	2.040	0.641
Luxembourg	0.019	0.002	0.004	0.001
Netherlands	28.274	3.377	10.697	3.358
Portugal	0.318	0.038	0.098	0.029
Spain	3.236	0.386	1.120	0.352
United Kingdom	141.824	16.937	45.860	14.397
Total	242.338	28.941	79.346	24.909
Pacific Rim				
Australia	69.500	8.300	35.220	11.057
Hong Kong	8.670	1.035	2.409	0.756
Japan	58.970	7.042	17.701	5.557
South Korea	6.467	0.772	2.106	0.661
Philippines	10.270	1.226	5.989	1.880
Singapore	15.925	1.902	7.009	2.200
Taiwan	9.183	1.097	2.938	0.922
Total	178.985	21.375	73.462	23.062
Other Nations				
Canada	364.371	43.515	143.381	45.012
Brazil	14.406	1.720	5.563	1.746
India	15.270	1.824	4.129	1.296
Mexico	14.786	1.766	9.823	3.084
Switzerland	7.192	0.859	2.833	0.889
Total	416.025	49.684	165.729	52.028
Grand Total	837.348	—	318.537	—

Source: Chandler B. Grannis, "Balancing the Books: U.S. Export Ratios; World Figures Reported," *Publishers Weekly,* 2 June 1989, 42–45.

Table 5.6 / Comparative Economic Data: Europe in 1988

Category	West Germany	France	U.K.	All Common Market Nations	U.S.A.
Percent of World's Gross National Product	4.8	4.2	4.1	22.1	25.9
Percent of GNP Spent on Defense	3.2	4.1	5.3	3.3	6.6
Govt. Deficit as Percent of GNP	-2.0	-1.6	0.3	-2.9	- 1.7
Inflation Rate Dec. 1987- Dec. 1988	1.6	3.1	6.8	4.4	4.4
Population, 1988 (in millions)	61.0	55.6	56.8	323.4	243.8
Unemployment Rate, 1988	8.7	10.3	8.7	10.3	5.5
Personal Savings Percentage Rate, 1988	13.3	12.0	3.8	n/a	4.0

Source: Karen Elliot House, "The '90s and Beyond: Europe's Global Clout Is Limited by Divisions 1992 Can't Paper Over," *Wall Street Journal*, 13 February 1989, A1, A10; Philip Revzin, "Europe Will Become Economic Superpower as Barriers Crumble," *Wall Street Journal*, 23 January 1989, A1, A4; and John Paxton, ed., *The Statesman Yearbook: 1988–1989* (New York: St. Martin's Press, 1988), xv-xxx, 3–58.

categories. In addition, its currency hardly has an impressive value internationally.

However, there is keen interest in both the United States and Canada in Russian journals; so Russia could develop a "bartering" system with publishers in the U.S. and Canada whereby rights to covet ed Soviet publications could be exchanged for U.S. periodical or journal titles. These existing business hurdles have already been addressed effectively by a few creative publishing executives, including Simon Michael Bessie and Martin Levin.

The following table (5.7), drawing on material cited in note 33, provides a brief comparison among the U.S., the Common Market countries, and Russia since 1980.

Table 5.7 / U.S., Common Market, and U.S.S.R. (1987 Data)

Category	U.S.	Common Market	Percent of U.S.	U.S.S.R.	Percent of U.S.
Population	243.8 million	326.6 million	133.96%	284.0 million	116.49%
GNP (in billions of 1987) U.S. dollars	$4,436.1	$3,782.0	85.25	$2,375.0	53.54
Per Capita GNP 1987	$18,200	$11,690	64.23	$8,360	45.93
GNP Growth Rate (Percentage increase)					
1966–1970	2.8	4.6	5.1		
1971–1975	2.3	3.0	3.1		
1976–1980	3.3	3.0	2.2		
1981–1985	3.0	1.5	1.8		
1987	2.9	2.9	0.5		
Total Labor Force	121.6 million	143.0 million	117.60	154.8 million	127.30

Source: Karen Elliot House, "The '90s and Beyond: Europe's Global Clout Is Limited by Divisions 1992 Can't Paper Over," Wall Street Journal, 13 February 1989, A1, A10; Philip Revzin, "Europe Will Become Economic Superpower as Barriers Crumble," Wall Street Journal, 23 January 1989, A1, A4; and John Paxton, ed., The Statesman Yearbook: 1988–1989 (New York: St. Martin's Press, 1988), xv-xxx, 3–58.

WHAT IMPACT WILL 1992 HAVE ON U.S. BUSINESS PUBLISHERS?

After reviewing all of the *available* information (as of 1 February 1990) about the Common Market's planned or proposed trade policies, along with relevant economic data, it appears that a U.S. or Canadian business publishing firm with an existing operating unit or units in a Common Market nation or nations (e.g., Dow Jones, Dun and Bradstreet, the Thomson Corporation, Hearst, etc.) should not experience many problems as of 31 December 1992. Conversely, Common Market-based publishing corporations with units in the United States or Canada (e.g., Maxwell, Hachette, Bertelsmann AG, Viking-Penguin, Reed, Elsevier, Springer-Verlag, etc.) should find "business as usual" to be the standard operating procedure as of 1992.

However, far too many "ifs" exist to present many definitive statements, especially with the rapid changes taking place in Russia and Eastern Europe. This was readily apparent at the June 1989 American Booksellers Association (ABA) annual meeting in Washington, D.C. During one of the ABA sessions, a panel of publishing experts addressed the "potential" impact of 1992 on global publishers, and it was abundantly clear that no consensus was reached by these individuals.

Ellis Levine from Random House, a Newhouse property, tackled the thorny issue of U.S. books exported to a Common Market nation and then later forwarded into the United Kingdom, a process that would seriously undercut sales of the same book by the U.K. publisher. Marcella Berger from Simon and Schuster, owned by Paramount, worried about subsidiary rights of U.S. books, especially the vulnerable mid-list book, in this new business climate. Roland Algrant from Hearst Books wondered about the all-important issue of intellectual property and copyright laws and proposed ECC guidelines.[34]

In the end, these panelists discussed a series of "what ifs." Few real conclusions were bantered about at the convention because no one knew for sure what really will take place. The same is true for business periodicals!

However, one general observation can be made, even during this period of inevitable transition and uncertainty. It appears that all will not be sanguine for U.S. or Canadian publishing firms lacking ties to any Common Market nation. The major problem will be the licensing of U.S. or Canadian business properties in Europe. These firms will find the road a bit rocky, if not inac cessible. Unless U.S. or Canadian business publishing corporations develop effective business relations with a European publishing firm, most likely in the U.K., or purchase part or all of an existing publishing firm in a Common Market nation, then they could experience a sharp drop in profits from exports to Europe.

So will United States or Canadian business publishing firms be closed out of the critically significant European market as of 1992? They could. However, in this question one finds the clear *assumption* that the Common Market nations will be able to work together. Obviously they have the ability to do this; and the Levitt-Blumenthal-Wriston "technology" thesis presents an exceptionally persuasive argument that this indeed will occur. Yet this author believes that their thesis, through remarkably cogent, is nonetheless flawed.

As of February 1990, these Common Market states have yet to address effectively a plethora of major problems that will limit, and possibly undermine, any attempts to create a united, effective economic bloc by the early to mid-1990s. These include the following items.

Despite heroic efforts in the recent past to ameliorate historical tensions in Europe, nationalism still lingers behind the scenes and generates a plethora of tensions and concerns.

Many Common Market nations have a "socialist" orientation. Unless the "capitalists" (primarily in the U.K.) and the "socialists" (led for the most part by France) can mend their fences, real unity on many critically important economic and social issues will be exceptionally difficult to achieve.

The Common Market lacks a central currency, although the French initiative to create a real European currency and a "central bank" just might succeed in spite of strong British opposition.

Union and nonunion wage scales, hours, and general terms and conditions of employment vary dramatically throughout Western Europe. This situation will lead ultimately to more industrial work being done in Spain, Italy, and Greece than in costly West

Germany. This situation has already generated a significant amount of unrest among labor leaders, and this "sword of Damocles" will hover over attempts at European unity for the foreseeable future.

Only optimists believe that the famed bureaucracies of Europe will disappear as if by wizardry at the stroke of midnight on 31 December 1992.

Lastly, there is no natural political leader of Europe. The U.K. might try to achieve this position, as will France or West Germany. Yet no one nation or individual has emerged in Europe that all of the others will follow.

Europe will and indeed *must* remain a major market for U.S. business publishing products generated in the U.S. and Canada because of a series of major economic events.

The business magazine industry has sustained major business reverses since 1987. The Wall Street crash of October 1987 led to a major reduction in advertising lineage in many business publications, especially those covering financial services sectors. This was followed by additional sharp declines in periodical advertising revenues in 1988–1989; and advertising rate cutting became a scourge, a veritable plague that decimated profits and confidence at many of this nation's leading business magazines. The consensus among key advertising leaders is that future reductions in advertising revenues must be anticipated at least through the 1990–1991 period, if not into 1992–1993.

These problems were exacerbated by the intense competition exerted by other electronic forms of communications, namely cable television and videotape rental films, which will unquestionably intensify in the next three to five years.[35]

However, as of 1992, it appears that "business as usual" will be the European Common Market business framework that the United States and Canada will confront; and publishing firms must be prepared to participate in this burgeoning global market. Failure to develop effective strategic plans will prove to be a costly error for publishing firms already facing stiff competition and lagging sales revenues and profit margins at home.

A PACIFIC RIM "COMMON MARKET"?

So will publishers in the United States and Canada ever face the dilemma of being closed out of an Asian equivalent of Europe's Common Market? As of 1990 the prospects of a Pacific Rim economic bloc, patterned on Europe's trade regulations, appeared to be a remote possibility before the year 2000 for of a number of reasons.

First, Japan is an immensely wealthy nation, purchasing some of the world's finest buildings, manufacturing corporations, and art works. They have done this because of a shortage of high-yielding investment opportunities in Japan. Ironically they have committed many of their resources to "non-liquid" ones. After all, you cannot move the Pan Am Building out of New York City.

As strong as Japan is economically, it remains exceptionally vulnerable from an economic point of view since it is so dependent on exporting products rather than consuming a majority of them within Japan. A worldwide depression or even a relatively mild though long-lasting recession would be felt rather quickly in Japan.

This means that Japan could be adversely affected if trade restrictions were created against its products in, for example, the United States. So if Japan sought to establish trade restrictions against the United States in a Pacific Rim common economic market, Japan could suffer severe economic reversals in the U.S.

Second, Japan could encounter steep opposition if it ever sought to become the economic leader in an Asian common market.[36] The death of the Japanese emperor in 1989 highlighted the plight that many Asians have in dealing with Japan in the 1990s. Most Asian nations were occupied by Japan during World War II; and intense debates took place in January 1989 in many of these states regarding whether an official delegation, and on what level, should be sent to the emperor's funeral services in late February 1989.

China is the next strongest Asian nation; and it might seek to play the dominant role in an EEC. Yet two significant problems stalk China. All of the data reveals conclusively that it is a rather weak nation economically. The following table (5.8) out lines the

Table 5.8 / U.S.A., Japan, and China: 1988 (in billions of dollars)

	U.S.	Japan	Percent of U.S.	China	Percent of U.S.
Population (millions)	243.8	120.0	49.2	1,100.0	451.2
GNP	$4,436.1	2,800.0	63.1	368.0	8.3
GNP Growth Rate (Percentage Increase)	2.9	4.0	—	11.2	—
Inflation Rate (Percentage Increase 1988)	3.7	0.1	—	9.2	—
Total Labor Force millions)	121.6	60.0	49.3	510.0	419.4
Life Expectancy (in years)	75.0	78.0	+4.0	68.0	-9.3
U.S. Exports to	n/a	$27.0	—	5.3	—
U.S. Imports from	n/a	$88.0	—	8.3	—

Source: Mike Van Horn, *Pacific Rim Trade: The Definitive Guide to Exorting and Investment* (New York: AMACOM, 1989), 300–304.

economic status of Japan and China in relation to the United States.[37]

Perhaps more importantly, political and military events in Beijing, China in the period stretching from April through June 1989 exposed the fact that the existing political hierarchy in China cannot provide the type of dynamic and respected leadership needed to create and administer an Asian economic community.

Winston Lord, formerly president of the influential Council on Foreign Relations and U.S. ambassador to China from November 1985 until April 1989, addressed this key issue in a recent article on "China and America: Beyond the Big Chill" in *Foreign Affairs.* Lord maintains that even "the most cold-blooded observer would have difficulty justifying the Chinese government's policies since June [1989]."[38] The direct impact of these political events on China's economic infrastructure will be immense. Lord remarks that "economic pressure on the regime will intensify. Before this spring [of 1989] there were already serious problems: an overheated economy, inflation, unemployment, bottlenecks in energy, raw materials and transportation, and income disparities. Rampant nepotism and corruption were souring the populace. All of this has now been compounded by the dislocation of recent months."[39]

The global response to the Chinese regime's handling of the student rebellion has been harsh. "In a few brief months, the Chinese leaders have lost the respect, confidence, and credibility they had garnered during the past decade [of the 1980s]."[40]

Alan M. Webber fashioned his intriguing article "The Case of the China Diary" from the excerpts of a diary written by Geoff Parker, a textile executive who worked in China. "Incredible news from Beijing [in April–June 1989]. We watch on CNN at the Hilton. Thousands of students killed. . . . Everything is at a standstill in Shanghai; buses pulled across roads and public transportation shut down. . . ."[41]

Other important and highly critical books about China's debacle have flowed from publishers at a rapid rate, including a remarkable book by Michael Fathers and Andrew Higgins entitled *Tiananmen: The Rape of Peking;* Scott Simmie and Bob Nixon's *Tiananmen Square;* the International League for Human Rights and the Ad Hoc Group on Human Rights in China's *Massacre in Beijing: The Events of 3–4 June, 1989 and Their Aftermath;* and Harrison E. Salisbury's *Tiananmen Square: Thirteen Days in June.* Jonathan Mirsky's review of these and other books in the *New York Review of Books* is perhaps the best overview of the troubles that engulfed China in 1989.[42]

Lastly, while South Korea, Taiwan, Singapore, and Honk Kong have posted impressive economic results in the last ten years, they have not exhibited the political or diplomatic acumen needed to lead a fragmented group of East Asian nations into a coordinated and complicated economic endeavor. South Korea is an interesting case. Its manufacturing efforts are indeed impressive, as Ira C. Magaziner and Mark Patinkin illustrate in their *Harvard Business Review* article "Fast Heat: How Korea Won the Microwave War."[43] Yet its image in the international publishing world has been badly tarnished because of its tolerance of book pirating operations, a problem that also has plagued Taiwan and far too many other East Asian nations.[44]

In addition Hong Kong will revert back to Chinese control by the end of the 1990s, which effectively nullifies its chances to play a major role in economic consolidation discussions.[45]

Australia stands alone as the most reasonable and respected leader in the entire Pacific Rim region. Its business statistics are impressive: a population of 16.2 million people; an annual growth rate in its Gross National Product of 5 percent; no budget deficit; and a +$1.7 billion trade balance.[46] However, it remains to be seen whether this dynamic nation can handle such a demanding role.

Consequently, all of the available economic and political information indicates clearly that there is no unified Pacific Rim economic block, merely a collection of about thirteen nations all anxious to excel. Creating a version of the EEC in this part of the world in the 1990s will be an exceptionally difficult task; after all, it has taken the Western Europeans almost thirty-five years to reach their current level of achievement. A similar time period just might be required for their Asian counterparts.

However, the Pacific Rim is a major +$179 million book market (with a healthy 19.35 percent market share) for U.S. book publishing companies. As long as English remains the primary language in the expanding business, scientific, and technical fields, it is likely that these Pacific Rim nations will continue to need books, professional and technical journals, periodicals, and software produced in the United States.

It appears that the majority of U.S. and Canadian publishing companies, at least through the year 2000, with existing (or planned) business connections in this region should find business in the 1990s to be as difficult, demanding, and competitive as it was in the 1980s. This means that the prospects look bright for book publishing executives who are able to manage in turbulent times and seek to cultivate strong market ties with these dynamic, complex, and important nations in the Pacific Rim.

NOTES

1. Philip Revzin, "United Front: Europe Will Become Superpower As Barriers Crumble," the *Wall Street Journal*, 23 January 1989, A1, A4.

Also see Kevin Cote, "1992: Europe Becomes One," *Advertising Age*, 11 July 1988, 46; Kevin Cote, "1992 Means Restructuring," *Advertising Age*, 3 October 1988, 46; John F. Magee, "1992: Moves Americans Must Make," *Harvard Business Review* 67 (May-June 1989): 78–84; Eric G. Friberg, "1992: Moves Europeans Are Making," *Harvard Business Review* 67 (May-June 1989): 85–89; Nan Stone, "The Globalization of Europe: An Interview with Wisse Dekker," *Harvard Business Review* 67 (May-June 1989): 90–95; and Raymond Vernon, "Can the U.S. Negotiate for Trade Equality?" *Harvard Business Review* 67 (May-June 1989): 96–103. Other useful works include Thomas M. Hout, Michael Porter, and Eileen Rudden, "How Global Companies Win Out," in Richard G. Hamermesh, ed., *Strategic Management* (New York: Wiley, 1983), 35–49; Karen Elliot House, "The '90s and Beyond: Europe's Global Clout Is Limited by Divisions 1992 Can't Paper Over," *Wall Street Journal*, 13 February 1989, A1, A10; Philip Revzin, "Europe Will Become Economic Superpower as Barriers Crumble," *Wall Street Journal*, 23 January 1989, A1, A4; and John Paxton, ed., *The Statesman's Yearbook: 1988–1989* (New York: St. Martin's, 1988), xv-xxx, 3–58. Also see "Europe's Houdini Trade," the *Economist*, 6 May 1989, 9–10; "International," *Publishers Weekly*, 30 June 1989, 54–61; "International Booksellers Meet," *Publishers Weekly*, 30 June 1989, 56; "Talking about 1992," *Publishers Weekly*, 30 June 1989, 58; "Debut for the AAP International Trade Group," *Publishers Weekly*, 30 June 1989, 60. Also see Vivienne Menkes, "London '89: A Growing Internationalism," *Publishers Weekly*, 5 May 1989, 33–36; "1992 and All That," *Publishers Weekly*, 3 February 1989, 21–28; W. Gordon Graham, "The Shadow of 1992," *Publishers Weekly*, 23 December 1988, 24–26.

2. John Paxton, ed., *The Statesman's Yearbook: 1988–1989* (New York: St. Martin's 1988), 352–64, 602–08, 749–57, 771–80. Also see Raymond J. Waldman, *Managed Trade: The New Competition between Nations* (Cambridge, Mass.: Ballinger, 1988); Gilbert R. Wenham, *International Trade and the Toyko Round Negotiation* (Princeton, N.J.: Princeton University Press, 1987); and Sumner N. Levine, ed., *The Dow Jones-Irwin Business and Investment Almanac: 1989* (Homewood, Ill.: Dow Jones-Irwin, 1989), 675–90.

3. Theodore Levitt, *The Marketing Imagination* (New York: Free Press, 1983), 20.

4. W. Michael Blumenthal, "The World Economy and Technological Change," *Foreign Affairs* 66 (1988): 535, 545.

5. Roger B. Smith, "Global Competition: A Strategy for Success," in *The Global Marketplace*, ed. James M. Rosow (New York: Facts on File, 1988), 33–52; Donald B. Marron, "The Globalization of Capital," in *Global Marketplace*; James E. Olson, "Toward a Global Information Age," in *Global Marketplace*, 93–110.

6. Walter B. Wriston, "The State of American Management," *Harvard Business Review* 68 (January-February 1990): 80.
7. Ibid., 81.
8. Walter B. Wriston, "Technology and Sovereignty," *Foreign Affairs* 67 (1987): 67.
9. M. Panic, *National Management of the International Economy* (New York: St. Martin's, 1988), 37.
10. Felix Rohatyn, "America's Economic Dependence," *Foreign Affairs* 69 (1989): 54.
11. Sir Michael Butler, *Europe: More Than a Continent* (London: Heinemann, 1988), 27–49.
12. Levitt, *The Marketing Imagination*, 20–21.
13. Ibid., 28.
14. John Palmer, *Europe without America? The Crisis in Atlantic Relations* (New York: Oxford University Press, 1988), 7–27.
15. Robert A. Scalapino, "Asia's Future," *Foreign Affairs* 66 (1988): 85–89. Also see Robert A. Scalapino and Hongkoo Lee, eds., *Korea-U.S. Relations: The Politics of Trade and Security* (Berkeley: Institute of East Asian Studies, University of California, 1989), 1–49; and Robert A. Scalapino, et al., eds., *Pacific-Asian Economic Policies and Regional Interdependence* (Berkeley: Institute of East Asian Studies, University of California, 1989), 1–8, 54–89.
16. Peter Drucker, "Japan's Choices," *Foreign Affairs* 65 (1985): 923, 929.
17. R. Taggart Murphy, "Power without Purpose: The Crisis of Japan's Global Financial Dominance," *Harvard Business Review* 67 (March-April 1989): 74.
18. Ibid., 81.
19. Ibid., 81.
20. Roger Lowenstein, "Japan Market Woes Raise Fears of Pullback in U.S.," *Wall Street Journal*, 19 January 1990, C1. Also see James Sterngold, "Tokyo's Wary Money Managers," *New York Times*, 22 January 1990, D1; and Kenneth N. Gilpin, "Japanese Rate Surge Felt in U.S.," *New York Times*, 22 January 1990, D1.
21. Michael R. Sesit, "Japan Banks Seen Cutting LBO Role after Campeau," *Wall Street Journal*, 19 January 1990, C1.
22. Kamran Kashani, "Beware the Pitfalls of Global Marketing," *Harvard Business Review* 67 (September-October 1989): 91, 92–98.
23. Michael Schrage, "A Japanese Giant Rethinks Globalization: An Interview with Yoshihisa Tabuchi," *Harvard Business Review* 67 (July-August 1989): 71.
24. Michael E. Porter, *Competitive Strategy: Techniques for Analyzing Industries and Competitors* (New York: Free Press, 1980), 3–33; 275–99; Michael E. Porter, "How Competitive Forces Shape Strategy," *Harvard Business Review* 57 (March-April 1979): 137–45; Kenichi Ohmae, *The Mind of the Strategist* (New York: Penguin, 1988), 163–278; Keni-

chi Ohmae, "Planting for a Global Harvest," *Harvard Business Review* 67 (July-August 1989): 136–45; Kenichi Ohmae, "The Global Logic of Strategic Alliances," *Harvard Business Review* 67 (March-April 1989): 143–54; and Theodore Geiger, *The Future of the International System: The United States and the World Economy* (Boston: Unwin Hyman, 1988), 5–21.

25. *Business Publication Rates and Data,* 24 January 1989, 1784. *The 1988 MagazineWeek 500* (Natick, Mass.: MagazineWeek Partners, 1988), 1–12, 65.

26. Robin Kamen, "N.J. Publishing Houses for Sale," *The Record,* 9 February 1989, C1, C11. For additional information about this topic, see David A. Ricks, *Big Business Blunders: Mistakes in Multinational Marketing* (Homewood, Ill.: Dow Jones-Irwin, 1982); Roger E. Axtell, *Dos and Taboos around the World: A Guide to International Behavior* (New York: John Wiley & Sons, 1986); and Gavin Kennedy, *Doing Business Abroad* (New York: Simon & Schuster, 1985).

27. Susan P. Douglas, C. Samuel Craig, and Warren J. Keegan, "Approaches to Assessing International Marketing Opportunities for Small- and Medium-Sized Companies," *Columbia Journal of World Business* (Fall 1982): 26–32. Also see Michael R. Czinkota and George Tasar, *Export Development Strategies: U.S. Promotion Policy* (New York: Praeger, 1982); Nigel Percy, *Export Strategies: Markets and Competition* (Winchester, Mass.: Allen & Unwin, 1982); Franklin R. Root, *Foreign Market Entry Strategies* (New York: AMACOM, 1982); *Exporting from the United States* (Rocklin, Calif.: Prima Publishing, 1988), 11–16; and Raul Kahler, *International Marketing* (Cincin- nati, Ohio: Southwestern Publishing, 1983). Also see Susan Douglas and C. Samuel Craig, *International Marketing Research* (Englewood Cliffs, N.J.: Prentice-Hall, 1983). Also see Ursula Springer, "Selling Your Scholarly Books Overseas: Some Practical Tips for Non-Experts," *SSP Letter* 11 (1989): 5–6, 12; Ann Reinke Strong, "Marketing Journals Internationally," *SSP Letter* 11 (1989): 7–8; Robert F. Winter, "Measures of the Book Industry: 1982–1988," *Trends Update* 8 (1989): 1–8; Fred Kobrak, "The International PSP Market: An Update," *Publishers Weekly,* 10 November 1989, 44–45.

28. Also see R. Strobaugh, "How to Analyze Foreign Investment Climates," *Harvard Business Review* 48 (September-October 1969): 100–108; P. Carr, "Identifying Trade Areas for Consumer Goods in Foreign Markets," *Journal of Marketing* (October 1978): 76–80; R. Moyer, "International Market Analysis," *Journal of Marketing Research* (November 1968): 353–60.

29. U.S. Department of Commerce, International Trade Administration, *1989 U.S. Industrial Outlook* (Washington, D.C.: GPO, 1989), 37-1–37–12. Also see William Lofquist, "Statistical Series: U.S. Book Industries," *Book Research Quarterly* 4 (Summer 1988): 71–75.

30. Chandler B. Grannis, "Balancing the Books: U.S. Export Ratios; World Figures Reported," *Publishers Weekly*, 2 June 1989, 42–45.

31. Ibid., 42–45.

32. U.S. Department of Commerce, International Trade Administration, *1989 U.S. Industrial Outlook* (Washington, D.C.: GPO, 1989), 37–1–37–12, 45–1–45–5. Also see the Center for Book Research, *Book Industry Trends 1988* (New York: Book Industry Study Group, 1988), 42–97. Statistical information about specific countries can be obtained from various agencies of the U.S. Department of Commerce, including U.S. Dept. of Commerce, Export Promotion Services, *Annual Worldwide Industry Review* (Washington, D.C.: GPO, 1989); *Country Trade Statistics* (Washington, D.C.: GPO, 1988); *Custom Statistical Service* (Washington, D.C.: GPO, 1989); and *International Market Research* (Washington, D.C.: GPO, 1988).

33. Karen Elliot House, "The '90s and Beyond: Europe's Global Clout Is Limited by Divisions 1992 Can't Paper Over," *Wall Street Journal*, 13 February 1989, A1, A10; Philip Revzin, "Europe Will Become Economic Superpower As Barriers Crumble," *Wall Street Journal*, 23 January 1989, A1, A4; and John Paxton, ed., *The Statesman's Yearbook: 1988–1989* (New York: St. Martin's Press, 1988), xv-xxx, 3–58. Also see "Europe's Houdini Trade," *The Economist*, 6 May 1989, 9–10.

34. "International," *Publishers Weekly*, 30 June 1989, 54–61; "International Booksellers Meet," *Publishers Weekly*, 30 June 1989, 56; "Talking about 1992," *Publishers Weekly*, 30 June 1989, 58; "Debut for the AAP International Trade Group," *Publishers Weekly*, 30 June 1989, 60. Also see Vivienne Menkes, "London '89: A Growing Internationalism," *Publishers Weekly*, 5 May 1989, 33–36; "1992 and All That," *Publishers Weekly*, 3 February 1989, 21–28; W. Gordon Graham, "The Shadow of 1992," *Publishers Weekly*, 23 December 1988, 24–26.

35. Karen Elliot House, "The '90s and Beyond: Though Rich, Japan Is Poor in Many Elements of Global Leadership," *Wall Street Journal*, 30 January 1989, A1, A8. Edward J. Lincoln, *Japan's Economic Role in Northeast Asia* (Washington, D.C.: University Press of America; New York: Asia Society, 1987); Michael Schrage, "A Japanese Giant Rethinks Globalization: An Interview with Yoshihisa Tabuchi," *Harvard Business Review* 67 (July-August 1989): 61–69.

36. Edward J. Lincoln, *Japan's Economic Role in Northeast Asia* (Washington, D.C.: University Press of America; New York: Asia Society, 1987); John K. Emerson, *The Eagle and the Rising Sun* (Reading, Mass.: Addison-Wesley, 1988), 163–75. Also see Chalmers Johnson, Laura D'Andrea Tyson, and John Zysman, *Politics and Productivity: How Japan's Development Strategy Works* (Cambridge, Mass.: Ballinger, 1989), 22–32; Kent E. Calder, *Crisis and Compensation: Public Policy and Political Stability in Japan, 1949–1986* (Princeton, N.J.: Princeton University Press, 1988), 188–211.

37. Mike Van Horn, *Pacific Rim Trade: The Definitive Guide to Exporting and Investment* (New York: AMACOM, 1989), 300–304.
38. Winston Lord, "China and America: Beyond the Big Chill," *Foreign Affairs* 68 (1989): 2.
39. Ibid., 5.
40. Ibid., 5. Also see Harrison E. Salisbury, *Tiananmen Diary: Thirteen Days In June* (Boston, Mass.: Little, Brown, 1989).
41. Alan M. Webber, "The Case of the China Diary," *Harvard Business Review* 67 (November-December 1989): 24.
42. Michael Fathers and Andrew Higgins, *Tiananmen: The Rape of Peking* (New York: Independent; Doubleday, 1989); Scott Simmie and Bob Nixon, *Tiananmen Square* (Seattle: University of Washington Press, 1989); and Jonathan Mirsky, "The Empire Strikes Back," *New York Review of Books*, 1 February 1990, 21–25.
43. Ira C. Magaziner and Mark Patinkin, "Fast Heat: How Korea Won the Microwave War," *Harvard Business Review* 67 (January-February 1989): 83–93.
44. David Kaser, *Book Pirating in Taiwan* (Philadelphia: University of Pennsylvania Press, 1969), 128–41, 147–50. Also see Jeffrey D. Sachs, ed., *Developing Country Debt and the World Economy* (Chicago: University of Chicago Press, 1988); Peter L. Berger and Michael Hsiao, *In Search of East Asian Development Model* (New Brunswick, N.J.: Transaction Books, 1988); Hans H. Indorf and Patrick M. Mayerchak, *Linkage or Bondage: U.S. Economic Relations with the ASEAN Region* (Westport, Conn.: Greenwood, 1989), 1–17; Frederick C. Deyo, ed., *The Political Economy of the New Asian Industrialism* (Ithaca: Cornell University Press, 1987), Roy Kim, ed., *New Tides in the Pacific: Pacific Basin Cooperation in the Big Four (Japan, PRC, USA, and USSR)* (Westport, Conn.: Greenwood, 1987); Michael T. Skully, *ASEAN Financial Cooperation: Developments in Banking, Finance, and Insurance* (New York: St. Martin's, 1985); *The Pacific Guide* (Saffron Walden, England: World of Information, 1987); Walter Galenson, ed., *Foreign Trade and Investment: Economic Growth in the Newly Industrialized Asian Countries* (Madison: University of Wisconsin Press, 1985).
45. Nijolas R. Lardy, *China's Entry into the World Economy* (Washington, D.C.: University Press of America; New York: Asia Society, 1987). Also see Jonathan R. Woetzel, *China's Economic Opening to the Outside World* (New York: Praeger, 1989), 23–49; E. E. Bauer, *China Takes Off: Technology Transfer and Modernization* (Seattle: University of Washington Press, 1986); James T. H. Tsao, *China's Development Strategies and Foreign Trade* (Lexington, Mass.: Lexington Books-D.C. Heath, 1987).
46. Van Horn's book is the best study on this complex topic, and his material on existing convoluted trade regulations and how to cope with them is clear and highly useful.

SIX

Advertising Management Cases

INTRODUCTION

In the following cases, key advertising management issues are identified. The problems in these cases are typical of the type advertising managers at business magazines and their associates must address, almost on a daily basis, in a careful and thoughtful manner.

All of these cases, which are based on actual events, were designed specifically to identify a problem and to stimulate class discussions *rather* than to illustrate either effective or ineffective handling of an advertising management situation. All of the names, addresses, locations, financial and marketing data, companies, publications, dates, etc., used in *all* of the following cases are fictional. *No* reference to any living or dead person is intended. This procedure was followed to protect the identity of the individuals, companies, and publications researched by the author.

The *Journal of Industrial Accident Prevention* (A)

The *Journal of Industrial Accident Prevention* (JIAP) was a business magazine with a successful history and a bleak future. In 1990 it was the number seven magazine (or book) in a field of eight titles. The following table outlines its position in this rather aggressive market niche; all of these periodicals were issued on a "controlled free" circulation basis.

Safety and Accident Prevention Periodicals: 1990

			Advertising			
Rank	Title	Frequency (Issues per Year)	Revenues (in millions of dollars)	Pages	CPM	Circulation
1	Agusto's Safety Digest	27	$50,493	4,628	$77.00	141,690
2	Fire Safety	52	27,477	2,744	101.15	92,978
3	Noren's Hygiene Directory	18	24,314	2,925	72.20	115,121
4	Hazards	12	10,429	1,488	120.30	58,271
5	Safety Equipment Monthly	12	10,347	1,400	60.57	122,010
6	Safety World	14	9,534	1,743	147.71	37,032
7	Journal of Industrial Accident Prevention	12	6,062	1,439	223.10	18,883
8	National Safety	12	4,806	668	70.64	101,802

JIAP was founded in 1948 in Pittsburgh, Pennsylvania, by Billy North, a recently discharged veteran of the United States Army Air Corps. Prior to his induction in 1941, North was an advertising sales manager for the old *Norden Business Systems* magazine. During World War II, North was a captain, and he was assigned to a wing of B-17 bombers as a flight safety officer at a variety of air fields in England. He developed an expertise in accident prevention.

When he returned to civilian life, North decided to launch JIAP. He was able to borrow $8,900 from Jerry May and $4,000 from Lou Limmer, friends from the Air Corps.

After many difficult years, JIAP was finally in the black in 1947, and North repaid all of his loans with interest in June 1950. Circulation was increasing at a steady 7 to 9 percent rate in the 1950s, and advertising revenues climbed an average of 5 percent per year throughout that decade.

The secret of JIAP's success was in the skilled sales force North created in the late 1940s. He hired only veterans, preferably former pilots with extensive air combat or Marines with battlefield experiences, who were aggressive individuals keenly interested in making high sales commissions. At that time the advertising agencies were filled with former service personnel; so North's sales force had a lot in common with the very people who were developing print campaigns and making decisions regarding which business periodicals would be selected.

By the late 1950s, this sales force was considered to be a rather successful one in this niche, and JIAP rose to the number three book in 1958. North fully expected to see it overtake *Fire Safety*, a feisty periodical then ranked number two.

However, in the 1960s the world seemed to be in disarray. The advertising agencies were filled with young college graduates who were not impressed with World War II war heroes who told long battle stories about their exploits. New publications about various U.S. governmental safety policies and related procedures appeared on the market, and JIAP's sales revenues increased at a modest 2 to 3 percent rate between 1963 and 1974. In 1975 JIAP sustained a staggering 6.1 percent drop in ad pages, a trend that continued well into 1976. By 1977 JIAP posted a small profit, and in 1978 North considered selling JIAP to a West German magazine company. Just before a deal was made, he backed out. He felt that he and his sales associates could turn around JIAP's bleak financial outlook. After all, he mused, "We won the war in 1945, and we certainly can get back on the track with JIAP."

For most of the 1980s, the "greed decade," JIAP posted small to respectable profits. Yet in October 1987 another drop in advertising pages took place. The following two years were also dismal, with declines of 4.1 percent in 1988 and 3.7 percent in 1989.

While many people approached the 1990s with optimism, JIAP's sales executives were a tired group of people in 1990. As of January 1990, twenty-one of the company's thirty-one salespeople were World War II vets who had been with North since the 1940s; and another eight saw aerial combat in the Korean War and joined the magazine in the mid-1950s. Only two of the sales executives were under the age of forty, and both of them were the grandchildren of long-time sales executives.

By 1 June 1990, JIAP had slipped to a dismal seventh ranking in its field; between January and May 1990, financial losses were running at $15,600 per month; and the periodical's market share was quickly eroding, prompting fears that it might slip into dead last place.

On 6 June 1990, North called a meeting of his entire sales force. He reviewed the data found in the table listed above, and he created two subcommittees to evaluate JIAP's current position and to develop a plan to save the publication.

The first subcommittee was chaired by Bob Kennedy, the vice-president of sales management; Kennedy had been a pilot in the Pacific during World War II. He was joined by Fritz Henrich, Max Alvis, Johnny Logan, and Tim Tolman.

The other subcommittee was slightly larger, and Dave Koslo, the company's best sales executive, was in charge. Woodie Held, Eddie Dyer, Joe Neale, Gary Neibauer, Bernie Allen, Bob Allen (two cousins), and Curry Foley also served.

North told them that "we need a big new push to recapture our lost position. Report back on 6 August 1990 with your recommendations."

The *Journal of Industrial Accident Prevention* (B)

Kennedy's subcommittee convened every morning at 9:00 (and ended promptly at 12:30) for three weeks, evaluating all aspects of

JIAP's operation. After some rather lengthy discussions that at times bordered on mayhem, they reached the following conclusions.

First, the media kit needed to be overhauled; it was last revised in 1971. Second, more cold calls needed to be made on the major advertising agencies. They just barely agreed that a sales-call quota system needed to be created and enforced. Third, Logan convinced Kennedy that the company needed to spend more money to cultivate potential and retain existing clients. They discussed an interesting variety of options, including participating in more golf outings and buying more season football, hockey, and baseball tickets for Pittsburgh's local teams. "All of us love the Steelers, and our clients want to see some games," Logan repeated endlessly during the stalemated discussions.

Kennedy also outlined in great detail the single advertising sponsor system developed by the *Journal of Contact Lens*. "Doug Flynn at *Contact Lens* created a single advertising sponsor plan that increased color ad pages by 11.8 percent in the first three months of 1990." Apparently Flynn was able to sell twenty four-color bleed pages to the Florence Optical Company, the nation's leading manufacturer of contact lenses and solutions, in the 24 April 1990 issue. "If that old sea dog can do it, we can."

This subcommittee voted unanimously to accept Kennedy's recommendations. Tolman was asked to write the subcommittee's report.

Koslo was in charge of the "other team"; and unlike Kennedy he eschewed meetings. "Either you work or you meet. I work." However, the Allens insisted that the subcommittee had to be convened so that they could review recent data about JIAP and the entire safety industry.

At the first meeting, Bernie Allen prepared an analysis of JIAP's seven competitors, including detailed material on CPM (cost per thousand), ad pages, number of color ad pages, circulation data, etc. This material was circulated to all subcommittee members. Bernie also outlined the 1989 Butka and Busse report on the safety industry. Butka and Busse was the nation's oldest business magazine marketing research company.

Bernie Allen recommended that JIAP consider a specialized

target marketing sales campaign "designed to sell 'advertorials' to companies manufacturing safety products." Allen pointed out that no safety periodical had adopted such a strategy. However, other business periodicals in a variety of markets had been rather successful with "advertorials."

"Advertorials" were in reality "special advertising supplements" or "special advertiser sections." The typical "advertorial" had a polished text and numerous four-color photographs. " 'Advertorials' can help us attract new advertisers and possibly convince existing advertisers to increase their purchases of [ad] space." Koslo seemed to like this idea, "especially if we could run one every three issues."

At the end of their deliberations, the Koslo team decided "to recommend an aggressive campaign to target the nation's fifteen leading safety manufacturing corporations and sell them on the idea of supporting advertorials in JIAP."

The *Journal of Industrial Accident Prevention* (C)

At the August 6 meeting, Billy North asked Kennedy to make a presentation outlining the recommendations of his committee. When Kennedy finished North thanked him for his thoughtful report, "which is filled with some great ideas that certainly should help us."

Koslo briefed the sales group about his team's plans.

North then told everyone that he would open the floor to questions before "we decide which plan to adopt." Members of the group asked a series of pithy questions; yet in the end the veteran sales executives seemed to be almost evenly divided between those who favored the Kennedy "hard sell" approach versus the Koslo "sophisticated target marketing" approach.

North asked Andy Carey, the youngest sales executive and the grandson of Johnny Logan, what he thought about the two plans. Carey had been with the company for four years, and he had impressed the seasoned sales execs with his thoughtful manner and ability to market JIAP to coal mine safety equipment manufacturers.

Carey was reluctant to enter into the fray since he did not want to alienate his grandfather; but North pushed him to "tell us what you think, Andy. You know all about marketing, since you studied it in college."

After trying to avoid what Andy knew would be anything but a tempting invitation, Carey reluctantly reviewed the key issues raised by the Kennedy-Koslo teams.

Carey maintained that the purpose of an effective marketing strategy was to satisfy the needs of a customer. "Hard selling is a clear indication that the customer really does not want or need what you are trying to sell." He told those present about a sales seminar he attended the previous August at the famous Magazine Institute conference in San Francisco. At the conference he listened to a "space sales pro outline his ideas on selling more ad pages."

"This fellow thought that effective selling was an 'attitude,' and that you had to manipulate the mind of the ad agency executive so that he or she would buy more space from you every month. He said we should use 'overkill' if necessary to engulf the potential client; we needed to think 'selling' twenty-four hours a day. He was rather honest with us, and he informed the audience that some of his best selling strategies materialized during his frequent vacations in Florida when he sat on a deserted beach at seven in the morning quietly drinking a bottle of beer."

The bottom line, according to this space pro, was to develop a gimmick, a new approach to capture the imagination of the agency people. "If you were trying to make a sales pitch to an agency representing an automobile replacement parts company, and you wanted them to buy three four-color ad pages this month instead of their usual one black and white page, rent twenty vans and circle the agency's building with them. Put signs on each van with your book's name and your 'big sales idea' or your 'sales slogan' on each vehicle. Push these agency people to remember your magazine's name. Send them special cards for birthdays, the fourth of July, Groundhog Day, or anything else. Fax them messages; send singing clowns to thank them for their interest in your company. Send flowers to all of the secretaries. Hire a high school band and entertain the employees when they enter or leave their office building. If need be make up anniversaries and send them cakes.

Do not let them forget you! Keep your name in front of them all of the time."

Carey rejected this approach; and he also maintained that although the "old boy" sports network of golf outings, football games, etc., has a place in society, it would be foolish "to believe that these events will convince agency people, especially those individuals who are not that interested in professional or recreational sports, that our magazine deserves their support. All this does, in reality, is fill the coffers of the people who own the teams. It also reinforces the belief within the advertising agency world that we are nothing more than 'tired old people' clinging onto promotions, rather than the substance of our periodical's editorial content, to sell space."

As for the notion that single sponsor issues might be the salvation of the magazine, Carey also rejected this approach. "Too many people who read single sponsor magazines think that the periodical's editorial staff prepared the advertorial. There is an implied relationship between our editorial and their advertising clutter. This makes us responsible, at least to the average reader, for what is 'said' in the ads, as if we endorse the product. I do not believe that this approach has merit. In fact, single sponsor issues degrade the importance and significance of what this business magazine stands for, which is the importance of *industrial safety* and not a *particular industry safety manufacturer* in the workplace."

As for advertorials, consumer magazines have been telling "agency people for decades that business publications are 'whores' who use editorial copy to hype a new product released by Company X *only* because Company X bought eight ad pages. This false image of our industry exists; and if we play the cheap advertorial game, we will lose our credibility. The top of the line consumer periodicals can afford to run advertorials because they have a strong image; business publications lack this type of reader acceptance, because of the reasons I just mentioned. Advertorials might be a necessary evil; but we do not need them."

Carey finished with an interesting summation. "I believe that it is imperative that we address the following questions. Should we develop a more effective marketing 'reach' for our customers through the use of in-store related promotions? Should we package some of our best safety articles into books that could be sold or given away by our customers? Should we develop a series of innovative safety videocassettes or CD-ROMs? Must we change the way we view the needs of the customer and offer 'extras' such as point-of-purchase displays?"

North and all those present were impressed with Carey's eloquent presentation. North asked Carey what he would do to correct JIAP's drift.

What recommendations do you believe Carey should make?

THE MARKETING MANAGEMENT PROCESS

The Oxbridge Business Journal

The Oxbridge Business School was established in 1903 with a $5 million gift from the William Bruce Corporation, then the nation's leading manufacturer of paints and related products. Oxbridge was not the country's first business school; but it quickly became the largest and best graduate school training general business leaders.

The business school's relationship with the university's other undergraduate, graduate, and professional schools was at best strained. Many influential professors in the faculty of arts and sciences believed that "business trade school training was best left to the entrepreneurial types on Madison Avenue or on Wall Street."

The typical U.S. university was created in the eighteenth century to educate ministers and teachers, not "tradesmen." So when the business school began to expand after World War I, and the first group of instructors were presented for tenure, loud cries of unrest were heard up and down Arthur Avenue in the Bronx, the location of the college's faculty club. "These are not scholars; these people do not understand scholarship and research."

Nevertheless, while the business school did obtain tenure for its instructors, this vicious debate left Francis Ferrell (the dean) and his associates deeply concerned about the rancor. Business studies were indeed a new academic discipline in the United States, lacking the formal academic trappings long associated with liberal arts and science departments. In addition there was no scholarly association or scholarly journal servicing business school professors; and, as with anything new in the academic community, strenuous efforts were needed to disprove the critics.

To address this severe problem, Ferrell asked William Devery (the assistant dean of instruction) to "create a first-rate scholarly journal that will publish serious research findings in accounting, finance, and managerial sciences." Devery launched the journal in 1929, hardly an ideal time to begin a questionable business venture. Fortunately, the business school provided the journal with a significant amount of financial support, including free space, an adequate supply of secretarial and research staff, and superb editors and publishers (who were granted release time from teaching and research).

Devery was a patient man, and he was well aware of the rigorous nature of scholarly pursuits since he had been initially trained as an economic historian at Oxbridge. Devery was able to create a viable editorial board, and the quarterly quickly became the preeminent business journal in the United States.

In 1941 Devery retired, and, in the next forty years, a series of outstanding editors led the journal to new heights. Some of the more prominent ones included William Donovan (1941–1945), Edward Huggins (1949–1960), and the legendary Arthur Lennox Jones (1972–1981).

Efforts were made in the late 1940s to broaden the readership base of the review. So a major effort was made to reposition the magazine as "must reading" for all intelligent managers, not just for business school professors. By the early 1950s, this strategy paid off, and the journal was viewed as the nation's most important business periodical. Aside from an impressive collection of subscribers, the various editors made sure that major business leaders, usually presidents of the country's leading banks and large manufacturing companies, contributed pithy articles. This policy reassured the readership that the "ivory tower" types did not dominate the editorial content of the publication.

Each year the journal generated a surplus of funds, which the business school utilized to support its extensive research activities. All concerned parties seemed eminently pleased with this arrangement.

However, random readership surveys in the 1980s (1982 and

1985) revealed the unsettling fact that far too many business leaders purchased the journal as a "coffee table" book; few of them actually read it. These findings triggered concern about the long-term future of this "cash cow." This issue was carefully monitored; and when circulation, advertising revenues, and advertising pages dropped significantly in 1988 and 1989, the editorial board (comprised of fifteen senior members of the business school's faculty) responded.

At the quarterly business meeting of the editorial board, Paul Minner (the editor) was asked for his suggestions to address this serious problem. He outlined the steps he believed were needed to stop the decline. The primary one, according to Minner, was to hire a first-rate advertising manager. "After all Aaron Robinson [the current director of advertising] has been ill for the last seven months, and it appears that he will not be able to rejoin the journal. We need a full-time director able to develop effective ties with the nation's advertising agencies."

Clarence Huber (the senior member of the journal's editorial board) disagreed. "This is a stodgy journal with little editorial or artistic appeal to the readers. We need to redesign it and change our editorial direction." Other members of the board discussed a myriad of would-be solutions, including cutting the advertising rate card, increasing circulation, cutting the circulation base to make the readership's demographics more appealing to Madison Avenue's number crunchers (many of whom were trained at Oxbridge), raise the subscription price, curtail the reduced subscription policy, and, lastly, bring in new editorial and publishing leadership.

If you were a member of the editorial board, would you follow the suggestion of the editor and bring in a new advertising director to "stop the hemorrhaging"?

Green's Book News

Green's Book News was the oldest, most prestigious weekly business magazine servicing the eclectic book industry in the United States. It was one of seventeen business periodicals owned by the

Grant Publishing Company of Philadelphia. Other Grant magazines covered the medical-healthcare, sports management, interior design, and direct marketing fields.

As of 30 January 1990 *Green's Book News* had two viable competitors. The following table outlines the positions of these weekly paid subscription publications at the end of 1989.

The Book Trade Business Periodical Industry in the United States

Rank	Title	Revenues (in millions of dollars)		Total	CPM	Circulation
		Advertising	Subscription			
1	Green's Book News	$11,014	$4,043	$15,047	$48.48	95,700
2	National Book Journal	6,973	1,028	8,001	178.06	50,830
3	Book Industry Times	4,710	645	5,354	79.07	76,073

In 1989 the book industry in the United States sustained heavy losses. Returns of high-priced hardcover books set records, as did mass market trade paperbacks. Profit margins at almost every U.S. publisher declined dramatically, and red ink was evident at far too many houses. Book publishers finally began to confront the hidden problem of managerial and editorial incompetence.

There were other major changes. The bottom line dictated sharp reductions in book advertising campaigns, almost all of which was spent in the three publications listed above.

By February 1990 Marie Martin, the director of advertising at *Green's*, began to feel pressure from the publisher to "stimulate some additional sales revenues. We are 10.4 percent behind last year's totals." Martin reviewed the list of advertisers who had purchased space in the last six months, and she began to call on the key advertising agencies who developed ads for book clients to ascertain what could be done to "prime the advertising pump."

She was told that book unit sales were off and advertising budgets had been reduced significantly. The prognosis for 1990 and 1991 was dismal at best. So it was not likely that these book companies, many of which were apparently under siege, would become generous with their already-slashed ad budgets.

Martin called a meeting of her sales staff to review the industry's economic climate and to develop an effective marketing campaign. Roberta Santorini suggested that the magazine consider approaching agencies representing companies selling products and services to the book publishing industry to determine if any of these firms might want to advertise in *Green's*. The magazine had a long-standing policy to accept display advertisements only from book companies; classified ads could be placed by manufacturers, head hunters, etc., in the back of the magazine.

Roberta maintained that "editors, publishers, and authors in the book industry purchase millions of dollars worth of supplies and products each year. Just think how much money these people spent in 1989 on fax machines, computers, messenger services, etc. We should be allowed to approach the agencies representing these manufacturers and convince them that the best way to position their products in the book industry would be with four color ads in *Green's*."

Santorini also reminded those present that "Grant's other sixteen periodicals report on many important fields. We should try to develop some synergy with them. Readers of these magazines certainly purchase books; so why not try to develop an advertising campaign for book publishers so that they could advertise their latest, or backlist, books in these Grant publications? Another option would be to create a carefully designed card deck system for readers of these magazines. This extra service should be of interest to book publishers in their quest to maximize sales."

Judith Sloan disagreed. "*Green's* is the number one book industry magazine; and we must maintain this position. If we consent to allow this dangerous abandonment of our principles and run nonbook advertisements, our readers will question our integrity. After all we are perceived to be a 'literary' journal reporting on the world that transmits culture and ideas to our citizens. We must maintain our image."

If you were Marie Martin, what would you do?

ADVERTISING MANAGEMENT STRATEGY

The Stein Publishing Company (A)

The Stein Publishing Company was a diversified United States-based global corporation active in books, magazines (consumer and business), electronic databases and CD-ROM products, and miscellaneous publishing (annuals, directories, etc). A review of its 1990 annual report revealed the size and significance of this corporation. All of the following figures are in United States dollars.

The Stein Publishing Company: Financial Highlights 1990 (in thousands of dollars except share data)

For the Year	1990	1989	Percent Change
Operating Revenue	$2,334,839	$2,149,766	+9
Operating Profit	417,943	302,053	+38
New Income	210,406	141,537	+49
Net Income per Share	2.78	1.80	+54
Dividends per Share	.76	.64	+19
Return on Stockholders' Investment	18.4%	12.90	—
Capital Expenditures	213,596	191,895	+11
Common Stock Price Range:			
High	43.00	49.76	—
Low	33.75	28.38	—
Close	37.88	39.50	—
At Year End Stockholders' Investment	1,188,480	1,094,943	+9
Total Assets	2,941,582	2,758,395	+7
Shares Outstanding	74,826,300	76,289,349	-2

A careful analysis of this corporation's financial documents indicated that its track record for the last ten years, 1981–1990, was quite impressive.

The Stein Publishing Company: Operating Revenues, Profits and Net Income, 1981–1990 (in millions of dollars)

Year	Revenues	Profits	Net Income
1990	$2,335	$417.9	$210.4
1989	2,149	302.1	141.5
1988	2,022	281.3	292.9
1987	1,931	241.4	123.8
1986	1,790	188.5	103.1
1985	1,584	145.7	69.3
1984	1,428	23.3	23.9
1983	1,403	138.3	89.1
1982	1,231	136.9	78.0
1981	1,103	139.8	70.1

In 1990 Stein Publishing had four publishing units. The following table reveals the strength of the book and periodical divisions and the obvious weakness of its miscellaneous publishing operations.

The Stein Publishing Company: Operating Results, 1981–1990 (in thousands of dollars)

Year	Books	Periodicals	Electronic Databases and CD-ROMs	Miscellaneous Publishing
1990	$505,729	$1,561,717	$462,550	$(195,157)
1989	485,276	1,465,668	385,023	(186,201)
1988	466,231	1,355,486	378,181	(178,285)
1987	384,723	1,350,543	384,723	(172,755)
1986	322,082	1,270,532	322,082	(158,246)
1985	260,083	1,134,826	260,083	(153,246)
1984	205,991	1,038,363	205,991	(132,856)
1983	154,086	1,020,522	154,086	(131,552)
1982	125,963	920,664	125,963	(148,963)
1981	105,537	853,385	105,537	(161,280)

The following table outlines the operating profits generated by these four publishing units.

The Stein Publishing Company: Operating Profits, 1988–1990 (in thousands of dollars)

Year	Books	Periodicals	Electronic Databases and CD-ROMs	Miscellaneous Publishing
1990	$77,754	$263,734	$99,154	$(22,699)
1989	62,858	192,001	73,009	(25,815)
1988	65,537	200,297	33,126	(17,650)

The following table outlines Stein's capital expenditures for 1988 through 1990.

The Stein Publishing Company: Capital Expenditures, 1988–1990 (in thousands of dollars)

Year	Books	Periodicals	Electronic Databases and CD-ROMs	Miscellaneous Publishing
1990	$14,449	$126,022	$73,125	$80,000
1989	41,116	99,477	51,303	73,000
1988	13,802	92,327	41,597	60,000

In spite of certain financial reverses posted by the miscellaneous publishing unit, overall this is an incredibly stable corporation generating impressive profits over a ten-year period.

The Stein Publishing Company (B)

Veston G. "Bunky" Stewart was the senior vice president for marketing and advertising at the Stein Publishing Company. He was in charge of the periodical division, which included both consumer and business magazines.

For some time Stewart was concerned about the shrinking operating revenue base of his business magazines, which had posted six straight years of declines. On 3 July 1990, Anthony L. Collins, the president of the company, instructed Stewart that he had to address this vexing problem and make a presentation and recommendation(s) at the 30 September 1990 meeting of the company's board of directors. "Tell us about the current position of Stein's business magazines and what prudent steps we should consider to correct this decline."

In preparation for this meeting, Stewart reviewed a number of financial documents, including the following table.

The Stein Publishing Company: Operating Revenues for the Periodicals Division, 1981–1990 (in millions of dollars)

Year	Consumer Magazines	Percent of Operating Revenues	Business Magazines	Percent of Operating Revenues
1990	$1,180	75.5	$381	24.5
1989	1,112	75.9	354	24.1
1988	1,012	74.6	344	25.4
1987	1,002	74.2	348	25.8
1986	929	73.1	341	26.9
1985	809	71.3	326	28.7
1984	723	69.7	316	30.3
1983	722	70.7	298	29.3
1982	661	71.8	260	28.2
1981	621	72.8	232	27.2

Clearly the operating profits generated by consumer magazines easily outdistanced Stein's business titles, which indicated that the company's return on investment in business magazines was not impressive. Equally unsettling was the fact that the corporation was investing significantly more money into capital expenditures for business publications than for its consumer titles. The following table outlines these trends.

The Stein Publishing Company: Operating Profits and Capital Expenditures, 1981–1990

| | Consumer Magazines | | Business Magazines | |
Year	Percent of Total Operating Profits	Percent of Total Capital Expenditures	Percent of Total Operating Profits	Percent of Total Capital Expenditures
1990	83	21	17	79
1989	81	21	19	79
1988	80	23	20	77
1987	78	24	12	76
1986	73	23	27	77
1985	71	26	29	74
1984	68	28	32	72
1983	70	27	30	73
1982	72	25	28	75
1981	73	28	27	72

For the last four years, Stein had been active in acquiring both consumer and business titles. So the total number of Stein's magazines varied yearly, as did the ratio of consumer to business titles. By 30 June 1990 Stein owned and operated twenty-nine business and ten consumer magazines in the United States.

Stewart decided to evaluate the business magazines using the Boston Consulting Group's (BCG) market share matrix.

Star	Question Mark
Cash Cow	Dog

So he placed Stein's twenty-nine periodicals into the following matrix.

Star	Question Mark
U.S. Machine Shop	*Life Insurance Agent*
Monthly Maritime News	*Diesel New York Glass Digest*
Global Commerce Reporter	*High Tech Ceramics*
	Natural Gas Journal
	U.S. Upholstery News
	American Fire Protection
	Journal of Fire Safety
Cash Cow	**Dog**
Tax Monthly Review	*Education Monthly*
Journal of Tax Management	*Dairy Farm Monthly*
American Grain Industry	*Ewen's Candy News*
New York Engineering	*Vending Machine Digest*
East Coast Engineering	*Chemical Industry Times*
Concrete Monthly	*American Camps*
	Stadium Management
	Auditorium Management
	Marina Management News
	Tire Dealer Management
	Gas Station Management
	Professional Designer

Stewart decided to review a computer print-out outlining the CPM, circulation, and advertising revenues and pages for all of Stein's business magazine competitors. He then wondered if the "dogs" could be helped? Could they sell enough advertising to improve their profits?

After a substantial analysis, Stewart came to the sad conclusion that "we face a flat or declining advertising market in the United States in the next few years. Our consumer titles are clearly outpacing our business ones in terms of profits; and I believe that the time has come for us to sell our entire stable of twenty-nine business magazines. We should use the funds derived from this sale to support our efforts in the electronic database and CD-ROM market. Business magazines have a place, an important one, in our society. Stein Publishing, on the other hand, will be better off by withdrawing from this market."

Do you believe that Stewart's recommendation was prudent?

MARKETING RESEARCH

U.S. Wine

U.S. Wine was established in 1897 by Roy Joiner. Originally a newsletter catering to the needs of small bars and liquor stores in California and Nevada, in 1912 the newsletter's format was changed to a weekly business magazines servicing the entire west coast. Advertisement revenue grew 400 percent between 1912 and 1918, and the book became a "controlled free" periodical in late December 1918.

Ownership of the magazine passed to Joiner's son Haydel in 1919. During Prohibition the periodical ceased operation, and Haydel moved to Cleveland, Ohio, where he obtained a marketing position with Hamilton and Jeffcoat (H & J), the nation's leading manufacturer of consumer soap and food products. Haydel demonstrated a keen grasp of the consumer advertising market, and he rose through the ranks quickly, emerging as a regional sales manager by 1931.

When Prohibition ended during the administration of Franklin D. Roosevelt, Haydel made the difficult decision to leave H & J and bring back *U.S. Wine.* Haydel was unquestionably on a fast track with H & J; yet he loved the business magazine industry, and his strong entrepreneurial spirit convinced him that he could make more money managing his own product "rather than making the H & J stockholders a stack of money."

Under Haydel's careful stewardship, *U.S. Wine* became the number one book in a crowded field of over thirty periodicals. It remained a "controlled free" publication, and its annual advertising revenues grew at an impressive 12.5 percent rate in the 1940s, a pace that was exceeded in the 1950s (+13.7 percent) and the 1960s (+12.8 percent).

Haydel died in 1970, and his two children, Ferguson and Anne, assumed the reigns of power. Ferguson died in an automobile accident in 1972; and Anne, then fifty-two years old, became president and chief operating officer. Anne was a gifted manager, and she pushed *U.S. Wine* into the number one book, with a sizable market share by 1980.

The Wine Periodical Industry in the United States: 1980

Ranking	Title	Advertising Revenues (in millions of dollars)	Advertising	Average CPM	Circulation
1	U.S. Wine	$34,300	6,082	$41.11	137,189
2	Wine Media	29,937	3,742	65.82	121,537
3	Wine Bulletin	17,378	3,165	40.03	137,191
4	Spirits Wine	15,934	2,993	88.55	60,121
5	Wine Business	12,802	1,588	76.84	88,481

During the early to mid-1980s, the wine industry was revolutionized with the introduction of "wine coolers." The public seemed enchanted with this new product, and wine manufacturers rushed to capitalize on this new development with a significant advertising blitz. While the bulk of all advertising dollars went into television in 1985, over $130 million was spent on print campaigns. Business periodicals captured a 34 percent share of these expenditures.

Yet wine coolers quickly faded in popularity. *Advertising Age* reported in the 11 September 1989 issue that "significant sales declines in imports and wine coolers last year [1988] helped push down total wine industry volume sales 3 percent to 561.4 million gallons, a major drop from 581.3 million gallons in 1986."

Apparently America's thirst for wine peaked in 1985. Per capita consumption hovered at the 2.27 gallon mark in 1988, down from the 2.42 gallon record established in 1985. The prognosis for 1990 was hardly upbeat; *Advertising Age* predicted flat sales, with the possibility of a modest 2–3 percent decline in total sales if the economy sustained even a mild recession.

Advertisers responded to this downturn and curtailed ad placements. *U.S. Wine* sustained a 13 percent decline in ad revenues, and a 12 percent drop in pretax profits, in 1986. This problem was exacerbated by the general decline in advertising revenues in 1987, triggered by the October 1987 Wall Street stock market crash. *U.S. Wine*'s 1987 ad revenues were off an additional 11 percent; this was followed by declines in 1988 (-16.1 percent) and 1989 (-7.5 percent).

In January 1990 Anne stepped down as president, and she appointed her daughter Robin as the new president and CEO. Robin majored in marketing in college, and she was determined to recapture *U.S. Wine*'s lost advertising luster. She had extensive discussions with Curtis Simmons, the company's director of advertising sales. Together they evaluated the existing market and created a three-year strategic plan for *U.S. Wine*. They targeted the highly lucrative 43 million gallon "fortified or enriched wine" niche, which did not have a tradition of advertising in business magazines.

Fortified or enriched wines were sold in small pint glass containers for approximately $1.50 in skid row districts of inner cities; 1989 annual sales were estimated to be in the $500 to $510 million range. These wines were rather sweet with a high alcohol content, often reaching 18 to 20 percent. The alcohol content of normal table wines traditionally were significantly lower, generally in the 8 to 9 percent range. They were cheap and potent wines, providing a fast high. Some individuals were reported to consume up to one gallon of these fortified wines each day.

The major fortified wine brand names were rather exotic, reflecting the interests of the clientele: "Big Joe" (usually called "BJ" on the street), "Truck Stop" (generally referred to as "diesel"), "Frisco Pete" (its ribald street name cannot be mentioned in this case), "Gold Coast" (also known as "gold), and the ubiquitous "Greenpoint" ("greenie" to its legions of fans).

These highly profitable fortified wines were manufactured by the leading wine vintners in the United States, although all of these companies eschewed any public ties with their skid row products. These companies included San Remo, Oakland Wine, and Wines of Upland.

Robin and Simmons made sales presentations to all of the Madison Avenue advertising agencies that represented the major vintners; and Robin was able to convince these ad executives that a carefully orchestrated selective binding advertising campaign in *U.S. Wine* could open new markets for these wines in ninety major cities with large concentrations of inner-city convenience and liquor stores that currently did not stock the enriched wines. Robin's market survey indicated that these wines should be able to increase unit sales between 13.2 and 15.2 percent by October 1990. She sold over one hundred ad pages covering the period March–October 1990; and she delivered on her pledge. By 1 November 1990 all of the wine companies that participated in this advertising campaign posted sharp increases in unit pint sales in the seven key markets, which included San Francisco, Los Angeles, Chicago, Boston, New York, and Miami. The bottom line at *U.S. Wine* was also enhanced; ad revenues were up a steady 11.8 percent between March and October 1990.

In February 1990 a Baptist minister in San Francisco began a campaign against the sale of these cheap wines in inner cities. Television and consumer news weeklies highlighted this movement, and the nation's various alcoholic rehabilitation organizations gave their support. The leading professional marketing organizations castigated publicly the sale "of products designed to enslave citizens in a hopeless web of despair."

By June 1990 the president of the United States attacked the sale of fortified wines. "These wines have a horrible impact on the nation's homeless, and I urge the U.S. business community to cease the manufacture and sale of this dangerous product."

During the company's annual sales meeting, Anne asked why *U.S. Wine* decided to "capitalize on the misery of countless millions of unfortunate people by initiating this demonic [advertising] campaign. Profits generated through the misery of women and children cannot be justified. I am embarrassed that *U.S. Wine* is involved in this cancer." She recommended that the magazine cease immediately the targeting and printing of ads for fortified wines.

What should Robin do?

ANALYZING MARKET OPPORTUNITIES

The Mall

The Mall was a controlled circulation weekly business magazine covering the nation's ubiquitous shopping malls and shopping centers. In early 1990 this periodical had three principal rivals. The following table outlines the advertising revenue situation at these publications.

Shopping Center Business Publications in 1989

Rank	Title	Frequency	Advertising Revenues ($1,000)	Pages	CPM	Circulation
1	U.S. Malls	52	$19,784	2,504	$104.02	75,940
2	Shopping Mall Weekly News	52	9,500	2,800	82.75	41,000
3	Mall Reports	52	5,597	819	79.87	85,545
4	The Mall	52	4,970	1,597	79.52	39,139

The Mall had been running a distant fourth in a four book market since 1985, and, with the projected decline in advertising revenues in the 1990s for the U.S. business magazine industry, Herman Thomas "Tommy" Davis, the owner of *The Mall*, decided that something must be done to reverse this negative trend. So he decided to fire John Kruk, the periodical's long time Director of Advertising and Sales. "It was time for a change. Johnny had worked for us for twenty-three years, and he was like my brother; but business is business. He had to go."

After several weeks of searching for a successor, Davis hired George Lee Anderson. For the past ten years, Anderson had been involved with advertising sales at *The Cincinnati Soap Journal*, one of the nation's best and most lucrative business periodicals. Anderson was a seasoned professional in the area of advertising; yet he was not familiar with *The Mall*'s advertising niche.

Anderson spent the first two weeks on the job at *The Mall* reviewing the operations of the publication; and he was horrified at what he found. The magazine had experienced a dramatic decline in advertising revenues and pages in the last five years. The following chart outlines this trend.

Advertising Analysis: 1985–1989

Year	Advertising Revenues	Percent Change	Advertising Pages	Percent Change
1989	5,109	− 6.7	1,597	− 9.0
1988	5,451	− 2.7	1,740	− 8.4
1987	5,598	− 5.4	1,887	− 9.7
1986	5,900	− 8.0	2,070	− 13.0
1985	6,372	—	2,339	—

The Mall had sustained a total decline of $1.263 million in advertising revenues between 1985 and 1989 (off − 19.82 percent). Advertising pages dropped 742 pages (− 31.72 percent).

Anderson then reviewed the files of the seven principal sales executives at *The Mall*.

Sales Personnel: 1989

Name	Territory	Education	1989 Sales
Stone, Jeffrey G.	Missouri	High School	$415,000
Baumgartner, Ross	Illinois	High School	397,000
Fannin, Clifford	Ohio	High School	384,000
Darwin, Danny	Texas	High School	365,000
Kester, Richard	Kansas	Junior College	359,000
Pipgras, George	Iowa	High School	324,000
Orth, A.L.	Indiana	College	305,000

As he read through the sales personnel fines, Anderson noticed that while all seven averaged seventeen years sales experiences with business magazines, only one of them (Kester) had been with *The Mall* for more than three years. The magazine had a poor record in keeping talented sales representatives. The annual turnover rate in the sales department averaged fourteen percent between 1985–1989. Anderson found copies of the employment advertisements that his predecessor had placed in a variety of periodicals, mainly the two national advertising magazines, looking for new employees. The company had spent $40,000 between 1985 and 1989 advertising for new employees; he was not able to ascertain what the company had lost in terms of sales revenues, strained relations with existing or potential customers, and administrative time because of this needless revolving.

Anderson made it a point to interview all seven of the best sales representatives to ascertain why advertising sales had been declining and why the magazine had such an unreasonable turnover rate. In addition he combed through all of the business periodicals that covered the magazine, advertising, and related industries.

Anderson discovered that this was a group of moderately educated sales representatives who had worked at tiny to small periodicals before joining *The Mall*. Their sales commission averaged seven percent; there was no in-house sales training system, and the sales department's budget was totally inadequate even by small magazine standards. The company did not provide research support on potential clients, and the "best" sales executives were given territories only in the middle sector of the United States.

His analysis also turned up some critically important pieces of information about the magazine's competitors. *U.S. Malls*, the leading magazine in its niche, had started a FAX advertising service for its customers. *U.S. Malls* operated a broadcast FAX transmission network that had the capability to transmit thousands of FAX messages simultaneously. While FAX services were viewed with a healthy amount of skepticism in certain advertising circles and was yet to carve out a clearly defined market, it appeared that FAX services would eventually challenge many business magazines. The fact that the number one book in this niche had committed countless thousands of dollars to create this FAX system made Anderson worry about the fact that *The Mall* had not even discussed this possibility or developed any type of strategic planing operating unit.

Shopping Mall Weekly News, which was owned by the *Passeau Grouppe SA* from France, had announced a "value-added" option six months ago. This plan enabled *Shopping Mall Weekly News* to inform all of its advertisers about the following items: (1) how one advertiser's ad did in comparison with ads from competitors in the same issue, (2) general trends in the marketplace, (3) key statistical data on readers and the magazine, (4) detailed research about the magazine conducted by neutral outside parties, (5) the results of face-to-face and focus group research with readers of the magazine about their perception of the effectiveness of *Shopping Mall Weekly News,* (6) the impact of other forms of advertising on the advertiser's customers, and (7) eleven customized research programs available for all advertisers.

Three months ago *Shopping Mall Weekly Reports* announced the "implementation of its global marketing strategy for the 1990s. As of December 31, 1992, *Shopping Mall Weekly Reports* will have national versions dealing with the dynamic shopping mall industry in Europe. Foreign language versions will be launched covering the important German, Italian, Spanish, Dutch, French, Danish, and Greek markets. Separate English language editions will created for the disparate English, Scottish, and both Irish markets. This will enable U.S. advertisers of *Shopping Mall Weekly Reports* to begin selling goods and services in the important $4.5 trillion Western European market with its important 323 million consumers . . . As of January 1, 1994, regional editions will be available for the Latin American and North African market. Four specific versions for the Pacific Rim [Japan, Australia, South Korea, and Hong Kong] will go on stream no later than January 1, 1995 . . . These editions will allow our advertisers to participate in what has become a truly global marketplace . . . "

Another bit of timely information surfaced during Anderson's search. *Mall Reports,* another competitor, had just announced plans to "launch the most exciting selective binding program servicing the shopping center industry." "Selective binding" was a process whereby targeted audiences could receive "customized" versions of the periodical.

In general, target groups were selected based on income, location, or industrial classification. *Mall Reports* announced that their "unique" binding procedures and ink-jet printing processes were connected with their "sophisticated computer network" in such a manner that advertisers could target their ads to ten specific cohorts: (1) the largest malls (those with more than 500 stores), (2) large malls (250–499 stores), (3) medium sized malls (100–249 stores) (4) small malls (50–99 stores), (5) very small malls (under 49 stores), (6) specialty malls (e.g., a shopping center comprised only of antiques stores), (7) upper scale urban or suburban malls with certain types of stores (e.g. Bloomingdale's) with high predetermined annual sales, (8) malls servicing inner cities, (9) malls with the greatest sales potential in the next two years, and (10) the top twenty malls (in terms of "quality" stores and annual sales revenues) in the United States (regardless of location).

While the start-up costs associated with the creation and implementation of such a selective binding operation were certainly high, advertisers participating in this program would pay a premium. *Mall Reports* had announced that the CPM for this special selective binding program would be $103.00, slightly **under** the CPM for the number one book. Anderson assumed that *Mall Reports*'s creative costing of this selective binding option would enable it to capture a significantly larger market share.

As for the future, *The Mall* had no college recruitment program; there was no tuition remission program for sales representatives to attend college or register for seminars at the Magazine Institute's annual seminar; and there were no in-house training programs to develop inexperienced sales representatives. To complicate matters, the health care program offered by the company was at best "average;" the pension plan required ten years of uninterrupted service before an individual could become vested; and in reality no incentive existed for anyone to stay at *The Mall*, which explains why twelve sales representatives had joined competing periodicals in the last five years.

If you were Anderson, what systems or procedures would you initiate to increase advertising revenues and pages within the next twelve months?

PROMOTING PRODUCTS

Clinton Construction Products

Clinton Construction Products was the major Canadian construction business publication. It was started in 1955 by Patricia Donahue, daughter of the legendary Patrick "Jiggs" Donahue (who created, after World War II, a collection of twenty business publications, many with editorial and sales offices in London and Scotland). Under Pat's expert direction, *Clinton* quickly implemented an effective niche marketing campaign, and the pretax profits of this book in the 1970s generally hovered in the twenty-three to twenty-six percent range.

By late 1988 *Clinton* began to experience some downturn in its market share. Several newer and more aggressive periodicals had entered this market, and they were able to offer "appealing" advertising rates (in essence rate cutting) to several of the major Western Canadian manufacturers of building materials.

In March 1990 Pat decided it was time to hire a new Director of Advertising and Marketing, and, after several months of interviewing, she selected Joseph McDonald, formerly of the small but highly influential *Alberta Business Forms* magazine. McDonald reviewed *Clinton*'s market, and he recommended that Pat consider a "creative and aggressive advertising strategy designed specifically to remind Canadian advertising agency executives that *Clinton Construction Products* still held the number share in this niche."

Pat was convinced that this strategy would generate a great deal of interest in *Clinton*'s and shake up what had been a moribund advertising philosophy at the magazine.

McDonald, a creative individual, called on Padgett and Padgett, Toronto's leading business magazine advertising agency to design the campaign. After about three weeks of work, Padgett and Padgett presented their media strategy; Pat accepted it.

Four different full pages of advertisements would be purchased, three in the *Canadian Advertising Weekly* (Canada's leading business magazine servicing the advertising community) and one in the *Maple Leaf Ad Weekly* (a weekly publication with a smaller circulation base; but this rather trendy publication apparently was the emerging favorite among Canada's younger media buyers). The ad copy was bold. A sample of the first ad is reprinted below; all dollar figures are in Canadian dollars.

| | | | TOP | PURCHASE |
| | | TOTAL | MANAGEMENT | DECISION |
RANK	PERIODICAL	CPM	CPM	MAKERS CPM
1.	Clinton Construction Products	$44.16	$31.06	$32.98
2.	Canadian Builder	$47.71	$32.72	$36.22
3.	Dominion Contractor	$49.18	$34.59	$36.42
4.	Building Trends	$50.84	$34.96	$38.11
5.	Renovation News	$51.75	$35.35	$38.20

UNBEATABLE ADVERTISING POWER *CLINTON CONSTRUCTION PRODUCTS* IS NUMBER ONE IN CANADA!

Note: These figures were based on published rates for a four-color page as of February 24, 1990 in the Building Construction Publications listed above. For information about *Clinton's Construction Products,* call David Oldfield, Sales Manager, at 519-555-3800, ext. 401.

The first ad (depicted above) ran on July 14, 1990. The next day Jiggs called Pat to caution her about the "damage this ad has done to her magazine's fine reputation." Pat was concerned, and she demanded to know what was wrong with it.

Her father had made it a rule not to interfere in Pat's periodical; but he was candid in his assessment of the ad. "First of all, does bragging about CPM really sell ad pages? Second, you gave free advertising to your competitors. Remember, if you spell their names right, they profited from it. Third, if you really are number one, the ad community knows it. All this [ad] shows is an arrogance reminiscent of the people who run the athletic teams in this part of the world. Lastly, the 'I Am the Greatest' ad approach never has worked; so why should it help you. I think you 'shot yourself in the foot'."

Pat was crushed, and she told her father that she would think over his comments before another ad ran. The next morning she called McDonald, and she reviewed all of her father's salient points.

If you were Pat, what would you do?

SALES PROMOTIONS

The Morrison Publishing Company

The Morrison Publishing Company was the largest business magazine company in North America. They owned forty-four business periodicals and numerous directories. Their strategic plan was simple: to acquire existing publications, rather than starting new titles, with strong market shares and annual sales revenue increases in the fifteen to twenty percent range.

Morrison purchased *New York Restaurant Weekly*, a small, New York City based business magazine in 1985; this periodical covered the restaurant supply business. The periodical was owned by Terry and Tom McDermott, brothers well into their seventies who founded the publication in 1938. This magazine had no weekly competition in New York City, employed an editorial staff of three (including the two brothers), six secretaries, and a part-time clerk who handled the numerous advertising space sales that literally "came in over the transom since we did not have any sales executive calling on advertising agencies." Paid circulation for the unaudited publication had hovered near the 10,000 mark since 1953. Pretax profits were slim, but the brothers were frugal; and they were happy with their magazine and lifestyle.

Tom died in 1982, and Terry decided to continue publishing the magazine "as a living tribute to Tom's memory." However, Terry became ill, and, since he did not have any heir (Tom died a bachelor), he decided to sell the magazine to Morrison. "They made me a fair financial offer [reported to be in the $1.5 million range], and they insisted that I stay on and run the magazine as Publisher."

In 1986 the magazine moved into the Morrison Building on East 10th Street, and the *New York Restaurant Weekly* was quickly incorporated into the Morrison marketing strategy. In January 1988 Cindy Manuel was named Publisher of the magazine, and Terry was promoted to Publisher Emeritus.

On December 11, 1988, Larry Owen, the Group Vice President of Institutional Magazines at Morrison, announced that "Morrison has created the most exciting business magazine advertising network in the United States. As of February 1, 1989, twelve of Morrison's institutional periodicals will offer advertisers the possibility of taking advantage of our outstanding demographics to purchase quality advertising space in three or more periodicals at a significant savings." The following chart outlined some of the discounts available through this advertising network.

The Morrison Action Advertising Network: The Premium Plan

Number of Color Pages In Each Magazine in Each Year	Number of Magazines and Discounts							
	3	4	5	6	7	8	9	10
1 Each	2%	3%	4%	5%	6%	7%	8%	9%
2 Each	3%	4%	5%	6%	7%	8%	9%	10%
3 Each	4%	5%	6%	7%	8%	9%	10%	11%
4 Each	5%	6%	7%	8%	9%	10%	11%	12%
5 Each	6%	7%	8%	9%	10%	11%	12%	14%*
6 Each	7%	8%	9%	10%	11%	12%	14%	15%
7–10 Each	8%	9%	10%	11%	12%	14%	15%	16%
11–25 Each	9%	10%	11%	12%	14%	15%	16%	17%

*No discount of 13% will be offered.

The magazines in the institutional group of publications included: *New York Restaurant Weekly, U.S. Restaurant Business, Institutional Glass Digest, U.S. Giftware Weekly, Foundary Technology and Trends, Architecture Journal, North American Industrial Purchasing, The Furniture Weekly, U.S. Fishing, Industrial Concrete, College Bookstore Weekly,* and *Car Battery Monthly.*

During the monthly advertising sales meeting at *New York Restaurant Weekly,* Bob Veale (a three year veteran from Morrison's *Car Battery Monthly* who had been transferred to the restaurant title) complained that "this Premium Package will be difficult to sell because potential advertisers in the food industry have only two publications on this list. Will manufacturers of industrial stoves want to buy [advertising] space in a car or furniture periodical?"

Angel Torres, also new to the restaurant book, agreed. "The magazines in this group are so different that it makes no sense to announce a network that cannot deliver the right reader mix."

Owen interrupted the discussion, and announced that "there is nothing wrong with this audience. Just take a close look, not a superficial one, at the demographics; and you will ascertain that this is indeed a superb reader group. They are devoted to their particular industry and publication, and they peruse advertisements very carefully. The editorial content is impressive; after all three of them were just nominated for the Seward Prize [the business magazine's equivalent of the Pulitzer Prize]. Our own research indicated clearly that these readers are frequent travelers, have an average household income of $71,000, ninety-two percent are male, seventy percent attended college, eighty-one percent own homes with a market value in excess of $210,000 (as of 1987), and over eighty-five percent are involved in purchasing items for their company. These twelve publication have a combined readership of 500,000 with a reach of 1.75 million. On the average each reader spends seventy minutes reading each issue."

Do you believe that the creation of this advertising network was a prudent move?

Olivares Supermarket Digest

Jose Oquendo was Vice President of Sales and Marketing for *Olivares Supermarket Digest,* one of the nation's five largest business publications serving the important supermarket niche. Oquendo was a firm believer in keeping up with the latest demographic and advertising data to avoid being lulled into thinking that growth and profits were inevitable.

While his magazine covered all aspects of the supermarket business, between 1987 and 1989 his periodical had been very successful in attracting advertisements in the following six major product groups. (This statistical material originally appeared in *Advertising Age* on 13 November 1989, page 32.)

U.S. Supermarket Product Groups Advertising-to-Sales Ratios: 1989

Industry	Advertising Dollars As A Percent of Sales	Advertising Dollars As A Percent of Margin	Annual Growth Rate
Canned and Frozen Fruits and Vegetables	6.9%	17.1%	7.3%

U.S. Supermarket Product Groups Advertising-to-Sales Ratios: 1989

Industry	Advertising Dollars As A Percent of Sales	Advertising Dollars As A Percent of Margin	Annual Growth Rate
Dairy Products	4.7%	14.6%	9.9%
Groceries and Related Products	1.5%	10.7%	10.6%
Ice Cream and Frozen Desserts	6.9%	25.6%	16.6%
Pharmaceutical Preparations	6.8%	10.1%	9.8%
Prepared Meat Products	6.9%	21.0%	8.7%

While all six categories had been profitable for his magazine in the past, and the national marketing data indicated clearly that these six groups were expected to continue to invest heavily in advertising in 1990, the share held by *Olivares Supermarket Digest* had been declining. This concerned Oquendo since his advertising rates and CPM were the best in the industry. He pulled out his copy of *Schoendienst's Advertising Rates* book, and he reviewed the published advertising data for his magazine and his four chief competitors.

Supermarket Periodicals: Rankings As of October 12, 1990

Rank	Periodical	Frequency	Advertising Revenues ($1,000)	Pages	CPM
1	*Olivares Supermarket Digest*	52	$67,425	6,002	$74.34
2	*Market Weekly*	52	49,000	4,156	88.07
3	*U.S. Markets*	52	28,699	5,421	103.20
4	*Supermarket Systems*	52	25,212	2,252	77.06
5	*The Aker Report*	52	21,183	2,937	101.91

Oquendo discussed this matter with his sales representatives, and then he compared the published advertising rates for these five periodicals.

Supermarket Periodicals: Full Page Black and White And Color Advertising Rates As of October 23, 1990

Rank	Periodical	Black & White Number of Times			Color Standard Color Rates		
		One	Three	Six	One	Two	Match Colors
1	Olivares Supermarket Digest	$4850	4750	4640	750	1350	1500
2	Market Weekly	4980	4850	4660	780	1410	1510
3	U.S. Markets	4870	4770	4670	800	1500	1600
4	Supermarket System	5000	4900	4800	820	1640	1700
5	The Aker Report	4950	4870	4800	770	1400	1550

After some additional research, it became apparent that his competitors were cutting their rate cards on a selective basis. Oquendo made an appointment to see Danny Leon, the President of the magazine, to discuss strategies that *Olivares* could consider.

Both of them agreed that the following announcement would be released to the various advertising magazines with copies mailed to all of *Olivares*'s advertisers. "As of December 2, 1990, *Olivares Supermarket Digest* will abandon its traditional procedure of releasing a published rate card. The magazine will negotiate specific individual rates for all of their valued advertisers. *Olivares,* one of this nation's oldest business magazines, believes that this approach will maximize savings for its customers."

Oquendo knew that this was a bold move, one that could help the magazine regain its top position among its competitors; yet he was well aware of the fact that this was a gamble that could fail since some potential advertisers would look only at the bottom line and eschew interest in the periodical's editorial quality and overall contribution to the supermarket industry.

Do you believe that Oquendo and Leon made the correct decision?

SALES MANAGEMENT

Carew's Hardware Weekly (A)

In the 1980s the home improvement (hardware) business became unbelievably popular, almost "trendy" by many standards because of the unusual impact of a very special television program. Starting in 1979 the nation's Public Broadcasting System (PBS; educational television) produced a show entitled "This Old House" that became the number one weekly show on the entire educational television system. In fact marathon running of "This Old House," generally between ten and fifteen episodes, became all the rage among PBS affiliates during their semi-annual fundraising campaigns.

Essentially a "do-it-yourself" program for the average home owner, the show was hosted by Bob Vila, a charismatic general contractor who seemed to make any home improvement, from dreadful plumbing tasks to mixing and pouring concrete, almost "fun" or least "educational." Vila was assisted by Norm Abram, the show's master carpenter. These two individuals showed average homeowners, willing to invest some capital and a great deal of sweat equity, how to remodel or repair a home.

While the show did not have any commercials, various home improvement manufacturing companies supported the show with financial grants and free supplies. Part of the charm or panache of the show revolved around Vila and Abram demonstrating various home improvement techniques using traditional tools and the latest products on the market. Their use of a new product stimulated sales of the item. Each weekend countless thousands of individuals would descend on home improvement or hardware stores and ask for the tool Norm or Bob used in last week's episode. Norm, Bob, and their tools became celebrities.

This type of public recognition was exceptionally rare in the home improvement business. Yet sales of home improvement products skyrocketed in the late 1980s. This should have been an advertising manager's dream; it turned out to be a nightmare.

The real problem confronting advertising managers at business publications was totally unexpected. Should the manufacturer of home improvement products, power tools for example, advertise in business magazines (and reach owners and employees of home improvement centers) **or** should ads be placed in general consumer magazines to influence the individuals (the average home owner) who were watching "This Old House" and might buy the product?

This problem surfaced in February 1990 when the Deasley & Essian Company, a $4 billion power tool manufacturing company, wanted to introduce a new line of heavy duty power tools, including: a high torque cordless 3/8" screwdriver, a 7 1/4" circular saw, a 1/3 horse power variable-speed jig saw, a 1 3/4 horse power plunge router, a 3 1/4" electric plane, a 1/3 horse power orbital sheet sander, a 3/8" variable-speed drill, a 3/8" reversible cordless drill, a palm grip sander, a 4 1/2" disc grinder, and a 3/8" cordless power wrench.

The Stanley Raymond Harris advertising company was selected to handle the account. Harris was an old line advertising firm in Boston, Massachusetts.

Craig Kusick was the Vice President of Advertising at *Carew's Hardware Weekly*, and, when he read about the new Deasley & Essian products, he decided to put Joe Lefebvre on the account. Lefebvre was hired by Kusick in September 1989 as an ad space sales executive. While totally inexperienced in space sales prior to 1989, Lefebvre had twelve years of retail experience at an athletic shoe company. Kusick maintained that "any aggressive kid can learn the basics of business magazine space sales. All you have to do is create a sales quota and then push the client and the agency representative to buy more space each month."

Lefebvre was a pleasant but not very sophisticated individual. He had a strong regional speech pattern, his dress was rather informal, he only knew a little about his own magazine's editorial content, and his comments about competing periodicals were harsh but shallow. Kusick originally assigned him the important lumber and wood panel accounts; and his work up until that point was rather good.

Kusick told Lefebvre to call on Arnold Hauser at the Harris

agency. "Arnie is an old pro at business magazine advertising, and you should be able to sell him one full page of black and white [ad space] in each of our next four issues. Arnie is a gem; he will help you."

Lefebvre called on Hauser on February 28, 1990; unfortunately, Hauser had retired in late 1988, and Harris had decided not to replace Hauser with another full time business magazine specialist. "It just did not pay to spend a great deal of money to train a business magazine advertising media buyer when there was more money to be made in consumer magazine or television placements. In addition we had trouble convincing anyone, even new employees, to work in this less than exciting magazine niche."

Lefebvre made his sales pitch to Sally MacKenzie, a young (twenty-five years old) media buyer who handled women's magazines at the agency. MacKenzie was a home owner, and she had a rather detailed knowledge of certain types of power tools. However, she was not familiar with *Carew's Hardware Weekly* or business-to-business advertising; so she was interested in hearing what this business magazine could do to advertise these new products. She wondered if this type of magazine had the necessary reach. She thought consumer magazines or possibly television might be a better allocation of scarce funds instead of a business magazine. Sally also questioned the magazine's demographics, CPM, and other related statistical issues.

MacKenzie later reported that "Lefebvre's presentation was unimpressive when compared with the consumer magazine advertising representatives I saw. He lacked confidence, he did not understand demographics or the standard statistical tools we generally employ, and he lacked the sophistication that inspired the necessary confidence in a media buyer unfamiliar with this type of advertising vehicle." She did not recommend any advertising expenditures in *Carew's* or any business magazine for the new cordless screwdriver.

When Kusick found out, he was depressed. "This was just the right type of account for our magazine." If you were Kusick, what steps would you take to make sure that his business magazine captured some of Harris' advertising recommendations in the future?

The following week Kusick called an emergency meeting of his entire sales staff to review the Harris disaster. After he made his presentation, he asked for comments and questions and suggestions from the team.

Lindsay Deal, the company's old sales pro from Brooklyn, New York criticized Kusick for "sending in an inexperienced, unseasoned kid. This was a major account, a perfect business-to-business advertising dream; and we failed to get the job. Next time make sure that one of the old 'pros' handles the call."

While agreeing partially with Deal, John A. "Jocko" Flynn (who handled the Rhode Island territory) felt that he had experienced this type of rejection in the past few years. "The [advertising] business is now filled some sophisticated sales representatives fresh out of college. This 'new breed' understands the ad business and the subtle nuances of dress, talk, style, etc.; and they just make a better presentation since they are pitching their magazine to a media buyer from the same background, with the same training, and probably from the same type of college. The times have changed; we need to change our sales style."

Walker Cooper, grandson of the founder of *Carew's* and one of the leading owners of the magazine, took another approach. "The old business magazine media buyers are gone from some [advertising] agencies, and they are being replaced with what could be viewed as a 'new breed.' I doubt if we could be successful just by changing our sales style. I believe that we must face reality and accept the fact that business magazines are becoming 'dinosaurs' in the publishing industry. We must consider diversifying into the consumer periodical market to capture exactly this type of advertising. Clearly, business magazines just will not be able to continue to hold onto this type of account in the future. After all fax machines, computers, and other office equipment are being advertised in consumer magazines and on television. Our days [as business space sales executives] are numbered."

Jerry Grote, from San Antonio, Texas, felt that "we can do something positive. Since the [advertising] agencies are filled with 'yuppies in training,' why not consider running special seminars in New York and at the annual Magazine Institute conference on the advantages of business-to-business advertising. We could invite these young media buyers [to our sessions] and sell them on business magazine advertising. Giving up and moving into consumer magazines is the foolish way to go."

What strategy do you believe *Carew's Hardware Weekly* should follow?

MARKETING AND SOCIETY

Grocery Store News

Grocery Stores News was a controlled circulation weekly business publication covering the grocery industry in the Pacific Northwest. This magazine had a long history as an iconoclastic publication "free from the shackles of advertising agency control and Madison Avenue influences." It withstood the business magazine consolidation of the late 1980s and remained the only periodical owned and managed by James Joseph "Nixey" Callahan, a former reporter for a Fitchburg, Mass. daily newspaper. Callahan was unquestionably a "free spirit" more at home with the sentiments of the 1960s than the "greed" generation of the 1990s.

However, even hippies grow old, and he was compelled to earn a living and pay his bills; and his biggest test of "principles versus profits" materialized during an especially unhappy ten day period in September 1990.

Tommy Long, Callahan's advertising manager, reported on September 15th that he had just sold a four page color advertisement supplement to the Smalley Air Ionizer Company. The following week (September 20th), Long called Callahan to inform him that the Dillhoefer Corporation (the nation's third largest pharmaceutical company) had purchased full page color ads in the next five issues for "Dentotrol," its leading mouthwash with "tartar controlling power;" lastly, the Cliftdon Company (the nation's largest manufacturer of frozen microwave dinners) decided to run seven full page color advertisements in the next ten weeks.

These ads represented a major influx of cash at a time Callahan was having troubles paying his bills each month. "Perhaps the tide has finally gone our way," Callahan thought to himself as he calculated the advertising revenues these placements would bring his magazine.

On the evening of September 25th, he was reading *The Riverside Report*, a highly respected "consumer rights" magazine produced by a group of journalism professors at Northern Wyoming State University. Within the first five pages of *The Riverside Report*, Callahan read detailed and disturbing articles about the three new companies scheduled to run ads in his periodical in the next two weeks.

The first one dealt with Dillhoefer.

"Of the top ten mouthwashes sold in the United States, Dentotrol captured a remarkable 23.1 percent share of the United States' $720 million mouthwash market in 1989. However, recent clinical tests conducted by the University of Southern Colorado indicated conclusively that Dentotrol does not contain any know tartar fighting substances."

Truth in advertising was one thing; selling ad space and paying bills was something else; and Callahan became ill as he finished this article.

The second piece was equally unsettling.

The "Nuclear Regulatory Commission announced last week that its Safety and Standards Board had voted nine to three to consider recalling 35,000 ionizers manufactured by the Dillhoefer Corporation. Such action could take place at the next scheduled meeting on October 31, 1990 of the full Nuclear Regulatory Commission. If the Commission does recall this product, Dillhoefer could be required to 'show cause' why is should not have its license to manufacturer this product revoked."

Callahan's "illness" quickly turned to panic.

The very mention of the word "cancer" has been known to damage if not destroy a product in the marketplace. Callahan found out that another U.S. Government regulatory agency was investigating paperboard and cardboard products manufactured by one of his advertisers, the Cliftdon Corporation.

"While patrons at *Lutece* [New York City's most famous French restaurant] rarely eat frozen microwave food products, countless millions of Americans consume these items each day. According to a press release issued by the Food and Drug Administration (FDA), *some* of these microwave food items might not always be safe for human consumption. The preliminary results of an exhaustive three month study supported by the

U.S. Institute of Health revealed that small 'trace elements' of benezene, a known cancer causing substance, might be released into frozen food products, especially pizza, during the microwave cooking cycle when these items are placed on chemically treated cardboard or paperboard substrates lined with special 'foils' designed to enhance the 'browning' effect of microwaving. While additional research is needed, the FDA plans to monitor this situation, and, possibly consider taking these 'browning' materials off the market."

Callahan was in a state of panic.

Callahan called Long that evening to discuss these articles. He was deeply concerned about the potential loss of much needed revenue. Callahan asked Long if they should cancel all of the advertisements placed by the companies mentioned in the articles. Long insisted that "as long as a person or a company is innocent until proven guilty in a court of law, we have an obligation to treat these companies as innocent persons; we should run the ads until the appropriate regulatory agency or court rules that the product or products must be taken off the market in order to protect the safety of American citizens."

If you were Callahan, what would you do?

Fosse's Industrial Purchasing Digest

James King was hired as Sales Manager of *Fosse's Industrial Purchasing Digest* in December 1989. Edward Leonard, the longtime owner of the magazine, had fired Charles Starr, the previous Sales Manager, for "conduct unbecoming an employee of this corporation." King was brought in to "clean up what had become a legal nightmare."

It was alleged that Starr allowed his sales personnel to participate in a series of highly questionably "sales tactics" involving advertising agency executives. These included: (1) presenting "gifts" to advertising agency executives (for example pens, umbrellas, and jackets with the Fosse logo on them), (2) giving meals, trips, and tickets to agency personnel, (3) providing "special treatment and favors" to agency people, and (4) seeking "inside information" about competing periodicals from these agency executives.

Should a magazine provide these items to advertising agency

sales personnel? Should a magazine have a clearly stated policy regarding "appropriate" and "inappropriate" promotion marketing tactics?

Fowler's Beverage Times

Bon Jour was France's leading mineral water. In the early 1970s, *Bon Jour* became the trendy rage among Los Angeles's "beautiful people" who seemed to ingest dozens of bottles each day. This product's fame spread throughout the United States when several widely quoted consumer magazines printed pieces about the water's "almost mystical properties."

In July 1990 *Bon Jour* held a commanding market share of the mineral market sold in the U.S. with a 42.5 share. *Minerva Blanc* was second with 12.9 percent. Seven other foreign and domestic waters fought it out for the remaining quarter of the market.

On July 14, 1990, a testing lab in Lower Bucks County, Pennsylvania detected small traces of a cancer causing chemical substance in two hundred bottles of *Bon Jour*. Additional tests revealed these same chemicals in eighty-six percent of the 612 lots that were tested.

The U.S. Department of Agriculture and the U.S. Food and Drug Administration began their own investigation of the problem, and they recommended that "this product be removed immediately from the consumer market." As word of the recommendation spread throughout the nation, executives at *Bon Jour* announced that they would "recall and destroy approximately 127 million bottles of the product." The costs associated with this draconian measure exceeded $56 million.

Bon Jour was bottled in France, and, after several weeks of detailed scientific study, engineers at the bottling plant determined the source of the chemical substance. "The error of a member of a cleaning crew allowed this foreign substance to enter the bottling cycle, thereby contaminating water in lots 22–6758–A through 22–8990L [approximately 989 million bottles of water]. Because of a detailed investigation, the company has adopted new procedures to clean the bottling equipment and to prevent any future contaminations."

In late August the Secretary of the Food and Drug Agency for the State of California announced that "in the future this product [*Bon Jour*] must cease using the terms 'sodium free' and 'naturally sparkling' unless scientific tests indicating that this product contains five milligrams or less of sodium per eight ounce serving [or less than 21.1 milligrams per liter] can be presented to substantiate these advertising claims . . . "

On September 15, 1990, *Bon Jour* marketing executives announced the launching of a new business magazine advertising campaign designed carefully to convince grocery store owners to restock the product.

Fowler's Beverage Times was the leading business magazine servicing small to medium sized grocery stores in the Northeastern section of the United States. This was one of the two principal markets for bottled mineral water in the country. Advertising agency executives at Parmelee and Leary PLC called Jack Bentley, *Fowler's* Vice President of Sales, to inform him that they wanted to purchase two pages of four color advertising space in *Fowler's* each week for the next six months. Up to that point, *Bon Jour* had never advertised in *Fowler's;* in fact, Parmelee and Leary had refused to place any advertisements for any of their clients in business magazines. "We only use top twenty consumer magazines." Crises have a way of making even anti-business magazine ad agency people interested in the power of specialized periodicals.

There was a problem; Bentley could not find any statements from health or safety experts indicating that *Bon Jour* was totally safe for human consumption and/or that the issues raised by the California Secretary of the Food and Drug Agency had been addressed. All he had were a series of press releases from *Bon Jour* stating that "all problems associated with this unfortunate incident have been corrected. The New *Bon Jour* is ready for the U.S. market."

Parmelee and Leary wanted to start running the ads in the next available issue of this weekly periodical; and *Fowler's* business managers wanted to accept the copy as quickly as possible since it was "found money, a gift from heaven."

Should Bentley allow these ads to run without an ironclad

guarantee from *Bon Jour* stating in writing that all of the health problems and related issues had been corrected?

McRae Business Times

McRae Business Times was a medium sized (paid circulation 18,000) periodical servicing business executives in New Jersey.

The magazine was privately owned by Hal McRae, who started it in 1968. Advertising revenues stood at the $4 million mark as of April 1, 1990 (the end of its business year), and McRae was told by his accountant that pretax profits should reach $600,000.

McRae made it a point to avoid trouble. "We are not in the same league as *Lonnett's*, *Commercial Times*, or *Colbert's Review*, the nation's three largest general "consumer business" periodicals". McRae's magazine was a respectable publication reporting on the various business and economic issues affecting New Jersey's business leaders. The only controversial editorial position the publication ever took dealt with the state's "medieval" car insurance problem.

On March 30, 1990, yet another oil spill took place on the Delaware River. Unfortunately, over 900,000 gallons of number two heating oil was released into the river when a tanker ran aground near the Morrisville, Pennsylvania-Trenton, New Jersey bridge. This was the fifth oil spill on this river since January 1, 1989. The New Jersey Department of Environmental Protection (DEP) estimated that, with this March 30th spill, over 1.7 million gallons of oil had been released into the Delaware since September 1, 1989. The DEP calculated that thousands of fish and birds "had been destroyed or severely injured because of the careless safety precautions of the Yost Oil Corporation and the Sankey Company." Yost and Sankey were responsible for all five oil spills, with Yost culpable for four of them.

There was a major public outcry against the Yost Oil Company for "negligence." The state's major wildlife organizations began a campaign to boycott Yost's gas stations and oil companies. In addition they planned a major demonstration at Yost's annual meeting, scheduled for April 16, 1990 in Cleveland, Ohio.

The public relations department at Yost decided that the company should buy full page black and white advertisements in New Jersey's principal daily newspapers and weekly and monthly magazines. The purpose of this advertising campaign was to reassure the citizens of New Jersey that "Yost was doing everything possible to clean up the [March 1990] oil spill, and that extensive precautions were being taken by the company to make sure that New Jersey would be spared any ecological losses because of this spill."

Gordon Slade was the advertising manager at *McRae Business Times*. On April 3, 1990, Slade received a fax from Yost's advertising agency notifying him that "Yost wants to purchase one full page black and white advertisement in your next four issues, copy to follow by April 5th, at your standard [advertising] rate." Slade faxed back the following reply. "We will be glad to accept your advertisement."

Should Slade and his magazine run this ad?

Domingo's Fashion News (A)

Domingo's Fashion News was one of seventeen business periodicals covering the highly competitive fashion industry in the United States. To a great degree this magazine mirrored the industry that it covered. It faced intense competition, sagging advertising revenues, and strong competition from foreign publications.

Jerry Scala, the Director of Advertising, devised a marketing strategy that he maintained "would help curtail our cash flow problems, increase ad pages, reposition the magazine, and move it up to the number eight book in the field." As of January 2, 1990, *Domingo's Fashion News* was ranked the number eleven periodical in its field.

Scala wanted to target the beleaguered fur industry, a marketing niche that *Domingo's* had never be able to cultivate. The fur industry had sustained a series of negative setbacks in 1989, and the prognosis for 1990 was equally bleak. In 1989 animal-rights activists had conducted highly visible demonstrations in New York, Paris, Chicago, Aspen, and London. The fur industry's economic underpinnings were shaken when two of the nation's leading fur manufacturers sought protection under Chapter 11 of the Bankruptcy Code in September 1989; and various television shows, including many of the top ranked shows, presented episodes attacking the fur industry's treatment of animals.

This anti-fur crusade had mounted an impressive attack, including the obligatory number of Hollywood celebrities picketing against furs; and two of the major business fashion periodicals announced in November 1989 that "we can no longer tolerate the barbaric killing of 45 million minks and countless millions of other creatures just to manufacture [fur] coats."

Scala reviewed this strategy with Mark Stevens, the publisher of *Domingo's*, and he was given the authorization to develop a major campaign.

Was it prudent of Scala and *Domingo's* publisher to target such an industry?

Domingo's Fashion News (B)

Before Scala could even begin to develop his strategy for the fur industry, Ernie Oravetz, an account executive at Klusman and Klusman (a small advertising agency) called him about their meeting that afternoon. "I have great news for you, Jerry. I have two new [fashion] accounts for you."

At the meeting Oravetz outlined the two four-color advertising campaigns his agency wanted to run in *Domingo's*. Jerry was shown the boards, and he was thrilled about the ad copy and photographs.

The first advertisement was for the Gionfriddo Corporation, one of Europe's leading shoe companies. The photograph in the ad depicted a nude woman standing in a shower dreaming of shoes. "Great ad, Ernie. We should be able to help you push thousands of shoes with this one."

The second one featured a nude woman trying on a pair of Donlin's Hosiery. "Another winner, Ernie."

Stevens reviewed the boards, and told Scala that "we are on our way to a big year with these ads."

Was it prudent for Scala and Stevens to run these ads?

Retailing Industry News

Retailing Industry News was a weekly business magazine published in Tampa, Florida. It was founded in 1947 by Alfredo Sima to service the burgeoning retail store business in the South-Eastern section of the United States. Sima also published eleven other weekly and monthly business periodicals and three newsletters covering the fast food, fashion, and construction industries.

All of Sima's publications were controlled free periodicals; so advertising revenues were of the utmost importance to Sima, especially display advertisements. Ad sales reached $27.8 million in 1986; by the following year *Retailing Industry News* topped $31.4 million in ad revenues. As of December 31, 1989, ad income grew to $40.5 million, ad the projection for 1990 was a solid increase of 8.7 percent.

Retailing Industry News employed fifty-four telephone operators who took display ads for customers; their standard work week was fifty hours. On the week-end ten or eleven operators worked twelve hour shifts answering the telephones. Ad copy was prepared by a group of highly experienced people; and the billing procedure was totally computerized.

Sima had very little contact with the daily operations at his magazines; he relied on his two sons. In fact he had decided in April 1990 to put his stable of titles up for sale so that he "could spend the rest of my time on this carth fishing and attending the track. Why not get the money and relax?"

Alfredo contacted Daniel Schatzeder in Houston to see if Schatzeder could sell the books for + $80 million. On June 8, 1990, Alfredo began preliminary talks with George Pearce, President of the Nelson Company (one of the nation's largest business publishers) about selling his periodicals for $81 million to Nelson. Discussions went smoothly, and on October 30, 1990, Alfredo and Pearce signed a contract to sell "any and all assets of the Sima Publishing Company to the Nelson Company for $76.8 million dollars."

At the September 1990 annual convention of business magazine publishers, Sima outlined the latest feature at *Retailing Industry News*, a display ad format called "What's New" (which had been developed by Manny Sima, his youngest son). The "What's Hot" feature generated a significant amount of interest and profit, and it became *the* industry place to announce the latest developments or inventions of interest to managers and owners of retail stores. In the period July through September 1990, literally dozens of these ads appeared touting the introduction of a variety of interesting products, including the famous "amazing vego-tec food processor for $19.95," an "all purpose chrome forty-five piece screwdriver and socket set" for $9.95, the "ultimate $39.00 graphite baseball bat," and the "$189.95 user friendly computer, including a color monitor."

In September 1990 the Better Business Service, the Tampa Police Department, the Florida State Police, and the Attorney-General of the State of Florida received over one hundred complaints from store owners who purchased products advertised in *Retailing Industry News*.

On October 2, 1990 Alfredo Sima denied in a letter to the Attorney-General "all allegations about advertising misrepresentation." He insisted that his sons screened and personally tested all products before an advertisement was accepted for publication.

However, the Attorney General wrote to Alfredo on October 13, 1990 that "it has come to my attention that agents for your publication did not exhibit due diligence in the acceptance of ads for certain products . . . that products were not analyzed or subjected to routine tests prior to publishing [ad] copy . . . and that certain ads vastly misrepresented the product's quality, use, and implied warranty of merchantability . . . ."

Alfredo quietly investigated the practices of the periodical's advertising department, and he ascertained that the allegations contained in the Attorney-General's letter were essentially correct. His sons did not screen or test any products prior to running ads for these products. In fact they rarely saw any products.

What should Alfredo do?

Bibliography

ADVERTISING MANAGEMENT

Abeele, P.B., and I. Butaye. "Pre-Testing the Effectiveness of Industrial Advertising." *Industrial Marketing Management* 9 (February 1980): 75–83.

Adams, William James, and Janet L. Yellen. "Commodity Bundling and the Burden of Monopoly." *Quarterly Journal of Economics* 90 (1976): 475–98.

"Ad Pages in Farm Publications for 9 Months, 1987–1986." *Advertising Age*, 12 October 1987, 94.

"Ad Pages up in April [1987]." *New York Times*, 29 May 1987, 13.

"Ad Rates Climb at *TV Guide* and *People* Weekly Magazines." *MagazineWeek*, 9 October 1989, 3.

"Ad Revenues by Group Publisher." *Advertising Age*, 24 October 1988, S17.

"Ad Spending by Leaders Ranked 101 to 200." *Advertising Age*, 21 November 1988, S2–S34.

"Ad Spending Due to Snap Back, Experts Say." *Los Angeles Times*, 14 April 1987, sec. 4, p. 9.

"Ad Spending Forecast for Top 100." *Advertising Age*, 10 March 1975, 3.

"Ad Spending Will More Than Double by 1985, Cox Study." *Advertising Age*, 10 March 1975, 47.

"Ad Spending Wise Forecast Top 100." *Advertising Age*, 10 March 1975, 2.

"Ads Offer Less Bang for Buck." *Advertising Age*, 26 November 1984, 55.

"Ads Stimulate the Economy." *Business and Society Review* (Fall 1985): 58–59.

"Ads-to-Sales Ratio Study Uncovers Big Hikes." *Advertising Age*, 24 October 1988, 49.

"Advertising as Percent of Sales." *Advertising Age*, 23 November 1987, S4.

"Advertising Effectiveness: Cross Brands." *Journal of the Market Research Society* 28 (January 1986): 15.

"Advertising Is Bigger Than Ever." *The Economist*, 9 March 1985, 78.

"Advertising Power Charts." *Advertising Age*, 26 December 1988, 10–13.

"Advertising-to-Sales Ratios, 1989." *Advertising Age*, 13 November 1989, 32.

"Advertising Volume in Business Publications." *Industrial Marketing* 67 (February 1982): 114–16.

"Ad Volume in Business Publications." *Industrial Marketing* 65 (August 1980): 91–92.

"Ad Volume in Business Publications." *Industrial Marketing* 66 (August 1966): 118–22.

"Agency Billings by Media." *Advertising Age*, 30 March 1988, 18–25.

Albion, Mark S., and Paul W. Farris. *The Advertising Controversy: Evidence on the Economic Effects of Advertising*. Boston: Auburn, 1981.

Alwitt, Linda F., and Andrew A. Mitchell. *Psychological Processes and Advertising Effects: Theory, Research, and Applications*. Hillsdale, N.J.: Lawrence Erlbaum Associates, 1985.

Ames, B. Charles. "Build Marketing Strength into Industrial Selling." *Harvard Business Review* 50 (January-February 1972): 48–60.

———. "Marketing Planning for Industrial Products." *Harvard Business Review* 46 (September-October 1968): 100–111.

———. "Trappings vs. Substance in Industrial Marketing." *Harvard Business Review* 48 (July-August 1970): 93–102.

"Archival Sources for Business History at the National Museum of American History." *Business History Review* 60 (Autumn 1986): 474.

Arndt, Johan. "Toward a Concept of Domesticated Markets." *Journal of Marketing* (Fall 1979): 69–75.

Arrigo, K. "Business Press: An Open Letter to My Friends, the [Advertising Sales] Reps." *Market and Media Decisions* 16 (September 1981): 90.

———. "Good Industrial Ad Program Is a Sound Investment, Not a Dubious Expense." *Industrial Marketing* 61 (June 1976): 140–41.

Association of Business Publishers. *The ARF/ABP Study: The Impact of Business Publication Advertising on Sales and Profits*. New York: ABP, 1987.

———. *Top Management's Role in Directing, Budgeting, and Evaluating Advertising Programs*. New York: ABP, n. d.

Audits and Survey Department, *Newsweek*. "How Professionals/Managers Read Business and Newsweekly Magazines: A Landmark Study-Phase II." *Newsweek*, 1986.

Azorin, H. "The Anatomy of a Print Sell." *Marketing Communications* 8 (December 1983): 30–32.

"Bank Magazines Still Bear Scars from October 19." *Publishing News,* Pilot Issue (July 1988): 13.

Bass, Frank M. "A New Product Growth Model for Consumer Durables." *Management Science* 15 (1969): 215–27.

————. "The Relationship between Diffusion Rates, Experience Curves, and Demand Elasticities for Consumer Durable Technological Innovations." *Journal of Business* 53 (1980): 551–67.

"Beauty Ads Boost Magazine-Radio Ad Dollars, Small Cost Push." *Marketing and Media Decisions* 19 (Fall 1984): 73–74.

Belkaoui, A., and J. M. Belkaoui. "Comparative Analysis of the Roles Portrayed by Women in Print Advertisements: 1958, 1970, 1972." *Journal of Market Research* 13 (May 1976): 168–72.

Blasko, B. J., and C. H. Patti. "The Advertising Budgeting Practices of Industrial Marketers." *Journal of Marketing* 48 (Fall 1984): 104–10.

Bogart, Leo. "Mass Advertising: The Message, Not the Measure." *Harvard Business Review* 54 (September 1976): 107–16.

————. *Strategy in Advertising: Matching Media and Messages to Markets and Motivation.* Chicago: Crain Books, 1984.

Bonoma, Thomas V. "Get More out of Your Trade Shows." *Harvard Business Review* 61 (January-February 1983): 75–83.

————. "Market Success Can Breed 'Marketing Inertia.' " *Harvard Business Review* 59 (September-October 1981): 115–21.

Bonoma, Thomas V., Gerald Zaltman, and Wesley J. Johnson. *Industrial Buyer Behavior.* Cambridge, Mass.: Marketing Science Institute, 1977, Report 77–117.

Borden, Neil H. "The Concept of the Marketing Mix." *Journal of Advertising Research* (June 1964): 2–7.

Brown, Herbert E., and Roger W. Brucker. "The Buyer Problem Foundation of Industrial Advertising." *Industrial Marketing Management* 5 (1976): 163–67.

Brown, Paul B. *Marketing Masters: Lessons in the Art of Marketing.* New York: Harper & Row, 1988.

Brown, R. G. "Sales Response to Promotions in Advertising." *Journal of Advertising Research* 14 (August 1974): 33–38.

"Budget Norms for Industrial Advertisers." *Sales and Marketing Management* 116 (8 March 1976): 22.

Burnett, John J. *Promotion Management: A Strategic Approach.* St. Paul, Minn.: West Publishing, 1984.

"Business Advertising." *Advertising Age,* 9 July 1980, S1–S24.

"Business-Professional Advertising." *Advertising Age,* 14 July 1982, M7–M26.

"Business Publications: How to Make Them Work Harder for You." *Sales Management* 114 (2 June 1976): 39–44.

"Buying Binges Pump up Magazine Gains." *Advertising Age,* 26 June 1989, S10.

Buzzell, Robert D., Bradley T. Gale, and G. M. Sultan. "Market Share: A Key to Profitability." *Harvard Business Review* 53 (January-February 1975): 97–107.

Carman, James M. "Evaluation of Trade Show Exhibitions." *California Management Review* 11 (1968): 35–44.

Chase, Dennis. "Y & R Group Holds on to Top Spot." *Advertising Age*, 21 April 1986, 63.

Choffray, Jean-Marie, and Gary L. Lilien. "Assessing Response to Industrial Marketing Strategy." *Journal of Marketing* (April 1978): 20–31.

———. "A New Approach to Industrial Market Segmentation." *Sloan Management Review* (Spring 1978): 17–29.

"Circulation Stagnates in Business Books." *Advertising Age*, 12 June 1989, S6.

Clark, Lindley H., Jr. and Alfred Malabre, Jr., "Economists Fret over Consumer Outlays." *Wall Street Journal*, 3 August 1988, 6.

Clarke, D.G. "Econometric Measurement of the Duration of Advertising's Effect on Sales." *Journal of Marketing Research* 13 (November 1976): 345–57.

Cleaver, Joanne Y. "Magazine Rate Card More of a Wild Card." *Advertising Age*, 30 November 1987, S22–S23.

Coen, Robert J. "Ad Spending Outlook Brightens." *Advertising Age*, 15 May 1989, 2.

———. "A Mixed-Bag Future." *Advertising Age*, 24 May 1989, 68.

"Coen Sees U.S. Ad Spending Slowdown: Cuts Growth Outlook to 7.6%." *Advertising Age*, 30 June 1986, 6.

Collins, Kevin B. "An Examination of the Role of Advertising in Competition Using a Time-Varying Aggregate Markov Model of Consumer Behavior." Ph.D. diss., University of Wisconsin-Madison, 1988.

"Consumer vs. Trade Advertising: Ads Should Stimulate Sales or Stock." *Product Marketing: Cosmetic and Fragrance Retailing* 4 (June 1985): 28.

Corey, E. Raymond. "Key Options in Market Selection and Product Planning." *Harvard Business Review* 53 (September-October 1975): 119–28.

Cote, Kevin. "Uncertain Future Plagues Marketers Planning for 1992." *Advertising Age*, 5 June 1989, 1, 42.

Council of Economic Advisors. *Economic Indicators, January 1988*. Washington, D.C.: GPO, 1988.

Cox, William E., Jr., and Luis V. Dominguez. "The Key Issues and Procedures of Industrial Marketing Research." *Industrial Marketing Management* 8 (1979): 81–93.

Cravens, David W., Gerald E. Hills, and Robert B. Woodruff. *Marketing Decision Making*. Homewood, Ill.: Richard D. Irwin, 1980.

Crimp, Margaret. *The Marketing Research Process*. Englewood Cliffs, N.J.: Prentice-Hall, 1985.

Dash, Minati. "Pricing and Advertising Policies for an Innovation." Ph.D. diss., New York University, 1982.

Davidow, William H., and Bro Uttal. *Total Customer Service: The Ultimate Weapon.* New York: Harper & Row, 1989.

Day, George S., Allan D. Shocker, and Rajendra K. Srivastava. "Customer-Oriented Approaches to Identifying Product Markets." *Journal of Marketing* (Fall 1979): 8–19.

de Kluyver, Cornelis A. "Innovation and Industrial Product Life Cycles." *California Management Review* 20 (1977): 21–33.

Dhalla, N. K. "Assessing the Long-Term Value of Advertising." *Harvard Business Review* 56 (January-February 1978): 87–95.

Donaton, Scott. "Business Publishers Caught in Vicious Rate-Cutting Trap as Big Shakeout Looms." *Advertising Age*, 12 June 1989, S1.

———. "*Forbes* Readies Push into Europe." *Advertising Age*, 16 October 1989, 36.

Dougherty, Philip H. "Smaller Gain for Ads in '88 Is Predicted." *New York Times*, 16 June 1988, D23.

———. "Trade Ads Aids Sales, Study Says." *New York Times*, 16 October 1986, 48.

Dreier, Ted. "Does Your Image Match Your Ads?" *ABA Banking Journal* 77 (October 1985): 148.

Drucker, Peter. *The Effective Executive.* New York: Harper & Row, 1967.

———. *Management: Tasks, Responsibilities, Practices* New York: Harper & Row, 1974.

———. *The New Realities.* New York: Harper & Row, 1989.

———. "The Ten Rules of Effective Research." *Wall Street Journal*, 30 May 1989, A22.

Duke, Judith S. *The Technical, Scientific, and Medical Publishing Market.* White Plains, N.Y.: Knowledge Industry Publications, 1985.

Edel, Richard. "Growth Robust for Promo Shops." *Advertising Age*, 4 April 1988, S1–S2.

Edell, J. A., and R. Staelin. "The Information Processing in Print Advertisements." *Journal of Consumer Research* 10 (July 1983): 45–61.

Endicott, R. Craig. "'86 Ad Spending Soars." *Advertising Age*, 23 November 1987, S2.

———. "Media Companies Post Robust Growth." *Advertising Age*, 27 June 1988, S2–S3.

———. "Sales Surge 11% for Media Giants." *Advertising Age*, 29 June 1987, S2.

———. "Y & R Maintains Its Lead." *Advertising Age*, 20 March 1989, 3.

———. "Y & R Stays on Top Despite Solid Run by Saatchi." *Advertising Age*, 29 March 1989, 1, 8, 70.

Ewen, Stuart. *Captains of Consciousness: Advertising and the Social Roots of the Consumer Culture.* New York: McGraw-Hill, 1976.

Fajen, Stephen R. "More for Your Money From the Media." *Harvard Business Review* 56 (September-October 1978): 113–21.

Fox, Stephen. *The Mirror Makers: A History of American Advertising and Its Creators*. New York: Vintage, 1985.

Freeman, Cyril. "How to Evaluate Advertising's Contribution." *Harvard Business Review* 40 (July-August 1962): 137–48.

Fueroghne, Dean Keith. *"But the People in Legal Said . . . ": A Guide to Current Legal Issue in Advertising* Homewood, Ill.: Dow Jones-Irwin, 1989.

Gale Research, *The Gale Directory of Publications*. Detroit, Mich.: Gale Research, 1987.

"Getting the Most from Your Direct Response Advertising: A Look at Current Bank Practices." *Bank Marketing* 18 (June 1986): 14.

"Global Media and Marketing." *Advertising Age*, 14 December 1987, 53–65.

Goding, C. A. "Bridging Gaps for Tomorrow's Marketers." *Industrial Marketing* 62 (October 1980): 92.

Greco, Albert N. *Business Journalism: Management Notes and Cases*. New York: New York University Press, 1988.

Green, Paul E., and Yoram Wind. "New Way to Measure Consumer's Judgments." *Harvard Business Review* 53 (July-August 1975): 107–17.

Greenberger, Martin, ed. *Electronic Publishing Plus*. White Plains, N.Y.: Knowledge Industry Publications, 1985.

Greenhouse, Steven. "Europe's Buyout Bulge." *Wall Street Journal*, 5 November 1989, 1, 6.

Haley, Russell I. "Benefit Segmentation: A Decision-Oriented Research Tool." *Journal of Marketing* (July 1968): 30–35.

Hall, William K. "Survival Strategies in a Hostile Environment." *Harvard Business Review* 58 (September-October 1980): 75–85.

Hanssens, D. M. and B. A. Weitz. "Effectiveness of Industrial Print Advertisements across Product Categories." *Journal of Marketing Research* 17 (August 1980): 294–306.

Harris, Richard Jackson, ed. *Information Processing Research in Advertising*. Hillsdale, N.J.: Lawrence Erlbaum, 1983.

"Has the Business Press Turned the Corner?" *Media Decisions* 12 (May 1977): 76–78.

Healey, John S., and Harold Kassaryian. "Advertising Substantiation and Advertiser Response: A Content Analysis of Magazine Advertisements." *Journal of Marketing* 47 (Winter 1983): 139–43.

Herman, Tom. "Economists Expect Expansion to Continue for at Least a Year Despite a Faster Inflation Pace and Increase in Interest Rates." *Wall Street Journal*, 5 July 1988, 3.

Hirota, Janice M. "Cultural Mediums: The Work of 'Creatives' in American Advertising Agencies." Ph.D. diss., Columbia University, 1988.

Horowitz, Irving Louis. *Communicating Ideas: The Crisis of Publishing in a Post-Industrial Society*. New York: Oxford University Press, 1986.

Horton, Liz. "Business Titles Slip as Consumer Books Gain." *Folio*, January 1990, 16.

Hosman, D., and D. L. Fugate. "How To Develop an Industrial Advertising Budget for Smaller Companies." *Management Review* 70 (March 1981): 43–46.

"How Advertising and the Economy Work Together." *International Journal of Advertising* 5 (Winter 1986): 37.

Hunter, Margaret. "Pressured Publishers Cut Advertising Schedules." *Publishing News*, June 1989, 1, 52.

"Ideas & Trends: Who Buys . . . *Navy Times? Dirt Rider?*" The *New York Times*, 29 October 1989, sec. 4, p. 29.

"Is a New Product Hidden in Your Advertising Inquiries?" *Research and Development* (June 1985): 127.

Jackson, Barbara Bund. "Manage Risk in Industrial Pricing." *Harvard Business Review* 58 (July-August 1980): 121–33.

Johnston, Wesley J., and Thomas V. Bonoma. "Reconceptualizing Industrial Buying Behavior: Toward Improved Research Approaches." In Barnett A. Greenberg and Danny N. Bellenger, eds. *Contemporary Marketing Thought*. Chicago: American Marketing Association, 1977.

Kahn, George N., and Abraham Shuchman. "Specialize Your Salesmen!" *Harvard Business Review* 39 (January-February 1961): 90–98.

Kanter, Rosabeth Moss. *When Giants Learn to Dance: Mastering the Challenges of Strategy, Management, and Careers in the 1990s*. New York: Simon & Schuster, 1989.

Kelly, Keith. "Rizzoli Plans Push into U.S. Market." *MagazineWeek*, 30 October 1989, 1, 3.

Kist, Joost. *Electronic Publishing*. London: Croom Helm, 1987.

Kotler, Philip. "From Sales Obsession to Marketing Effectiveness." *Harvard Business Review* 55 (November December 1977): 67–75.

———. "Operations Research in Marketing." *Harvard Business Research* 45 (January-February 1967): 30–38.

Kotler, Philip, and Eduardo L. Roberto. *Social Marketing: Strategies for Changing Public Behavior*. New York: Free Press, 1989.

Krugman, Herbert E. "What Makes Advertising Effective?" *Harvard Business Review* 53 (March-April 1975): 96–103.

Lee, Haksik. "Moderating Roles of Involvement in Information Processing Routes and Message Acceptance for Differing Numbers of Ad Repetitions." Ph.D. diss., Michigan State University, 1987.

"Legal Publications: A New Growth Industry," *New York Times*, 19 August 1988, B5.

Levin, Gary. "Industries Back on Track." *Advertising Age*, 15 June 1987, S1.

Levitt, Theodore. "After the Sale Is Over . . . " *Harvard Business Review* 61 (September-October 1983): 87–93.

Levitt, Theodore. "Communications and Industrial Selling." *Journal of Marketing* 31 (April 1967): 15–21.

———. *Industrial Purchasing Behavior: A Study in Communications Effects.* Boston: Division of Research, Harvard Business School, 1965.

———. "The Morality of Advertising." *Harvard Business Review* 48 (July-August 1970): 84–92.

Lillien, Gary L., and J. D. C. Little. "Advisor Project: A Study of Industrial Marketing Budgets." *Sloan Management Review* 17 (Spring 1976): 17–31.

Lillien, Gary L., et al. "Industrial Advertising Effects and Budgeting Practices." *Journal of Marketing* 40 (January 1976): 16–24.

Lipman, Joanne. "Ad Spending to Rise 6.9% in '89, Coen Says in a Warmer Forecast." *Wall Street Journal,* 15 June 1989, B4.

———. "Estimate for '88 U.S. Ad Spending Is Sliced by Prominent Forecaster." *Wall Street Journal,* 16 June 1988, 28.

———. "Gap between Ad-Revenue Figures and Reality Grows." *Wall Street Journal,* 20 November 1989, B6.

———. "Meager Rise Forecast for '89 Ad Spending." *Wall Street Journal,* 13 December 1989, B6.

———. "Spending Forecast Augurs Ho-Hum 1990." *Advertising Age,* 12 December 1989, B5.

Lipman, Joanne, and Thomas R. King, "Ad Spending Expectations Turn Out To Be Too Great." *Wall Street Journal,* 21 August 1989, B1.

———. "Rate Hikes Fall off Pace as Poor Year Hits Pricing." *Advertising Age,* 28 November 1988, S1–S18.

———. "TV Forms Hot; Print, Outdoor Waver." *Advertising Age,* 30 November 1987, S2–S4.

Ljungren, Roy G. "Building More Business with Industrial Direct Mail Advertising." *Industrial Marketing Management* 5 (1976): 309–18.

Lorange, Peter, and Richard F. Vancil. "How to Design a Strategic Planning System." *Harvard Business Review* 54 (September-October 1976): 75–81.

MacAdams, Elizabeth A. "The Relationship between Attitude toward the Ad and Intention: A Quasi-Experimental Analysis." Ph.D. diss., University of Illinois-Urbana, 1988.

McCormack, Mark H. "What a Great Salesman." *Wall Street Journal,* 20 June 1988, 14.

"Magazines as the Mass Medium of the Future." *Marketing and Media Decisions* 17 (February 1982): 32.

"*MagazineWeek* 500," *MagazineWeek,* 23 October 1989, 26.

"Making Industrial Advertising Pay." *Sales and Marketing Management* 124 (19 May 1980): 71.

"The Measurement of Magazine Page Exposures." *Journal of the Market Research Society* 28 (April 1986): 145.

"Media Muscle: The Power in Numbers." *Advertising Age*, 9 November 1988, 66–67.

Meloche, Martin S. "The Effective Use of Price and Item Advertising in Retail Merchandising Strategy." D.B.A. diss., University of Kentucky, 1988.

Meyers, William. *The Image-Makers: Power and Persuasion on Madison Avenue*. New York: Times Books, 1984.

Mick, David G. "Levels of Compression in Consumers' Processing of Print Advertising Language." Ph.D. diss., Indiana University, 1987.

Moriarty, Rowland T. *Industrial Buying Behavior: Concepts, Issues, and Applications*. Lexington, Mass.: Lexington Books, 1983.

Morrill, John E. "Industrial Advertising Pays Off." *Harvard Business Review* 48 (March-April 1970): 4–14.

Morse, R.C. "Business-Industrial Videotext: Now's the Groundfloor for the Silent Salesman." *Industrial Marketing* 67 (October 1982): 42–43.

Mueller, Barbara. "Multinational Advertising: An Examination of Standardization and Specialization in Commercial Messages." Ph.D. diss., University of Washington, 1987.

Murray, Alan. "Greenspan Signals Higher Interest Rates." *Wall Street Journal*, 14 July 1988, 2.

Murrow, David. "Bertelsmann Tops in Euro Media." *Advertising Age*, 27 November 1989, 102.

"National Ad Spending by Category." *Advertising Age*, 27 September 1989, 8.

"National Measured Ad Spending." *Advertising Age*, 28 September 1988, 156.

"New Proof of Industrial Ad Values." *Market and Media Decisions* 16 (February 1981): 64–65.

"A New Threat to the Freedom to Advertise: Report on Developments in the United States." *International Journal of Advertising* 6 (Winter 1986): 67.

Newton, Derek A. "Get the Most out of Your Sales Force." *Harvard Business Review* 47 (September-October 1969): 130–43.

1988 MagazineWeek 500. Natick, Mass.: MagazineWeek Partners, 1988.

Ogilvy, David. *Confessions of an Advertising Man*. New York: Atheneum, 1981.

———. *On Advertising*. New York: Vintage, 1985.

Ogilvy, David, and Joel Raphaelson. "Research on Advertising Techniques That Work—And Don't Work." *Harvard Business Review* 60 (July-August 1982): 14–19.

"100 Leading Media Companies." *Advertising Age*, 29 June 1987, S3.

"100 Leading Media Companies by Revenue." *Advertising Age*, 27 June 1988, S6.

"100 Leading Media Companies by Revenue." *Advertising Age*, 26 June 1989, S2.

Ostheimer, Richard H. "Magazine Advertising during Recessions." *Journal of Advertising Research* 20 (December 1980): 11–16.

Parker, W. "How To Measure Your Advertising Sales Productivity." *Industrial Marketing* 68 (February 1983): 54–55.

Patterson, Perry W. "Economic and Marketing Aspects of the Business Press." Chicago: Crain Communication, 1984.

Patti, Charles H. "Evaluating the Role of Advertising." *Journal of Advertising* 6 (1977): 30–35.

———. "Role of Advertising in the Adoption of Industrial Goods: A Look at the Raw Materials Industry." *Journal of Advertising* 8 (Fall 1979): 38–42.

Peterson, R. A. and R. A. Kerin. "Female Roles in Advertisements: Some Experimental Evidence." *Journal of Marketing* 41 (October 1977): 56–63.

Piersol, Robert J. "Accuracy of Estimating Markets for Industrial Products by Size of Consuming Industries." *Journal of Marketing Research* 5 (May 1968): 147–54.

"Playboy Beats *Penthouse* with Hungary Launch." *MagazineWeek,* 20 November 1989, 7.

Pollman, A. W. and M. L. McBain. "Cost per Reader of Industrial Ads." *Journal of Advertising Research* 20 (July 1980): 51–54.

"Print Spending by 100 Leaders." *Advertising Age,* 28 September 1988, 10.

"The Promotion of Tobacco in Victorial England." *Journal of Marketing* 20 (1 December 1986) 5.

Publishers Information Bureau. *PIB: Magazine Advertising Pages and Dollars Gain in First Six Months of 1988.* New York: PIB, 1988.

Reilly, Patrick. "Trade Journals Riding Rebound of U.S. Industry." *Advertising Age,* 16 May 1988, 50.

Reynolds, William H. "More Sense about Market Segmentation." *Harvard Business Review* 43 (September-October 1965): 107–14.

Richards, Jeff I. "A Foundation for Theory and Assessment of Deception: The Legal and Behavioral Situs of Advertising Misrepresentation." Ph.D. diss., University of Wisconsin-Madison, 1988.

Richmond, D., and T. P. Hartman. "Sex Appeal in Advertising." *Journal of Advertising Research* 22 (October-November 1982): 53–61.

Ries, Al, and Jack Trout. *Marketing Warfare.* New York: McGraw-Hill, 1986.

———. *Positioning: The Battle for Your Minds.* New York: McGraw-Hill, 1981.

Riser, Earlene A. "A Content Analysis of Women in Pharmaceutical Advertisements." Ph.D. diss., Texas Woman's University, 1987.

Risley, George. *Modern Industrial Marketing.* New York: McGraw-Hill, 1972.

Roberts, Johnnie L. "Forecast Lowered for '88 Spending On Newspaper Ads." *Wall Street Journal,* 3 August 1988, 24.

Robinson, Patrick J., Charles Faris, and Yoram Wind. *Industrial Buying and Creative Marketing.* Boston: Allyn and Bacon, 1967.

Rosenberg, Larry J., and Elizabeth C. Hirschman. "Retailing without Stores." *Harvard Business Review* 58 (July-August 1980): 103–12.

Rothenberg, Randall. "Job Shuffle at Industry Publications." *New York Times,* 2 August 1989, D18.

———. "Shifts in Marketing Strategy Jolting Advertising Industry." *New York Times,* 3 October 1989, A1, D23.

"A Sampling of Interest-Rate and Economic Forecasts." *Wall Street Journal,* 6 July 1988, 37.

Scanlon, S. "Striking It Rich with Industrial Ads." *Sales and Marketing Management* 122 (18 July 1979): 39–44.

Scheiner, Edward C. "The Effects of Visual Complexity in Print Advertising Design on Looking Time, Arousal, and Ratings of Interestingness and Pleasingness." Ph.D. diss., Michigan State University, 1987.

Schmalensee, Richard. "Product Differentiation Advantages of Pioneering Brands." *American Economic Review* 72 (1982): 349–65.

Schneiderman, Ron. "A New Industry Springs Up: Europe 1992." *New York Times,* 26 November 1989, F16.

Sebastian, Pamela. "Data Likely to Signal Mounting Inflation." *Wall Street Journal,* 8 August 1988, 18.

———. "Robust Economy Raises Inflation Fears." *The Wall Street Journal,* 11 July 1988, 22.

"Second 100 Leading National Advertisers." *Advertising Age,* 23 November 1987, S2–S14.

Serafin, Raymond. "Magazines See Red Flag." *Advertising Age,* 10 July 1989, 3, 52.

Shapiro, Benson P., *Industrial Product Policy: Managing the Existing Product Line.* Cambridge, Mass.: Marketing Science Institute, 1977. Report 77–110.

———. "Manage the Customer, Not Just the Sales Force." *Harvard Business Review* 52 (September-October 1974): 127–36.

Shapiro, Benson P., and Thomas V. Bonoma. "How To Segment Industrial Markets." *Harvard Business Review* 62 (May-June 1984): 104–10.

Shapiro, Benson P., and Stephen X. Doyle. "Make the Sales Task Clear." *Harvard Business Review* 61 (November-December 1983): 72–77.

Shapiro, Benson P., and Barbara B. Jackson. "Industrial Pricing to Meet Customer Needs." *Harvard Business Review* 56 (November-December 1978): 119–27.

Shapiro, Benson P., and John Wyman. "New Ways to Reach Your Customers." *Harvard Business Review* 59 (July-August 1981): 103–10.

Shaw, Christopher J. H. M. "Buying and Selling Magazines: Innovation and Expansion." *Folio,* June 1988, 192.

Sheth, Jagdish N. "A Model of Industrial Buyer Behavior." *Journal of Marketing* 37 (October 1973): 50–56.

Shriver, Donald W., Jr., and Ralph S. Robinson, Jr. "The Case of the Constant Customers." *Harvard Business Review* 46 (July-August 1968): 150–55.

Smyth, Richard C. "Financial Incentives for Salesmen." *Harvard Business Review* 46 (January-February 1968): 109–17.

Soley, L.C., and L.N. Reid. "Industrial Ad Readership as a Function of Headline Type." *Journal of Advertising* 12 (1983): 34–38.

Speck, Paul S. "On Humor and Humor in Advertising." Ph.D. diss., Texas Tech University, 1987.

Standard Rate and Data Service. *Business Publications Rates And Data*. Part 1. Wilmette, Ill.: Standard Rate and Data Service, 24 July 1988.

Steinbrink, John P. "How to Pay Your Sales Force." *Harvard Business Review* 56 (July-August 1978): 111–22.

Stern, B.L., et al. "Magazine Advertising: An Analysis of Its Information Content." *Journal of Advertising Research* 21 (April 1981): 34–39.

Stevenson, T. H. and L. P. Swayne. "Comparative Industrial Advertising: The Content and Frequency." *Industrial Marketing Management* 13 (May 1984): 133–38.

"Study Uncovers Major Industrial Ad Influences." *Advertising Age*, 15 March 1976, 33.

Swinyard, Alfred W., and Floyd A. Bond. "Who Gets Promoted?" *Harvard Business Review* 58 (September-October 1980): 6–11.

"Taking the Business-Industrial Message to the Streets." *Business Marketing* 69 (April 1984): 128–29.

"Technology Titles Rake in Revenue." *Advertising Age*, 12 June 1989, S6.

Thompson, Joseph W., and William W. Evans. "Behavioral Approach to Industrial Selling." *Harvard Business Review* 47 (March-April 1969): 137–51.

Tilles, Seymour. "How to Evaluate Corporate Strategy." *Harvard Business Review* 41 (July-August 1963): 111–21.

"Top 100 Agencies by Gross Income." *Advertising Age*, 30 March 1988, 6–14.

"Top Ten by Print Media." *Advertising Age*, 29 March 1989, 83.

"Top 25 Business Pub[lication] Advertisers." *Advertising Age*, 28 September 1988, 20.

"Top 25 Farm Publication Advertisers." *Advertising Age*, 28 September 1988, 24.

"Tops in the Trades." *Advertising Age*, 12 June 1989, S2.

"Total U.S. Advertising Dollars by Media."*Advertising Age*, 28 September 1988, 158.

"U.S. Billings by Region." *Advertising Age*, 30 March 1988, 88.

U.S. Department of Commerce, Bureau of the Census. *County Business Patterns 1986: New York*. Washington, D.C.: GPO, 1986. 122–31.

U.S. Department of Commerce, Bureau of the Census. *1982 Census of*

Manufacturers: Newspapers, Periodicals, Books, and Miscellaneous Publishing. Washington, D.C.: GPO, 1985. 27A-6–27A-11.

U.S. Department of Commerce, Bureau of the Census. *1977 Census of Manufacturers: Newspapers, Periodicals, Books, and Miscellaneous Publishing.* Washington, D.C.: GPO, 1980. 27A-6–27A-11.

U.S. Department of Commerce, International Trade Administration. *1989 U.S. Industrial Outlook.* Washington, D.C.: GPO, 1989. 17–20.

U.S. Department of Labor. *Employment Projections for 1995: Data and Methods.* Washington, D.C.: GPO, 1986. 39, 41–45.

U.S. Department of Labor. *Occupational Employment in Manufacturing Industries.* Washington, D.C.: GPO, 1985. 45–50.

Van Esch, Linda Ann. "An Experimental Investigation Of Mixed-Media Advertising Effects." Ph.D. diss., York [Canada] University, 1987.

van Leer, R. Karl. "Industrial Marketing with a Flair." *Harvard Business Review* 54 (November-December 1976): 117–24.

Vernon, Raymond. "Gone Are the Cash Cows of Yesteryear." *Harvard Business Review* 58 (November-December 1980): 150–55.

von Hippel, Eric. "Successful Industrial Products from Customer Ideas." *Journal of Marketing* (January 1978): 39–49.

Walker, Arleigh W. "How to Price Industrial Products." *Harvard Business Review* 45 (September-October 1967): 125–32.

Wallace, Van. "Turnabout Fair Play for Some Publishers." *Advertising Age,* 15 June 1987, S10.

Weaver, Laurie. "Rates Bending, but Will They Break?" *Advertising Age,* 28 November 1988, S1–S2.

Webster, Bryce. *The Power of Consultative Selling.* Englewood Cliffs, N.J.: Prentice-Hall, 1987.

Webster, Frederick E., Jr. "Communication and Diffusion Processes in Industrial Markets." *European Journal of Marketing* 5 (1971): 178–88.

———. "Informal Communication in Industrial Markets." *Journal of Marketing Research* 7 (1970): 186–89.

———. "Modeling the Industrial Buying Process." *Journal of Marketing Research* 2 (1965): 370–76.

Weinstein, S., et al. "Brain-Activity Responses to Magazine and Television Advertising." *Journal of Advertising Research* 20 (July 1980): 57–63.

Weinstock, Neal. "Leaner Times Bedevil Business Magazines." *Advertising Age,* 20 June 1988, S24–S25.

Wendt, Lloyd. *Wall Street Journal: The Story Of Dow Jones and the Nation's Business Newspaper.* New York: Rand McNally, 1982.

Wind, Yoram, and Richard Cardozo. "Industrial Market Segmentation." *Industrial Marketing Management* 3 (1974): 153–66.

Wilson, Aubrey, ed. *The Marketing of Industrial Products.* London: Hutchinson, 1965.

Yankelovich, Daniel. "New Criteria for Market Segmentation." *Harvard Business Review* 42 (March-April 1964): 83–90.

Zemke, Ron, and Dick Schaaf. *The Service Edge.* New York: New American Library, 1989.

Ziegenhagen, M.E. "When Management Does Not Believe in Advertising." *Business Marketing* 69 (July 1984): 81–82.

FINANCE

Affiliated. *1987 Annual Report.*

Anderson, A. Donald. "Hollywood's Version of Trade Wars." *New York Times,* 7 August 1988, sec. 3, p. 4.

Bulkeley, William M., and Daniel Akst. "Affiliated Publications' Billboard Unit Agrees to Acquire *Hollywood Reporter." Wall Street Journal,* 26 January 1988, 42.

Capital Cities/ABC. *1987 Annual Report: 10–K.*

Cowan, Alison Leigh. "Harcourt Considers Asset Sale." *New York Times,* 13 August 1987, sec. 4, p. 6.

Crist, Steven. *"Racing Form:* Trifecta for Murdoch?" *New York Times,* 11 August 1988, D1, D18.

Crossen, Cynthia, and John Marcom, Jr. "Macmillan Receives $80–a-Share Offer from Maxwell, topping Bass Group Bid." *Wall Street Journal,* 22 July 1988, 3.

Dagnoli, Judann. "Murdoch's Reach Extends into FSIs [Free Standing Inserts]." *Advertising Age,* 22 August 1988, 3.

Dow Jones & Company. *1987 Annual Report: 10–K.*

Eichenwald, Kurt. "Murdoch Agrees to Buy *TV Guide* in $3 Billion Sale by Annenberg." *New York Times,* 8 August 1988, 1, D3.

Esler, Bill. "Maxwell Measures Up." *Graphic Arts Monthly,* August 1988, 54, 60–61, 64.

Fabrikant, Geraldine. "Harcourt: A Vulnerable Giant." *New York Times,* 20 May 1987, sec. 4, p. 3.

———. "Harcourt Gains in Debenture Fight." *New York Times,* 23 June 1987, sec.4, p. 6.

———. "Harcourt's Loss Narrows. " *New York Times,* 12 August 1988, D16.

———. "Industry Confident Murdoch Can Finance *TV Guide* Deal." *New York Times,* 9 August 1988, D1, D18.

———. "Macmillan Profit Falls 10 Per Cent." *New York Times,* 12 August 1988, D16.

———. "Maxwell Is Joining Fight for Macmillan." *New York Times,* 22 July 1988, D1.

———. "Salomon Cites Stake in Harcourt." *Wall Street Journal,* 20 June 1987, sec.1, p. 37.

————. "$334.1 Million Sale of Two Harcourt Units." *New York Times,* 19 November 1987, sec.4, p. 4.

Feldstein, Martin F., ed. *The U.S. in the World Economy.* Cambridge, Mass.: National Bureau of Economic Research, 1987. 49–53.

"The *Fortune* 500." *Fortune,* 25 April 1988, D15–D21.

Gerard, Jeremy." *TV Guide's* Power over the Air." *New York Times,* 11 August 1988, D1, 18.

Gulf & Western. *1987 Annual Report: 10–K.*

"Harcourt Sale of Units Near." *New York Times,* 9 October 1987, sec.4, p. 4.

"Harcourt Sets Layoffs of 750 at Theme Parks." *New York Times,* 25 August 1988, D4.

"Harcourt to Sell Magazine Unit." *New York Times,* 24 August 1987, sec.4, p. 7.

Henderson, Bruce D. *Henderson on Strategy.* New York: Mentor, 1979.

Hicks, Jonathan P. "McGraw-Hill." *New York Times,* 20 July 1988, D19.

Isler, Erika. "M-H [McGraw-Hill] Axes 1,000 Jobs." *MagazineWeek,* 18 December 1989, 1, 4.

"The International 500." *Fortune,* 1 August 1988, 436.

International Thomson. *1987 Annual Report.*

Jones, Alex S. "The Journal Gets a New Order." *New York Times,* 1 February 1988, D1, D3.

————. "Murdoch's *Post:* Futile Battle or Missed Opportunity?" *New York Times,* 7 March 1988, B1, B2.

Kelly, Keith J. "Times-Mirror Chiefs Mull Multi-Media Buy at N.Y. Pow Wow." *MagazineWeek,* 18 December 1989, 2.

Kneale, Dennis. "Capital Cities Net Rose 14 percent for Second Quarter." *Wall Street Journal,* 25 July 1988, 22.

————. "Macmillan Board Rejects Maxwell Bid, Calling $2.34 Billion 'Inadequate.' " *Wall Street Journal,* 29 August 1988, 14.

Knight-Ridder. *1987 Annual Report: 10–K.*

"Knight-Ridder." *Wall Street Journal,* 25 July 1988, 22.

Landro, Laura. "Simon & Schuster Becomes a Publishing 'Juggernaut': G & W Fuels Unit's Growth with Buying Spree, Focusing on Education." *Wall Street Journal,* 17 December 1987, 6.

Lohr, Steve. "Britain's Maverick Mogul." *New York Times Magazine,* 1 May 1988, 52, 53, 80, 82, 107, 108.

McDowell, Edwin. "$1.7 Billion Bid Given Harcourt." *New York Times,* 19 May 1987, sec.4, p. 6.

————. "Major Reorganization Begun by McGraw-Hill." *New York Times,* 30 June 1988, D22.

McGraw-Hill. *1987 Annual Report: 10–K.*

Macmillan. *1987 Annual Report: 10–K.*

Marcom, John, Jr. "Britain's Maxwell Is a Press Baron Who's Always on Deadline." *Wall Street Journal,* 19 November 1987, 27.

"Maxwell Plea on Harcourt." *New York Times,* 17 June 1987, sec.4, p. 4.

"Maxwell Signs Paper Deal." *Printing Impressions News Edition,* 1 July 1988, 18.

Meyers, William H. "Murdoch's Global Power Play." *New York Times Magazine,* 12 June 1988, 18–19, 20–21, 36, 41, 42.

"Murdoch the Amazing." Viewpoint Editorial *Advertising Age,* 15 August 1988, 16.

"News Corp.'s Operating Profits Rises 7 Percent for Year," *MagazineWeek,* 11 September 1989, 10.

"Profit Profile: *Business Week." MagazineWeek,* 20 April 1988, 5.

"Profits Jump 20 Percent at McGraw-Hill." *New York Times,* 20 April 1988, D22.

Reilly, Patrick. "Murdoch Buy Stacks off the Racks." *Advertising Age,* 15 August 1988, 1, 62.

———. "Trade Journals Riding Rebound of U.S. Industry." *Advertising Age,* 16 May 1988, 50.

Robb, Gregory A. "Macmillan Rejects Bid of Maxwell." *New York Times,* 27 August 1988, 31.

Roberts, Johnnie L. "McGraw-Hill Is Streamlining Its Organization." *Wall Street Journal,* 30 June 1988, 1.

———. "McGraw-Hill Stock Declines; Revamp Cited." *Wall Street Journal,* 1 July 1988, 22.

———. "Murdoch's News Corp. Will Buy Triangle Publications for $3 Billion." *Wall Street Journal,* 8 August 1988, 3.

———. "Murdoch to Sell off Reuters Stake, Land in Australia, U.K. to Pay for Triangle." *Wall Street Journal,* 10 August 1988, 3.

Roberts, Johnnie L., Laura Landro, and John Marcom, Jr. "Rupert Murdoch Takes His Biggest Risk So Far in Purchasing Triangle." *Wall Street Journal,* 9 August 1988, 1, 16.

Ross, Philip E. "Founder Regains Helm at HBJ Publications." *New York Times,* 19 November 1987, sec.4, p. 2.

Salwen, Kevin G. "McGraw-Hill Once Again Attracts Rumors after More Than Two Years of Speculation." *Wall Street Journal,* 23 August 1988, 51.

Sandler, Linda. "Shares of Murdoch's News Corp. Are Clouded by Australian Accounting, Critics Contend." *Wall Street Journal,* 16 August 1988, 53.

Scardino, Albert. "How Murdoch Makes It Work." *New York Times,* 14 August 1988, sec. 3, pp. 1, 5.

Shames, Laurence. *The Big Time: The Harvard Business School's Most Successful Class and How It Shaped America.* New York: Harper & Row, 1986.

Smith, Randall. "McGraw-Hill Stock Rises on Takeover Rumor Despite Publisher's Steep $5 Billion Price Tag." *Wall Street Journal,* 16 February 1988, 71.

Thau, Richard. "Murdoch's *Premiere* Leads the Pack in Booming Movie Title Market." *MagazineWeek*, 18 December 1989, 5.

Times-Mirror. *1987 Annual Report: 10–K.*

Wayne, Leslie. "A Family Defends Its Dynasty," *New York Times*, 24 July 1988, sec.3, pp. 1, 6.

INTERNATIONAL MARKETING

Axtell, Roger E. *Dos and Taboos around the World: A Guide to International Behavior.* New York: John Wiley & Sons, 1986.

Bauer, E. E. *China Takes Off: Technology Transfer and Modernization.* Seattle, Wash.: University of Washington Press, 1986.

Berger, Peter L., and Michael Hsiao. *in Search of East Asian Development Model.* New Brunswick, N.J.: Transaction Books, 1988.

Blumenthal, W. Michael. "The World Economy and Technological Change." *Foreign Affairs* 66 (1988): 535, 545.

"Book Sales Rise to 8.5 Percent to $13 Billion in 1988." *Publishers Weekly*, 29 September 1989, 13.

Butler, Sir Michael. *Europe: More Than a Continent.* London: Heinemann, 1988.

Calder, Kent E. *Crisis and Compensation: Public Policy and Political Stability in Japan, 1949–1986.* Princeton, N.J.: Princeton University Press, 1988. 188–211.

Carr, P. "Identifying Trade Areas for Consumer Goods in Foreign Markets." *Journal of Marketing* (October 1978): 76–80.

Center for Book Research. *Book Industry Trends 1988.* New York: Book Industry Study Group, 1988.

Cote, Kevin. "1992: Europe Becomes One." *Advertising Age*, 11 July 1988, 4.

———. "1992 Means Restructuring." *Advertising Age*, 3 October 1988, 46.

Czinkota, Michael R., and George Tasar. *Export Development Strategies: U.S. Promotion Policy.* New York: Praeger, 1982.

"Debut for the AAP International Trade Group." *Publishers Weekly*, 30 June 1989, 60.

Deyo, Frederick C., ed. *The Political Economy of the New Asian Industrialism.* Ithaca, New York: Cornell University Press, 1987.

Douglas, Susan P., and C. Samuel Craig. *International Marketing Research.* Englewood Cliffs, N.J.: Prentice-Hall, 1983.

Douglas, Susan P., C. Samuel Craig, and Warren J. Keegan. "Approaches to Assessing International Marketing Opportunities for Small- And Medium-Sized Companies." *Columbia Journal of World Business* (Fall 1982): 26–32.

Drucker, Peter. "Japan's Choices." *Foreign Affairs* 65 (1985): 923, 929.

Dunn, William. "Selling Books." *American Demographics*, October 1985, 40–43.

Emerson, John K. *The Eagle and the Rising Sun.* Reading, Mass.: Addison-Wesley, 1988.

"Europe's Houdini Trade." *Economist,* 6 May 1989, 9–10.

Exporting from the United States. Rocklin, Calif.: Prima Publishing and Communications, 1988.

Fathers, Michael, and Andrew Higgins. *Tiananmen: The Rape of Peking.* New York: Independent/Doubleday, 1989.

Friberg, Eric G. "1992: Moves Europeans Are Making." *Harvard Business Review* 67 (May-June 1989): 85–89.

Galenson, Walter, ed. *Foreign Trade and Investment: Economic Growth in the Newly Industrialized Asian Countries.* Madison: University of Wisconsin Press, 1985.

Geiger, Theodore. *The Future of the International System: The United States and the World Economy.* Boston: Unwin Hyman, 1988.

Gilpin, Kenneth N. "Japanese Rate Surge Felt in U.S." *New York Times,* 22 January 1990, D1.

Graham, W. Gordon. "The Shadow of 1992." *Publishers Weekly,* 23 December 1988, 24–26.

Grannis, Chandler B. "Balancing the Books: U.S. Export Ratios: World Figures Reported." *Publishers Weekly,* 2 June 1989, 42–45.

———. "Titles and Prices, 1988: Final Figures." *Publishers Weekly,* 29 September 1989, 24–27.

House, Karen Elliot. "The '90s and Beyond: Europe's Global Clout Is Limited by Divisions 1992 Can't Paper Over." *Wall Street Journal,* 13 February 1989, A1, A10.

———. "The '90s and Beyond: Though Rich, Japan Is Poor in Many Elements of Global Leadership." *Wall Street Journal,* 30 January 1989, A1, A8.

Hout, Thomas M., Michael Porter, and Eileen Rudden. "How Global Companies Win Out." in *Strategic Management,* edited by Richard G. Hamermesh. New York: Wiley, 1983. 35–49.

Indorf, Hans H., and Patrick M. Mayerchak. *Linkage or Bondage: U.S. Economic Relations with the ASEAN Region.* Westport, Conn.: Greenwood, 1989.

"International." *Publishers Weekly,* 30 June 1989, 54–61.

"International Booksellers Meet." *Publishers Weekly,* 30 June 1989, 56.

Johnson, Chalmers, Laura D'Andrea Tyson, and John Zysman. *Politics and Productivity: How Japan's Development Strategy Works.* Cambridge, Mass.: Ballinger, 1989.

Kahler, Raul. *International Marketing.* Cincinnati, Ohio: Southwestern, 1983.

Kamen, Robin. "N.J. Publishing Houses for Sale." *Record,* 9 February 1989, C1, C11.

Kaser, David. *Book Pirating in Taiwan.* Philadelphia: University of Pennsylvania Press, 1969. 128–41, 147–50.

Kashani, Kamran. "Beware the Pitfalls of Global Marketing." *Harvard Business Review* 67 (September-October 1989): 91, 92–98.

Kennedy, Gavin. *Doing Business Abroad*. New York: Simon & Schuster, 1985.

Kim, Roy., ed. *New Tides in the Pacific: Pacific Basin Cooperation in the Big Four (Japan, PRC, USA, and USSR)*. Westport, Conn.: Greenwood, 1987.

Kobrak, Fred. "The International PSP Market: An Update." *Publishers Weekly*, 10 November 1989, 44–45.

Lardy, Nijolas R. *China's Entry into the World Economy*. Washington, D.C.: University Press of America/New York: The Asia Society, 1987.

Levine, Sumner N., ed. *The Dow Jones-Irwin Business and Investment Almanac: 1989*. Homewood, Ill.: Dow Jones-Irwin, 1989.

Levitt, Theodore. *The Marketing Imagination*. New York: Free Press, 1983.

Lincoln, Edward J. *Japan's Economic Role in Northeast Asia*. Washington, D.C.: University Press of America/New York: Asia Society, 1987.

Lofquist, William. "Statistical Series: U.S. Book Industries." *Book Research Quarterly* 4 (Summer 1988): 71–75.

Lord, Winston. "China and America: Beyond the Big Chill." *Foreign Affairs* 68 (1989): 2.

Lowenstein, Roger. "Japan Market Woes Raise Fears of Pullback in U.S." *Wall Street Journal*, 19 January 1990, C1.

Magaziner, Ira C., and Mark Patinkin. "Fast Heat: How Korea Won the Microwave War." *Harvard Business Review* 67 (January-February 1989): 83–93.

Marron, Donald B. "The Globalization of Capital." in *The Global Marketplace*, edited by James M. Rosow. New York: Facts on File, 1988.

Mcnkes, Vivienne. "London '89: A Growing Internationalism." *Publishers Weekly*, 5 May 1989, 33–36.

Mirsky, Jonathan. "The Empire Strikes Back." *New York Review of Books*, 1 February 1990, 21–25.

Moyer, R. "International Market Analysis." *Journal of Marketing Research* (November 1968): 353–60.

Murphy, R. Taggat. "Power without Purpose: The Crisis of Japan's Global Financial Dominance." *Harvard Business Review* 67 (March-April 1989): 74.

"1992 and All That." *Publishers Weekly*, 3 February 1989, 21–28.

Ohmae, Kenichi. "The Global Logic of Strategic Alliances." *Harvard Business Review* 67 (March-April 1989): 143–54.

———. *The Mind of the Strategist*. New York: Penguin, 1988.

———. "Planting for a Global Harvest." *Harvard Business Review* 67 (July-August 1989): 136–45.

Olson, James T. "Toward a Global Information Age." in *The Global Marketplace*, edited by James M. Rosow. New York: Facts on File, 1988.

The Pacific Guide. Saffron Walden, England: World of Information, 1987.

Palmer, John. *Europe without America? The Crisis in Atlantic Relations.* New York: Oxford University Press, 1988.

Panic, M. *National Management of the International Economy.* New York: St. Martin's, 1988.

Paxton, John, ed. *The Statesman's Yearbook: 1988–1989.* New York: St. Martin's, 1988.

Percy, Nigel. *Export Strategies: Markets and Competition.* Winchester, Mass.: Allen & Unwin, 1982.

Porter, Michael E. *Competitive Strategy: Techniques for Analyzing Industries and Competitors.* New York: Free Press, 1980.

————. "How Competitive Forces Shape Strategy." *Harvard Business Review* 57 (March-April 1979): 137–45.

Revzin, Philip. "Europe Will Become Economic Superpower as Barriers Crumble." *Wall Street Journal,* 23 January 1989, A1, A4.

Ricks, David A. *Big Business Blunders: Mistakes in Multinational Marketing.* Homewood, Ill.: Dow Jones-Irwin, 1982.

Rohatyn, Felix. "America's Economic Dependence." *Foreign Affairs* 69 (1989): 54.

Root, Franklin R. *Foreign Market Entry Strategies.* New York: AMACOM, 1982.

Sachs, Jeffrey D., ed. *Developing Country Debt and the World Economy.* Chicago: University of Chicago Press, 1981.

Salisbury, Harrison E. *Tiananmen Diary: Thirteen Days in June.* Boston: Little Brown, 1989.

Scalapino, Robert A. "Asia's Future." *Foreign Affairs* 66 (1988): 85–89.

Scalapino, Robert A., and Hongkoo Lee, eds. *Korea-U.S. Relations: The Politics of Trade and Security.* Berkeley: Institute of East Asian Studies, University of California, 1989.

Scalapino, Robert A., et al., eds. *Pacific-Asian Economic Policies and Regional Interdependence.* Berkeley: Institute of East Asian Studies, University of California, 1989.

Schrage, Michael. "A Japanese Giant Rethinks Globalization: An Interview with Yoshihisa Tabuchi." *Harvard Business Review* 67 (July-August 1989): 71.

Sesit, Michael R. "Japan Banks Seen Cutting LBO Role after Campeau." *Wall Street Journal,* 19 January 1990, C1.

Simmie, Scott, and Bob Nixon. *Tiananmen Square.* Seattle: University of Washington Press, 1989.

Skully, Michael T. *ASEAN Financial Cooperation: Developments in Banking, Finance, and Insurance.* New York: St. Martin's, 1985.

Smith, Roger B. "Global Competition: A Strategy for Success." In *The Global Marketplace,* edited by James M. Rosow. New York: Facts on File, 1988.

"Spending on Books to Reach $29.4 Billion in 1993, Study Shows." *Publishers Weekly,* 30 June 1989, 24.

Springer, Ursula. "Selling Your Scholarly Books Overseas: Some Practical Tips for Non-Experts." *SSP Letter* 11 (1989): 5–6, 12.

Sterngold, James. "Tokyo's Wary Money Managers." *New York Times*, 22 January 1990, D1.

Stone, Nan. "The Globalization of Europe: An Interview with Wisse Dekker." *Harvard Business Review* 67 (May-June 1989): 90–95.

Strobaugh, R. "How to Analyze Foreign Investment Climates." *Harvard Business Review* 48 (September-October 1969): 100–108.

Strong, Ann Reinke. "Marketing Journals Internationally." *SSP Letter* 11 (1989): 7–8.

"Talking about 1992." *Publishers Weekly*, 30 June 1989, 58.

Tsao, James T. H. *China's Development Strategies and Foreign Trade.* Lexington, Mass.: Lexington Books-D.C. Heath, 1987.

U.S. Department of Commerce. *Country Trade Statistics.* Washington, D.C.: GPO, 1988.

U.S. Department of Commerce. *Custom Statistical Service.* Washington, D.C.: GPO, 1989.

U.S. Department of Commerce. *International Market Research.* Washington, D.C.: GPO, 1988.

U.S. Department of Commerce, Export Promotion Services. *Annual Worldwide Industry Review.* Washington, D.C.: GPO, 1989.

U.S. Department of Commerce, International Trade Administration. *1989 U.S. Industrial Outlook.* Washington, D.C.: GPO, 1989.

Van Horn, Mike. *Pacific Rim Trade: The Definitive Guide to Exporting and Investment.* New York: AMACOM, 1989. 300–304.

Vernon, Raymond. "Can the U.S. Negotiate for Trade Equality?" *Harvard Business Review* 67 (May-June 1989): 96–103.

Waldman, Raymond J. *Managed Trade: The New Competition between Nations.* Cambridge, Mass.: Ballinger, 1988.

Webber, Alan M. "The Case of the China Diary." *Harvard Business Review* 67 (November-December 1989): 24.

Wenham, Gilbert R. *International Trade and the Toyko Round Negotiation.* Princeton, N.J.: Princeton University Press, 1987.

Winter, Robert F. "Measures of the Book Industry: 1982–1988." *Trends Update* 8 (1989): 1–8.

Woetzel, Jonathan R. *China's Economic Opening to the Outside World.* New York: Praeger, 1989, 23–49.

Wriston, Walter B. "The State of American Management." *Harvard Business Review* 68 (January-February 1990): 80.

———. "Technology and Sovereignty ." *Foreign Affairs* 67 (1987): 67.

MASS COMMUNICATIONS

Agee, Warren K. *Maincurrents in Mass Communications.* New York: Harper & Row, 1986.

Altschull, J. Herbert. *Agents of Power: The Role of the News Media in Human Events*. White Plains, N.Y.: Longman, 1984.

Compaine, Benjamin M. "The Expanding Base of Media Competition." *Journal of Communication* (Summer 1985): 81–97.

Czitrom, Daniel J. *Media and the American Mind*. Chapel Hill: University of North Carolina Press, 1982.

Dizard, Wilson P. *The Coming Information Age: An Overview of Technology, Economics, and Politics*. White Plains, N.Y.: Longman, 1982.

Epstein, Jason. "The Decline and Rise of Publishing." *New York Review of Books*, 1 March 1990, 8–12.

Hill, George H. *Black Media in America: A Resource Guide*. Boston: G.K. Hall, 1984.

Katzen, May. "A National Information Network." *Scholarly Publishing* (July 1988): 210–16.

Martin, L. John, and Anju Grover Chaudhary. *Comparative Mass Media Systems*. White Plains, N.Y.: Longman, 1983.

Mitchell, Craig. *Media Promotion*. Chicago: Crain, 1985.

Oakeshott, Priscilla. "The Impact of New Technology on the Availability of Publications." *Book Research Quarterly* (Spring 1985): 7–14.

Pool, Ithiel de Sola. *Technologies of Freedom*. Boston: Harvard University Press, 1983.

Rohrer, Daniel Morgan, ed. *Mass Media, Freedom of Speech, and Advertising*. Dubuque, Iowa: Kendall/Hunt, 1979.

Smith, Anthony. *The Politics of Information: Problems of Policy in Modern Media*. London: Macmillan, 1979.

Wimmer, Roger, and Joseph R. Dominick. *Mass Media Research*. Belmont, Calif.: Wadsworth, 1983.

PUBLISHING HISTORY

Center for Book Research, University of Scranton. *Book Industry Trends 1988*. New York: Book Industry Study Group, 1988.

Coser, Louis A., Charles Kadushin, and Walter W. Powell. *Books: The Culture and Commerce of Publishing*. Chicago: University of Chicago Press, 1985.

Crain, G.D., Jr., ed. *Teacher of Business: The Publishing Philosophy of James H. McGraw*. Chicago: Advertising Publications, 1944.

Davis, Kenneth C. *Two-Bit Culture: The Paperbacking of America*. Boston: Houghton Mifflin, 1984.

Elfenbein, Julius. *Business Journalism*. New York: Harper & Row, 1960.

Forsyth, David. *The Business Press in America: 1750–1865* Philadelphia: Chilton, 1964.

Greco, Albert N. "The Business Publishing Industry in the United States." Chapter 4 in *The Handbook of Business Publications*. edited by Iwao

Obe. Toyko. Japan: Nikkei Business Publications and Nihon Keizai Shimbun, 1989. In Japanese.

Johnson, Allen, and Dumas Malone., eds. *The Dictionary of American Biography*. vol. 6. New York: Scribner's, 1931.

Lemay, J. A. Leo, ed. *Benjamin Franklin: Writings*. New York: Library of America, 1987.

Mott, Frank Luther. *A History of American Magazines*. vol. *1, 1741–1850*. Cambridge, Mass.: Harvard University Press, 1966.

———. *A History of American Magazines*. vol. *2, 1850–1865*. Cambridge, Mass.: Harvard University Press, 1957.

———. *A History of American Magazines*. vol. *3, 1865–1885*. Cambridge, Mass.: Harvard University Press, 1967.

———. *A History of American Magazines*. vol. *4, 1885–1905*. Cambridge, Mass.: Harvard University Press, 1957.

———. *A History of American Magazines*. vol. *5, 1905–1930*. Cambridge, Mass.: Harvard University Press, 1968.

Peterson, Theodore. *Magazines in the Twentieth Century*. Urbana: University of Illinois Press, 1964.

Powell, Walter W. *Getting into Print*. Chicago: University of Chicago Press, 1985.

Richard, Lyon N. *A History of Early American Magazines: 1741–1789*. New York: Thomas Nelson, 1931.

Silverman, Kenneth. "From Cotton Mather to Benjamin Franklin." in the *Columbia Literary History of the United States*, edited by Emory Elliot. New York: Columbia University Press, 1988.

Tebell, John. *Between Covers: The Rise and Transformation of Book Publishing in America*. New York: Oxford University Press, 1987.

———. *A History of Book Publishing in the United States*, vol. *1, The Creation of an Industry 1630–1865*. New York: R. R. Bowker, 1972.

———. *A History of Book Publishing in the United States*. vol. *3, The Golden Age Between Two Wars, 1920–1940*. New York: R. R. Bowker, 1978.

MERGERS AND ACQUISITIONS

Anders, George. "Study by KKR Outlines Virtues of Buy-Outs." *Wall Street Journal*, 23 January 1989, C1, C9.

Arpan, Jeffrey S., Edward B. Flowers, and David A. Ricks. "Foreign Direct Investment in the United States: The State of Knowledge in Research." *Journal of International Business Studies* (Spring/Summer 1981): 137–54.

"Bank Magazines Still Bear Scars from October 19 [1987]." *Publishing News*, Pilot Issue (July 1988): 13.

Bartlett, Sarah. "Time Soars $9.25 amid Rumors." *New York Times*, 8 March 1989, D1, D17.

Bolick, Robert. "A European Beach-head: MIT Press's Oxford Editorial office." *Scholarly Publishing* 19 (April 1988): 130–35.

Brooks, John. *The Takeover Game.* New York: E. P. Dutton, 1987.

Clark, Lindley H., Jr., and Alfred Malabre, Jr. "Economists Fret over Consumer Outlays." *Wall Street Journal,* 3 August 1988, 6.

Cohen, Laurie P. "Maxwell to Buy for $750 Million Dun & Bradstreet Airline Guides." *Wall Street Journal,* 31 October 1988, B4.

"Corporate Profits Fell 18% in Third Quarter, for First Drop since '87." *Wall Street Journal,* 6 November 1989, A1.

Cowan, Alison Leigh. "For Business, the Thrills and Chills of Life with Debt," *New York Times,* 27 November 1988, Sec. 3, p. 5.

Dorfman, John R. "When a Stock Is in Play, Patience and a Little Study Can Pay." *Wall Street Journal,* 21 October 1988, C1, C23.

Eichenwald, Kurt. "Murdoch Agrees to Buy *TV Guide* in a $3 Billion Sale by Annenberg." *New York Times,* 8 August 1988, 1, D3.

"88: The Year of the Mega-Sale." *Folio,* February 1988, 111–12, 115–16, 120.

Gale Research. *The Gale Directory of Publications.* Detroit, Mich.: Gale Research, 1987.

Gerard, Jeremy. *"TV Guide's* Power over the Air." *New York Times,* 11 August 1988, D1, 18.

Graham, W. Gordon. "The Shadow of 1992." *Publishers Weekly,* 23 December 1988, 24–26.

Greco, Albert N. "University Presses and the Trade Book Market: Managing in Turbulent Times." *Book Research Quarterly* 3 (Winter 1987–1988): 34–53.

Green, Wayne E., and Sonya Steptoe. "Metropolitan Life Joins Backlash against Leveraged Buy-Outs." *Wall Street Journal,* 18 November 1988, C1, C21.

Greenhouse, Steven. "The Growing Fear of Fortress Europe." *New York Times,* 23 October 1988, 3–1, 3–24.

Hall, Robert E. "Economic Fluctuations." *NBER Reporter* (Summer 1989): 1–7.

Hamrin, Robert. *America's New Economy: The Basic Guide.* New York: Franklin Watts, 1988.

Hemp, Paul. "News International's Collins Bid Advances as Opponent Withdraws." *Wall Street Journal,* 5 January 1989, B4.

Herman, Tom. "Economists Expect Expansion to Continue for at Least a Year Despite a Faster Inflation Pace and Increase in Interest Rates." *Wall Street Journal,* 5 July 1988, 3.

Hersey, Robert D., Jr. "Greenspan Shuns Curb on Buyouts." *New York Times,* 27 January 1989, D1–D2.

Higham, Adrian. "Selling Abroad? Are We Doing Enough?" *Book Research Quarterly* 4 (Winter 1988–1989): 45–51.

Hilder, David B., and Randall Smith. "Time-Warner Deal Fuels Run-Ups in Other Media Issues: Proposed Stock Swap Could Be Vulnerable." *Wall Street Journal*, 7 March 1989, C1, C18.

Honomichel, Jack J. "Buyout Aftershocks among Lows of 1988." *Advertising Age*, 23 January 1989, 12.

"The International *Fortune 500.*" Fortune, 31 July 1989 291–310.

Kilborn, Peter T. "Brady Voices Concern over Takeover Debts." *New York Times*, 25 January 1989, D1.

Kneale, Dennis. "Time-Warner Pact May Be Fodder for Program Talks." *Wall Street Journal*, 8 March 1989, B1.

Kristol, Irving. "The War against the Corporation." *Wall Street Journal*, 24 January 1989, A20.

Kurtzman, Joel. "Prospects: Two Giants Become One." *New York Times*, 12 March 1989, Sec. 3, p. 25.

Landro, Laura. "Time's Nicholas Must Fuse Two Cultures." *Wall Street Journal*, 7 March 1989, B9.

———. "Time-Warner Merger Will Help Fend off Tough Global Rivals." *Wall Street Journal*, 6 March 1989, A1, A5.

Lipman, Joanne. "Time-Warner Deal May Yield One-Stop Shopping Possibility." *Wall Street Journal*, 7 March 1989, B7.

Little, Jane Sneddon. "The Financial Health of U.S. Manufacturing Firms Acquired by Foreigners." *New England Economic Review* (July-August 1981): 5–18.

———. "Foreign Direct Investment in New England." *New England Economic Review* (March-April 1981): 51–56.

———. "Foreign Direct Investment in the United States." *New England Economic Journal*, (November-December 1980): 5–22.

McDowell, Edwin. "Major Reorganization Begun by McGraw-Hill." *New York Times*, 30 June 1988, D22.

———. "Time-Warner Combination Joins Giants in Publishing." *New York Times*, 6 March 1989, D8.

Magee, John F. "1992: Moves Americans Must Make." *Harvard Business Review* 67 (May-June 1989): 78–84.

"Maxwell Seeking Stake in IDG Communications?" *MagazineWeek*, 31 October 1988, 1.

Menkes, Vivienne. "London '89: A Growing Internationalism." *Publishers Weekly*, 5 May 1989, 33–36.

"Mergers and Acquisitions Set Record in '88." *New York Times*, 31 January 1989, D19.

Moore, James P., Jr. "Highlights of the 1989 U.S. Industrial Outlook." in *1989 U.S. Industrial Outlook*. Washington, D.C.: GPO, 1989.

Moskowitz, Milton. *The Global Marketplace: 102 of the Most Influential Companies outside America*. New York: Macmillan, 1987.

Murray, Alan. "Brady Suggests LBOs Could Be Curbed by Shifting Tax Deductions to Dividends." *Wall Street Journal*, 25 January 1989, A4.

Murray, Alan. "Greenspan Signals Higher Interest Rates." *Wall Street Journal*, 14 July 1988, 2.

"The Next Recession: Just around the Bend?" *Wall Street Journal*, 6 March 1989, A1.

Norris, Floyd. "Behind the Wave of Leveraged Buyouts, High Profit Potential." *New York Times*, 21 October 1988, D13.

——. "In Media Merger, Tandem Control." *New York Times*, 6 March 1989, D6.

——. "Time and Warner Look to Europe and Pacific." *New York Times*, 7 March 1989, D22.

——. "Time Inc. and Warner to Merge, Creating Largest Media Company." *New York Times*, 5 March 1989, A1, A39.

"Plenty of Fish in Pond—Warner Wants to Swim In." *Wall Street Journal*, 7 March 1989, B1, B8.

"Profit Profile: *Business Week*." *MagazineWeek*, 20 April 1988, 5.

"Quarterly Review of Corporate Earnings: Second Quarter 1989." *Wall Street Journal*, 7 August 1989, A5–A14.

Reilly, Patrick. "Murdoch Buy Stacks off the Racks." *Advertising Age*, 15 August 1988, 1, 6.

Roberts, Johnnie L. "McGraw-Hill Is Streamlining Its Organization." *Wall Street Journal*, 30 June 1988, 1.

——. "McGraw-Hill Stock Declines; Revamp Cited." *Wall Street Journal*, 1 July 1988, 22.

Roberts, Johnnie L., Laura Landro, and John Marcom, Jr. "Rupert Murdoch Takes His Biggest Risk So Far in Purchasing Triangle." *Wall Street Journal*, 9 August 1988, 1, 16.

Rothenberg, Randall. "Time-Warner Bid for Global Marketing." *New York Times*, 6 March 1989, D11.

"A Sampling of Interest-Rate and Economic Forecasts." *Wall Street Journal*, 6 July 1988, 37.

Sandler, Linda. "Time-Warner Deal Fuels Run-Ups in Other Media Issues: But Terms Disappoint Some Time Holders." *Wall Street Journal*, 7 March 1989, C1, C2.

Scardino, Albert. "Companies Hope to Avoid Turmoil with Merger." *New York Times*, 5 March 1989, A38.

——. "How Murdoch Makes It Work." *New York Times*, 14 August 1988, sec.3, pp. 1, 5.

Sebastian, Pamela. "Robust Economy Raises Inflation Fears." *Wall Street Journal*, 11 July 1988, 22.

Smith, Randall, and George Anders. "Year of the Megadeals Is upon Us." *Wall Street Journal*, 21 October 1988, C1, C22.

Smith, Randall, and Laura Landro. "Time Inc. Shares Soar on Rumors That a Hostile Bidder May Emerge." *Wall Street Journal*, 8 March 1989, C1.

Smith, Randall, James A. White, and Thomas E. Ricks. "Wall Street Fears

Grow That Congress Will Out Brake on LBOs." *Wall Street Journal*, 16 January 1989, C1, C15.

Spencer, Edson W. "Capital-Gains Shift Could Curb LBO [Leveraged Buy-Outs] Break-Up." *Wall Street Journal*, 27 January 1989, A14.

Standard & Poor's. "Harcourt Brace Jovanovich." *Standard NYSE Stock Reports*, 21 October 1989, 1096K-97K.

———. "News Corp." *Standard NYSE Stock Reports*, 21 October 1988, 1314–15.

Tolchin, Martin, and Susan Tolchin. *Buying into America: How Foreign Money Is Changing the Face of Our Nation*. New York: Times Books, 1988.

U.S. Department of Commerce, Bureau of the Census. *1982 Census of Manufacturers: Newspapers, Periodicals, Books, and Miscellaneous Publishing*. Washington, D.C.: GPO, 1985.

U.S. Department of Commerce, Bureau of the Census. *1977 Census of Manufacturers: Newspapers, Periodicals, Books, and Miscellaneous Publishing*. Washington, D.C.: GPO, 1980.

U.S. Department of the Commerce, International Trade Administration, *1989 U.S. Industrial Outlook*. Washington, D.C.: GPO 1989.

Wallace, Anise C. "Behind the Boom in Takeovers: Enormous Capital Is Available to Buy Undervalued Assets." *New York Times*, 9 September 1988, C1.

Weldon, Peter. "Jovanovich of Harcourt Brace to Resign as Chief Executive, Names Caulo to Post." *Wall Street Journal*, 19 December 1988, B6.

"Why Fight Leveraged Buyouts?" *New York Times*, 28 November 1988, A24.

Zarnowitz, Victor. "Economic Outlook Survey: Second Quarter 1988." *NBER* [National Bureau of Economic Research] *Reporter* (Summer 1988): 11–14.

———. "Economic Outlook Survey: Third Quarter 1988." *NBER Reporter* (Fall 1988): 11–12. Zarnowitz, Victor. "Economic Outlook Survey: First Quarter 1989." *NBER Reporter* (Spring 1989): 11–12.

———. "Economic Outlook Survey: Second Quarter 1989." *NBER Reporter* (Summer 1989): 12–13.

Index

Bell and Howell, 115
Berger, Marcella, 202
Berne (Copyright) Convention, 194
Bertelsmann AG, 148, 169, 202. *See also* Bantam Doubleday Dell
Bessie, Simon Michael, 200
Beverage Industry Show Daily, 102. *See also* Edgell Communications
Billboard, 121
Billboard Information Network (BIN), 121. *See also* Affiliated Publications
Bill Communications, 67, 93
Black's titles, 105. *See also* McGraw-Hill
Blumenthal, W. Michael, 184, 202
Bond Buyer, 120. *See also* Thomson Corporation
Book Industry Trends 1988, 154
Book Research Quarterly, 9, 16, 44
Borowsky, Ned, 67–68
Boston Globe, 121. *See also* Affiliated Publications
Bradford, Andrew, 83
Bulletin of the Association for Business Communication, 44
Bureau of National Affairs (BNA), 44
Burstyn, Joseph, Inc. v. Wilson (343 U.S. 495, 503), 164
Business administration of periodicals, 88–89
Business Journalism: Management Notes and Cases, 89
Business publishing: advertising industry, 73–74, 127–48; advertising management cases, 214–62; advertising revenues, 51–52, 56, 65–68, 127–49; business outlook, 61–62, 70–78; business problems, 62–65; business versus consumer magazines, 68–70; case studies, 93–121; definition of business publishing, 40–44; "dinosaur" theory of publishing, 168–70; employment statistics, 38; European market, 198–205; foreign publishing firms in the U.S., 149, 171, 190–91; global publishing, 182–88; history, 82–92; magazine categories, 44–47; major publica-

tions, 56–61; market analysis techniques, 192–98; marketing research, 189–92; marketing training, 78; market share, 47–56, 76–77, 166–67; marketing in the Pacific Rim (Korea), 193–95; media corporations in U.S., 146–47; mergers and acquisitions, 156–63; mergers and acquisitions: public policy issues, 172–75; mergers and acquisitions: theories, 152–71; miscellaneous publishing, 27, 30–31; Pacific Rim, 205–8; periodicals 40, 46, 59–61, 75, 85–86; publishing industry: overview, 25–32, 43; publishing industry: research, 9–10; publishing industry in major states, 34; publishing in New York City, 32–36; publishing in U.S., 36–39; teaching business publishing, 1–8; teaching materials, 11–18, 21–22
Business Publication Rates and Data, 13, 45, 192. *See also* Standard Rate and Data Service
Business Week, 57, 69, 105. *See also* McGraw-Hill
Butler, Michael, 186
Byte, 105. *See also* McGraw-Hill

CableVision, 44
Cadence, 120. *See also* Thomson Corporation
Cahners-Reed, 90, 174. *See* Reed International PLC, 120–22
Capital Cities/ABC, 99–101
Capital Markets Report, 96. *See also* Dow Jones
Chesterton, G. K., 4
China, 206–8. *See also* Pacific Rim
Chronicle of Higher Education, 44
CNN, 207
Coen, Robert J., 62, 70–72, 75
Collins, 118, 167. *See also* Harper & Row; News Corporation
Columbia Journal of World Business, 193
Commerce Clearing House (CCH), 44, 93

Macmillan, 45, 102, 113. *See also* Maxwell Communications

Mad magazine, 61. *See also* Time Warner

Madison Square Garden, 107. *See also* Paramount Corporation

Magaziner, Ira C., 207

MagazineWeek, 13, 105

MagazineWeek 500, 40, 57, 59, 192

Manac Systems International, 109. *See also* Paramount Corporation

Manufacturing Systems, 101. *See also* Capital Cities/ABC

Marketing & Media Decisions, 65

Marron, Donald B., 184, 187

Martin v. Struthers (319 U.S. 141, 143), 164

Matthew Bender, 44

Maxwell, Robert, 45, 103, 106, 112–15, 119–20, 153, 169, 173

Maxwell Communications, 112–15

Mead, 93

Medical Economics, 44. *See also* Thomson Corporation

Mergers and Acquisitions, 153

Miller-Freeman, 120. *See also* Reed International PLC

Mintzberg, Henry, 13

Mirabella, 117. *See also* News Corporation

Modern Job Safety and Health, 108. *See also* Paramount Corporation

Money, 57. *See also* Time Warner

Moody's, 153

Mortgage-Backed Securities Information Service, 120. *See also* Thomson Corporation

Mosby, C. V., 99

Motor Age, 101. *See also* Capital Cities/ABC

Mott, Frank Luther, 11, 45, 83, 93

Munifacts, 120. *See also* Thomson Corporation

Murdoch, Rupert, 11, 111–12, 115–20, 153, 169

Murphy, R. Taggart, 187

National Directory of Magazines, 13

National Petroleum Times, 86

Neal Editorial Prize, 9, 101

New England Journal of Medicine, 44, 59, 85

News Corporation, 111, 116–18, 167, 174

Newsweek, 62, 69–70

New Woman, 117. *See also* News Corporation

New York, 117. *See also* News Corporation

New York City, 32–34

New Yorker, 39

New York Times, 12, 13, 95, 153

New York University, 91

Nexis, 44, 93

1934 Communications Act, 164

1927 Radio Act, 164

Norris, Floyd, 169

North American Publishing, 67

NYU Today, 44

O'Donnell, William, 55

Ogilvy, David, 69

Ohmae, Kenichi, 188

Olson, James E., 184

Pacific Rim, 130, 183, 189, 193–97, 205–8

Palmer, John, 186

Panic, M., 185

Paramount Corporation (formerly Gulf & Western Corporation), 107–9; Paramount Pictures, 107

Parents magazine, 148. *See also* Bertelsmann AG

Patinkin, Mark, 208

Pearson PLC, 93. *See also* Viking-Penguin

Pennwell, 93

Pergamon Holding Corporation, 115. *See also* Maxwell Communications

Perkins, Maxwell, 2

Penton, 93

PHINet, 109. *See also* Paramount Corporation

Piers, 110. *See also* Paramount Corporation

Plant Engineering, 121. *See also* Reed International PLC

Warner Communications, 117. *See also* Time Warner
Watson, Thomas, 7
Webber, Alan M., 207
Weinstock, Neil, 54
Western Railroad Gazette, 90
Whitney, 93
Who's Who, 114. *See also* Maxwell Communications
Wicks Communications, 102
William Collins PLC. *See* Collins
Williams and Wilkins, 93

Women's Wear Daily, 7, 101. *See also* Capital Cities/ABC
Wriston, Walter B., 184–85, 202

Yachting, 39
Year Book Medical Publishing, 98. *See also* Times-Mirror
Young and Rubicam, 40, 133

Zenger-Miller, 99
Ziff Communications, 93

About the Author

Professor Albert N. Greco is Associate Dean and Director of Publishing Studies, Gallatin Division, New York University.